"Brian Breuel writes clearly, tackles difficult technical subjects with ease, and has produced **A MUST READ FOR THOSE WHO WANT TO PRESERVE THE TRILLIONS OF DOLLARS OF WEALTH CREATED IN THE BULL MARKET OF THE LAST FIVE YEARS.**"

STEPHEN H. PANEYKO
Senior Executive Vice President, Summit Bank

"**THE GUY REALLY KNOWS HIS STUFF.** It is a fine guide for people who seek to preserve what they've worked so hard to build."

JOHN BACHMAN
Managing Principal, Edward Jones

"Brian H. Breuel has written **AN EXPERT PRACTICAL GUIDE TO KEEPING WHAT YOU HAVE EARNED.** Anyone concerned about their financial health today, their retirement, and their legacy for family, friends, and charity, will benefit from reading this book. This is **A STEP-BY-STEP, SOLUTION-ORIENTED GUIDE.** The book is organized according to real-world problems readers face in arranging their financial affairs. Brian H. Breuel's advice is specific, factual, and easy to understand. **I RECOMMEND IT WHOLEHEARTEDLY.**"

RON BROWN, CFP
Director of Planned Giving, Princeton University

"**ANYONE HOPING TO PRESERVE MORE OF WHAT THEY'VE EARNED CAN BENEFIT FROM THIS BOOK.** Well written, effective, and efficient . . ."

JOHN D. FIRESTONE
Partner, Secor Group

Staying
WEALTHY
Strategies for Protecting Your Assets

Also available from
BLOOMBERG PERSONAL BOOKSHELF

Smart Questions to Ask Your Financial Advisers
by Lynn Brenner

Investing in Small-Cap Stocks
by Christopher Graja and Elizabeth Ungar, Ph.D.

The Inheritor's Handbook
by Dan Rottenberg
(November 1998)

The New Commonsense Guide to Mutual Funds
by Mary Rowland
(October 1998)

A Commonsense Guide to Your 401(k)
by Mary Rowland

BLOOMBERG PERSONAL BOOKSHELF

Staying
WEALTHY

Strategies for Protecting Your Assets

BRIAN H. BREUEL

BLOOMBERG PRESS
PRINCETON

First edition published 1998
1 3 5 7 9 10 8 6 4 2

Breuel, Brian H., 1944–
        Staying wealthy: strategies for protecting your assets / Brian
    H. Breuel
            p.   cm.
        Includes index.
        ISBN 1-57660-022-X
        1. Estate planning–United States. 2. Finance. Personal–
    United States.   I. Title.
    KF750.Z9B74   1998
    332. 024'01- -dc21   98-16525
                                                                CIP

Acquired and edited by Jared Kieling
Icons by Mark Matcho
Book design by Don Morris Design

To the true inspiration for all
that I do that is worthy—
Shirley, Erin, Quinn, and Lucille

ACKNOWLEDGMENTS

I WOULD LIKE to thank Jared Kieling of Bloomberg Press for his meticulous and unselfish editing of the manuscript. He was involved from the conception of this project and has made this work readable through his insight and invaluable advice.

I would also like to thank Melissa Hafner and Christina Palumbo on the Bloomberg Press staff for their persistent efforts to wrap up the project.

Finally, thanks to my wife and partner for the encouragement and time away from the relationship to complete this writing, while pursuing a career more than full time.

INTRODUCTION

EALTH IS AS difficult to preserve as it is to create.

We struggle much of our adult life to accumulate enough money to retire. For most people, that involves 40 or more years of hard work, career shifts, family challenges, business successes, and business failures. Most likely, your successes outweigh your failures or you wouldn't be reading this book.

It's interesting that while many people are successful, even wealthy, by most standards, they don't feel completely secure. U.S. Trust Company, one of this country's oldest private-banking and money-management firms, conducted a survey of "wealthy" individuals during the mid-1990s. They defined wealthy as having a net worth of $3,000,000 or more, or having an adjusted gross income of $200,000. When this group was asked how they viewed themselves, only 19 percent believed they were wealthy. Sixty-eight percent described themselves as upper middle class.

Many wealthy people don't think they have a small fortune, even when they do. The primary reason for their pessimism is that there are so many threats to wealth today.

You probably think first of taxes. And you should. Federal, state, and local levies impede your ability to accumulate and compound significant wealth, and at your death, estate taxes can diminish what's left by as much as 55 percent. This is not to say that taxes are all bad. They educate our children, pave our roads, police our streets, and protect our shores. Oliver Wendell Holmes, the famous jurist, said, "Taxes are what we pay for a civilized society." However, that doesn't mean you should give away more than your fair share, at least not without getting a charitable deduction.

Probate expenses, poor health, creditors, and inflation are other familiar threats. Still others are not so obvious, such as outdated wills and trusts, excessive jointly owned property, the disability of a key employee, and living too long.

Staying Wealthy is about all these threats and what you can do to avoid, minimize, or neutralize them.

Most books on asset protection present a laundry list of solutions to tax- and estate-planning conundrums. Unfortunately, many of them don't take you deeply enough into a problem for you to know if the solution—such as an irrevocable life insurance trust—is something you should read about.

This book, by contrast, is organized by problem, to let you start where you are. For example, if you own a business, read Part 3, "Business Succession Problems," to see the kinds of challenges proprietors encounter. If you have assets in excess of $1,000,000, you are likely to face some tricky choices, so read Part 1, "Estate-Planning Problems." Divorced persons and those in the process of divorce can get ahead of their financial difficulties by reading *Problem 30,* "Separation and Divorce," in Part 5, "Family Problems." You'll find cross-references to related areas in the **SEE ALSO** section following each problem.

PART 1 of this book addresses estate planning. Tax troubles are just the beginning. Insufficient income for the heirs and a lack of cash to meet the expenses of the estate are more common among the wealthy than you'd think. Estate dilemmas frequently result from faulty distribution, such as leaving the wrong assets to the wrong heirs. *Problems 1 through 14* show how to avoid the pitfalls that await the estate owner.

Dying is not the only circumstance that triggers unpleasant wealth-preservation surprises. Living too long will raise financial issues for more and more Americans during the next century. When most people began their careers, they probably thought they would spend 10 or 15 years in retirement. However, if you are alive today at 65, your life expectancy is closer to 20 more years. And that's if you are average. What if you are in great health? **PART 2** helps you ensure that the blessings of longevity never turn into a burden.

For most business owners, the quality of their later life is going to depend on their ability to dispose of their business profitably. For their heirs, financial security may depend on the quality of whatever planning got done before the business owner's death or disability. **PART 3** highlights situations that can decimate the value of a business often built over a lifetime. Solutions are usually within their grasp, but most business owners haven't acknowledged how much the death or disability of themselves, their partners, or other key employees will cost them and their company.

Investments preoccupy many of us today. In an era when information is everywhere but common sense and sound advice are harder to come by, you need to choose vehicles that preserve your wealth not just throughout your lifetime, but possibly for future generations. Yet, too many people make long-term decisions over significant dollars based on two-minute interviews, magazine columns, or sound bites. Some investors diligently follow the recommendations of authors who know nothing about their individual needs, objectives, or risk tolerance. **PART 4** addresses obstacles to successful investing, including tax inflation, excessive expenses, poor asset allocation, mediocre asset management, and the lack of time to complete an investment plan.

Family problems—divorce, child support, "sandwich-generation" challenges, astronomical educational expenses, and the costs of assisted living—occupy a new role in planning today. **PART 5** gives you ways around them. While you can't always plan your way out of a divorce or the support of your parents, there are steps you can take to conserve assets for both divorced partners, pay for expensive educations, provide for aging parents, and ensure your children a share in your financial success.

Litigation has become not only a way of settling disputes, but also a weapon people use to punish their competitors and pressure their neighbors. Distinguishing "right from wrong" is beside the point in many lawsuits. Deciding these claims can be expensive, time consuming, and stressful. **PART 6** tells you how to minimize your exposure. You will also find help navigating the baffling world of insurance.

On a more positive note, there is today a growing commitment to charitable giving. As most astute philanthropists will tell you, the desire to share your wealth presents special challenges, and if you are going to be an effective donor you will need to plan your generosity. **PART 7**, devoted to charitable giving, assists you.

Finally, **PART 8** delves into the psyche of the superwealthy. Some of their disciplines and attitudes toward money are worth acquiring for your own portfolio of skills.

This book is as appropriate for someone still building up their net worth as it is for someone in retirement. Both can take advantage of the **RESOURCES** section at the back of this book and also lean heavily on the "Recommended Advisers" section at the end of each Problem. With so much at stake, don't overlook the importance of assembling a first-rate team to guide you through the entire wealth–creation/preservation cycle.

Finally, a note about the icons found in the "Recommended Advisers" section following every Problem. These icons, shown below, each highlight one of four financial professionals whose advice you may want to seek:

 Financial Planner

Insurance Agent

 Attorney

Tax Accountant

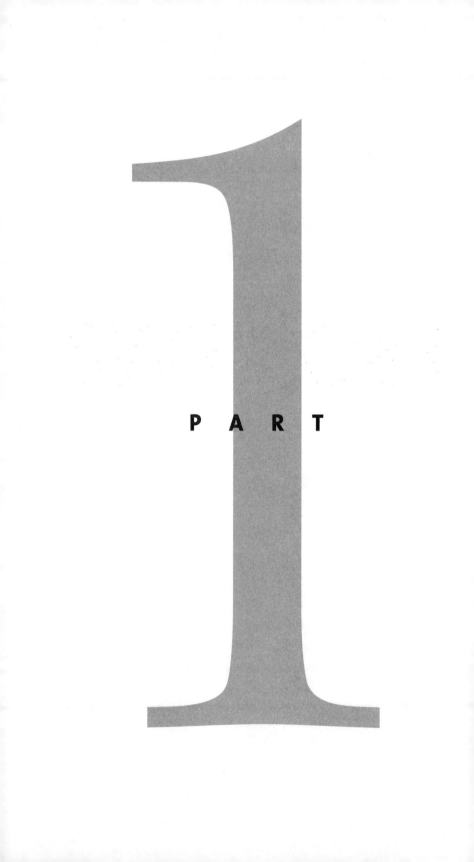

PART

1

Estate-
PLANNING
PROBLEMS

STATE-PLANNING problems rarely present themselves one at a time. They surface by the half-dozen, making it difficult to decide which one to tackle first. Related problems may overlap or spring from a common source. For example, failure to have a current will could result in assets passing to the wrong heirs, excessive expenses and delays in administering an estate, and shrinkage of the estate due to unnecessary taxes. Part 1 shows you where to get started.

The first and threshold Problem in this Part is the "Lack of a Current Estate Plan." In *Problem 1,* you'll learn what estate planning is and is not. You will see the importance of taking an active approach to planning not only your estate but your whole financial life. "Decision by indecision" can be a fatal flaw in an otherwise financially successful life.

An analogy often used by professional planners is that of a ship heading to sea with no plans or charts. The likelihood of the ship reaching its overseas destination is slim. So it is with your journey to financial independence and wealth preservation. Without a current plan, you're not likely to reach your goals.

PROBLEM 1

LACK OF A CURRENT ESTATE PLAN

The most common estate-planning problem by far is the lack of a current estate plan. You can fall into this trap by having no will, having an outdated will, or assuming that estate planning involves no more than having a will. Pretend you have one month to live and follow your assets through a hypothetical disposition at your death.

WHEN SOMEONE DIES without a valid will, they are said to die intestate. Each state has its own laws of intestate succession to protect surviving spouses and children. These laws, which vary significantly from state to state, impose a plan of distribution for your assets. This "plan" does not take into account the special needs of your spouse and children. Instead it distributes your assets as the state legislature deems fair for the average situation.

The consequences of *intestacy,* that is, dying without a valid will, are usually more complex than just following the state's plan of distribution, however. Some of the decedent's property may escape the laws of intestate succession. For example, property owned jointly with a right of survivorship will pass automatically to the survivor, who may or may not be the surviving spouse. Life insurance proceeds payable to a named beneficiary will pass by operation of the contract, and hence avoid the intestate succession plan of the state. Individual retirement accounts (IRAs) that name someone other than the spouse as the beneficiary will pass to that person, not to the marital partner as they might have under the state's plan. In the absence of a valid will, your assets will likely be distributed through a combination of these plans.

On top of these exceptions to intestate succession, some states have additional laws that create presumptions about how property is owned. Community-property states create a fiction that all property created during a marriage is actually owned jointly by the couple. This presumption overrides the facts of who earned what, and the surviving spouse receives at least half the assets. Some states provide for family allowances, which pay income or earmark assets for the children of the decedent. It would be purely coincidental if the state's plan of distribution matched your own.

What would happen if Mr. DeLay left a wife and six young children, no will, no other family, and everything titled in his name?

The answer would depend on the state where Mr. DeLay is *domiciled,* his permanent home. If he is governed by the state of Alaska and the six children are the offspring from his current marriage, then Mrs. DeLay inherits all of his assets. In New Jersey, his spouse would receive the first $50,000, the remainder being divided one-half for the spouse and one-half for the children. In Rhode Island, the real estate would be earmarked for the children and everything else split 50-50 between the spouse and children. In Tennessee, the spouse shares equally with each of the children, but is entitled to at least one-third; the difference between all of the assets and one-third could be a significant amount of money.

What happens if there are children from a prior marriage? What if the decedent favored some children over others, or one of the children needed special care because of health problems? Too bad. The state does not make exceptions to the "plan" in its statutes.

According to Paula Monopoli, professor of law at Southwestern University School of Law, 70 percent of Americans die without a will. And it isn't just the poor or the uninformed who duck that responsibility. She cites Pablo Picasso and Abraham Lincoln as among the famous who died intestate—and Lincoln was a lawyer!

Dying with an outdated will is as problematic as dying with no will at all. Countless American men had wills written in anticipation of being shipped overseas for military duty in Korea, Vietnam, or the Persian Gulf War. Changes in family status will make these wills obsolete. Statistically, over half of the marriages entered into during those years have ended in divorce. However, even for couples still happily married, the

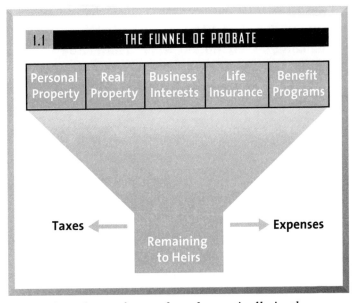

| 1.1 | THE FUNNEL OF PROBATE |

| Personal Property | Real Property | Business Interests | Life Insurance | Benefit Programs |

Taxes ← ... → Expenses

Remaining to Heirs

tax laws have changed so dramatically in the more than 25 years since Vietnam that significant tax benefits will be wasted under those old wills. Estate planning involves a lot more than having a current will. It is a process of making conscious and continual decisions about the accumulation, preservation, and ultimate disposition of everything you have earned and saved. This process involves gathering information, analyzing your assets and liabilities, identifying your needs and objectives and those of your heirs, and disposing of those assets during your lifetime as well as after your death.

The aim of estate planners should be the attainment of your needs and objectives in the most effective manner, considering both tax and nontax consequences along the way. Look at TABLE 1.1, *above*. The Funnel of Probate Table illustrates the planning opportunities you have if you make some sensible decisions now. Without planning, assets pass haphazardly, some through probate, others outside. Planning can eliminate the delays and expenses of probate and minimize taxes.

SOLUTIONS

◆ **Begin the estate-planning process now.** Commit to assembling a team of professionals to help you create a plan. The team should include an attorney, a tax accountant, and someone who understands insurance and investments, such as a highly experienced life insurance agent, financial planner, or stockbroker. You may be able to find one person with experience in all three areas.

◆ **Use the insurance/investment professional to run a hypothetical probate.** Select someone with the experience and the computer software tools to illustrate what happens under your existing estate plan. The experience necessary should include courses in estate planning. Interview potential planners and ask to see a sample report they would prepare. The computer software should be a program that illustrates the disposition of your estate under different scenarios and the tax consequences.

One of the advantages of using the planner for the analysis stage of the estate-planning process versus the attorney or accountant is that you can usually get the hypothetical probate completed without a large fee. A good estate-planning attorney could charge thousands of dollars just to gather your personal information and run hypothetical estate models for you. A good life insurance or investment professional could do the job for hundreds of dollars, or no fee at all.

◆ **Use an attorney to create your new plan.** Effective planning is not done in a vacuum and is rarely done alone. Most wealth-preservation strategies are complex and require the assistance of professionals. Don't throw away part of your fortune by hoping to avoid all fees and expenses. You may have heard the admonition, "Don't jump over dollars to get to dimes." The estate-planning process will cost a few thousand dollars in legal, accounting, and planning fees and insurance and investment-management expenses. It's worth it. Never draft your own will and trust documents. Leave do-it-yourself legal remedies to people with few assets to lose.

◆ **Review your estate plan after a divorce or remarriage.** Failure to change your old will could result in a windfall for an ex-spouse and a shortfall for your own children. If you are unmarried and have a live-in relationship, you especially need a will. The marriage bond protects a partner under state law; roommate status does not. If your relationship is intended to be like a marriage, you will have to make special provisions in a legal document, i.e., a will. Palimony suits are no way to ensure the efficient disposition of assets to either your "significant other" or your families.

◆ **Review your plan annually and as circumstances change.** Other events that require a planning review include the adoption of a child; the sale of controlling interest in a closely held business; a change in your state of domicile; buying a house or land in another state; major career moves; threatening changes in your health; anticipation of long-term care for yourself, your spouse, or a parent; and the death of a spouse or a child.

Remember, when you fail to plan, you are not leaving matters to chance. You're leaving them to the hodgepodge of laws of intestacy and contracts. The result is usually much more expensive and time consuming for your heirs than any investment you might make in planning now.

RECOMMENDED ADVISERS

Use your **accountant** to verify the value of your assets. Valuation challenges are discussed in *Problem 8.*

Use your **attorney** to discuss the solutions to estate-planning problems and to draft the documents necessary to implement your plan.

A **financial planner** cannot draft wills and trusts, but can save you some attorney's or accountant's fees by gathering your personal information, inputting it into a computerized hypothetical estate program, and showing you the disposition and tax consequences of your current plan.

SEE ALSO

◆ **Problem 2:** *The Estate-Tax Bite* to find out how an outdated will can result in unnecessary estate taxes at your death.

◆ **Problem 5:** *Excessive Joint Ownership with Spouses* to find out why jointly owned property is frequently the worst way to own your assets.

◆ **Problem 10:** *Improper Beneficiaries and Owners* to learn why the right beneficiary can make the difference between a successful plan and a planning disaster.

◆ **Problem 26:** *Finding the Best Financial Adviser* to locate experienced, competent advisers.

PROBLEM 2

THE ESTATE-TAX BITE

The federal and state estate tax taken out of many estates can consume half of the assets. Yet, some estates are so well-planned that the estate taxes are zero. Perhaps Justice Learned Hand of the U.S. Court of Appeals summed it up when he wrote, "There are two systems of taxation in our country: one for the informed and one for the uninformed." This discussion aims to put you in the first category.

THE *INTERNAL REVENUE CODE* (IRC)—the codification of tax laws in this country—imposes a tax on your right to transfer property. Called the *federal estate and gift tax,* it is actually a tax on the transfer of assets, rather than on the right to inherit or receive that property.

The estate-tax bite can be painful. Most Americans

don't realize *how* painful because they've heard they can pass $625,000 of assets tax free at their death, enough to shelter most estates from taxation. Indeed, Congress's Joint Committee on Taxation estimated that only 1.66 percent of all estates in 1997 would be taxable. Even before the passage of the Taxpayer Relief Act of 1997, the number of taxable estates was expected to increase to only 2.5 percent over the next decade. These percentages may seem low to you, except that it's your estate that may be taxed. With that in mind, let's look at this from the other direction.

The new law will increase the amount of assets that will escape the estate tax from $600,000 to $1 million, gradually from 1997 to the year 2006. However, that $600,000 tax threshold had not changed since its enactment into law in 1987. Since that time, inflation has increased 42 percent and the stock market has risen over 200 percent. The combination of these factors alone has elevated many middle-class families to estate-taxable levels. If the original $600,000 exemption had been indexed to inflation back in 1987, it would be close to the $1 million level today, not in 2006.

By the time the $1 million exemption becomes effective in 2006, an estate growing at 7 percent will have almost doubled in size. In 1995, over half of the estate tax returns filed were from estates under $1 million. The remaining half accounted for most of the $17.2 billion in estate-tax revenues paid last year. Critics of the tax may argue that it is a minor source of revenue for the Treasury—1.2 percent—and should be abolished, but that is little comfort if it includes up to 55 percent of your hard-earned wealth.

Understanding the calculation of the estate-tax credit, called *the unified credit,* will help you realize its potential in the planning process. The tax-free $625,000 allowed each taxpayer actually takes the form of a tax credit, rather than a deduction. A credit results in a greater tax break. In 1997, a tax credit of up to

1.2	THE ESTATE- AND GIFT-TAX TABLE

AMOUNT WITH RESPECT TO WHICH TENTATIVE TAX TO BE COMPUTED	THE TENTATIVE TAX IS
Under $10,000	18% of such amount
$10,000–19,999	$1,800 + 20% over $10,000
$20,000–39,999	$3,800 + 22% over $20,000
$250,000–499,999	$70,800 + 34% over $250,000
$500,000–749,999	$155,800 + 37% over $500,000
	[1998 tax credit bracket = $625,000 or 37%]
$750,000–999,999	$248,300 + 39% over $750,000
$1,000,000–1,249,999	$345,800 + 41% over $1,000,000
$1,250,000–1,499,999	$448,300 + 43% over $1,250,000
$1,500,000–1,999,999	$555,800 + 45% over $1,500,000
$2,000,000–2,499,999	$780,000 + 49% over $2,000,000
$2,500,000–2,999,999	$1,025,000 + 53% over $2,500,000
Over $3,000,000	$1,290,800 + 55% over $3,000,000

SOURCE: IRC

$192,800 was subtracted directly from the tentative tax due. By referring to the Gift and Estate Tax Table, TABLE 1.2, *above,* you will see that the tax on $600,000 is exactly $192,800, calculated as follows:

$600,000 taxable estate – $500,000 tax base = $100,000 excess
$100,000 excess over base x 0.37 tax rate = $37,000
$155,800 tax on base amount + $37,000 tax on excess = $192,800

By subtracting the tax credit of $192,800 from the tentative tax due of $192,800, the remaining tax due is zero.

The Taxpayer Relief Act of 1997 increases that $192,800 to $345,800 in the year 2006. The annual scheduled increases are shown in TABLE 1.3, *on the following page.*

I.3	ESTATE-TAX EXEMPTION INCREASES	
YEAR OF DECEDENT'S DEATH	**AMOUNT OF CREDIT**	**EFFECTIVE EXEMPTION AMOUNT**
1997	[$192,800]	$600,000
1998	[$202,050]	$625,000
1999	[$211,300]	$650,000
2000	[$220,550]	$675,000
2001	[$220,550]	$675,000
2002	[$229,800]	$700,000
2003	[$229,800]	$700,000
2004	[$287,300]	$850,000
2005	[$326,300]	$950,000
2006 and beyond	[$345,800]	$1,000,000

SOURCE: IRC

What happens to the next dollar of taxable assets in excess of $600,000? It is taxed at 37 percent, referred to as your *marginal tax bracket,* which operates the same as your personal-income-tax-bracket every April 15. You pay a flat dollar tax on a threshold amount, and then a fixed percentage of every dollar of taxable income above that threshold amount.

The marginal tax for estates and gifts peaks at 55 percent for taxable estates valued over $3,000,000. Most taxpayers will work for 40 or more years to accumulate their wealth. When they die, federal and state governments can take approximately half of that value within nine months, the time allowed for the payment of the estate tax. That is the equivalent of half a lifetime of hard work and stress wiped out by operation of the tax law. And yes, I did mention the state government.

Each state has its own version of an inheritance or estate tax. The federal estate-tax law allows the state to take a portion of the federal estate-tax for itself. However, some states do not limit their estate or inheritance tax to that federal share.

Daisy Crowder of Newport, Tennessee, complained

to her representatives in Congress that the tax could force her four children to liquidate the stoneworking and construction company that she and her husband, Charles, have built from scratch. They don't consider themselves wealthy, but the Internal Revenue Service (IRS) does. The Crowders are like most business owners, long on business value and short on liquid assets. "I started out living in little two-room shacks," Crowder said. "We work long hours still and struggle every day to pay our bills. It's not fair in the least to subject to estate taxes what's already been taxed in my lifetime." Fair or not, the IRS expects payment within nine months of death.

Is the situation hopeless? Hardly. Estate taxes are "essentially voluntary" according to George Cooper, professor of law at Columbia University. He believes that the only reasons the IRS collects any taxes at all are "taxpayer indifference" and "a lack of aggressiveness" by estate planners. According to Cooper, adequate loopholes exist to avoid the tax.

Whether you subscribe to Cooper's "voluntary-tax" theory or merely agree with Justice Hand's "informed" versus "uninformed" perception, you can reduce, and often eliminate, the bite.

SOLUTIONS

◆ **Decrease the size of your estate.** The *gross estate,* the starting point for the tax calculation, includes all the assets in which you have an ownership interest, such as real estate, stocks, bonds, mutual funds, life insurance proceeds or cash values, partnerships, closely held businesses, and personal property. These assets are generally included at their *fair market value*—what a willing buyer will pay to a willing seller, neither of whom is under a compulsion to act and each with a reasonable knowledge of the facts.

The lower the gross estate, the lower the tax. Does this mean you should simply give everything away right before you die? No. To start, Congress already thought of that angle and made the tax due at death a *unified estate and gift tax*. This means that the tax is levied against the combined total of the assets in your estate at your death *and* the gifts you made prior to your death. In other words, the tax-free $625,000 unified tax credit can be used during your lifetime and/or at your death.

◆ **Take advantage of the $10,000 annual gift-tax exclusion to help reduce your estate.** Each individual can, while still living, gift up to $10,000 each to an unlimited number of people each year, without those gifts counting against the unified tax credit or triggering a gift tax. Make certain you can comfortably part with the asset or income before you give it away. Generosity, like charity should begin at home. However, if you can live without the $10,000, whether from excess income or assets such as stocks, gifting will reduce the estate and can save a minimum of $.37 and a maximum of $.55 in tax for each $1.00 gifted. The higher your projected estate-tax bracket, the greater the tax savings. Not only are these annual gifts of $10,000 or less available in addition to the $625,000 estate- and gift-tax credit, they will also be adjusted for inflation after 1998, though only in increments of $1,000.

Does this mean you should never gift more than $10,000 per donee each year? No, it does not.

Consider gifting $625,000 of assets covered by the $192,800 unified credit if your assets permit. This technique will not only remove the assets from your taxable estate, but also the appreciation attributable to these assets between the date of the gift and the date of your death.

CASE STUDY

Ms. E. Nuff is a 70-year-old widow with an estate valued at $5,000,000, consisting mostly of blue-chip stocks and municipal bonds that give her an annual income of $200,000. If she needs only $50,000 per year to live comfortably, it would be safe to say that she has an income cushion. It might have made good sense to gift $625,000 of her assets to her heirs in 1997. She would have done well to select the assets likely to appreciate the most in the future. This would remove that appreciation from her estate. These would probably have been stocks that pay low or no dividends, leaving her the income-producing assets. For example, at 10 percent appreciation, that $625,000 would be worth $2,400,000 in less than 15 years. Assuming the tax rates stay the same, the extra $1,775,000 of growth in her estate ($2,400,000 – 625,000) would be taxed at 55 percent. That's an additional $980,000 in taxes. The gift of stocks equal to the unified credit of $625,000 in this case is used during the estate owner's lifetime to avoid paying $980,000 in estate taxes at death in 15 years.

Minimize the expenses, taxes, and losses to the estate. These items can all be claimed as deductions from the estate and will help reduce the tax bill. However, it is usually not sound policy to run up expenses as a way of reducing estate taxes. The expenses of the estate will be high enough that you won't want to add to the list, as you might be tempted to do on an income tax return.

It is an important objective in estate planning to be tax efficient in passing assets to the intended heirs. However, tax considerations should not come first. Jack Freeland, tax professor emeritus at the University of Florida College of Law, used to teach, "Never let the tax tail wag the dog." Determine how you want your assets to pass to your heirs. Then see if there are tax-efficient ways to make the transfers.

Use but don't overuse the marital deduction. The law allows a deduction from the gross estate for all of the assets passing to your surviving spouse. *Problem 5* explains how passing all your assets to your surviving spouse may unnecessarily increase the taxes due at the survivor's death.

Take advantage of the charitable deduction. The tax law allows you to deduct from your gross estate the full value of all assets passed to a qualifying charitable organization. The challenge is to benefit the charities you care about without impairing your family's ability to survive. These problems are addressed in Part 7.

RECOMMENDED ADVISERS

 Your **accountant** or **tax adviser** can counsel you on when to begin making gifts and how to value the assets in your estate.

 Your **attorney** will be responsible for creating and implementing an estate plan, including the drafting of wills and trusts and advising when to make gifts.

 Use a **planner** to compose a hypothetical probate, illustrating the projected taxes and expenses under various scenarios in the event of your death.

SEE ALSO

◆ **Problem 3:** *Insufficient Cash in the Estate.* Excessive taxes can put the estate in a cash bind.

◆ **Problem 4:** *What to Sell, What to Keep* about deciding which assets should be retained and which need to be sold to pay taxes and expenses.

◆ **Problem 8:** *What's It Worth: Valuation Problems with the IRS* to learn how disputes over the value of assets in the estate can create greater tax burdens.

PROBLEM 3

INSUFFICIENT CASH IN THE ESTATE

Why do so many estate owners die without providing adequate liquidity to pay their debts, expenses, and taxes? Easy answer. Estate owners usually position their assets to maximize their living needs, not their needs at death.

WHAT CAUSES THE liquidity squeeze? Illiquid assets, excessive expenses, and very little time to pay taxes.

Liquid assets are assets held in cash or those easily converted to cash. Cash in the mattress is the best example (although the worst investment). Savings accounts, money-market accounts, Treasury bills, and life insurance proceeds are highly liquid. Publicly traded stocks, bonds, mutual funds, and certificates of deposit (CDs) are easily convertible to cash, although commissions, penalties, and taxes may be generated by the conversion.

Much of the wealth in this country is *illiquid,* comprised of family businesses and real estate. The assets can certainly be sold. The problem is that they cannot be sold soon enough. Debts are due right away—probate expenses during the months or years in which the estate is being administered, and federal estate taxes at the end of nine months. Debbie Gillan learned about estate taxes the hard way. In 1984, she inherited 4,500 acres of her uncle's ranch in Hill County, Texas. The bad news was that the property generated a $1,700,000 estate-tax bill. In 1989, her father died and left her another 5,500 acres. This parcel added $565,000 to the tax bill. "I knew I'd probably go my entire life doing nothing more than paying off inheritance taxes," said Ms. Gillan. She mortgaged the farm to pay the taxes. Wayne Hayenga, a Texas A&M professor, believes that estate taxes could be due on up to 20 percent of the farms and ranches in Texas.

The second contributing factor to insufficient cash in the estate is that expenses during probate are almost invariably greater than the estate owner anticipated. For any estate large enough to pay taxes, it is wise to seek legal counsel, if for no other reason than to reduce the executor's personal liability for mismanagement of the estate. The executor will also have to open separate bank and often brokerage accounts for the estate, generating more fees and probably commissions. The sale of assets to pay debts and expenses often triggers commissions, as is usually the case with real estate, stocks, bonds, and some back-end-loaded mutual funds.

Debts must be paid before an estate can be closed. Debts include outstanding loans and personal bills, such as mortgage payments, electricity, automobile insurance, telephone, and tuition for college-age children. Let's not forget credit card debt—the entire balance due.

Third, taxes must be paid. The federal estate tax, due nine months from the date of death, is just the beginning. There are also state inheritance or estate taxes. (An inheritance tax is actually levied on the right to *receive* property, while the estate tax attaches to the right to *transfer* property.) The executor is likewise responsible for settling the unpaid income taxes of the decedent as well as the income taxes of the estate itself during the period of administration.

Throughout this difficult time, there is also an overriding consideration—the maintenance of the surviving family. While the executor is marshaling assets and determining what to sell and what to keep, the surviving spouse and children, if at home, need income to live.

Executors with family-owned businesses face additional challenges. Who will continue the business? If the decedent was a part-owner, what provisions have been made for the sale of that interest to the remaining owners? And how can the decedent's family continue to derive income from that business? Any one of these issues can cripple an estate and ruin a family's financial security.

Your executor will have a choice of four methods of paying estate taxes and expenses, listed here in order of desirability:

1 **Life insurance.** Payment from insurance proceeds purchased with estate taxes in mind.

2 **Cash.** Payment with cash assets from the estate.

3 **Sell assets.** Liquidate assets for cash.

4 **Borrow** from the government or a lender.

Each of these methods has advantages and disadvantages. The first alternative, using life insurance proceeds, is available only if you plan it in advance.

SOLUTIONS

◆ **When you walk through a hypothetical probate of your estate, see how much your death costs.** Take the initiative and meet with your attorney, accountant, and financial planner to anticipate how much cash will be needed, and match it with prospective sources.

◆ **Use discounted dollars to pay expenses and taxes, by purchasing life insurance.** Many smart planners have helped their clients fund future estate-tax liabilities by purchasing life insurance in the amount of the estimated taxes due. The cumulative premium expense is almost always less than the tax bill itself. Gene Kweeder of the Creative Financial Group in Newtown Square, Pennsylvania, says, "Life insurance buys flexibility." The estate owner can use the assets and income from these assets during his or her lifetime, because there will be adequate cash on hand at death to pay the bills.

◆ **As with all life insurance, you must qualify.** That means you must be insurable, and a physical exam will usually be required. If you wait until you know you have major health problems, it may be too late. Don't make assumptions about your insurability. An experienced life insurance professional will be able to find insurance for you, if it can be had.

◆ **When looking for an experienced life insurance agent, look for someone with decades of experience.** Also, ask about their industry credentials. A CLU (chartered life underwriter) designation identifies someone at least conscientious enough to pass a series of exams spanning the important areas of life insurance. You can locate CLUs by calling the American Society of CLU & ChFC [chartered financial consultant] in Bryn

Mawr, Pennsylvania. *(Check with the "Resources" appendix at the back of this book.)*

◆ **Make certain you do not own the insurance policy.** If you do, the entire proceeds will be included with your gross estate, magnifying the problem rather than solving it *(see Problem 10, Improper Beneficiaries and Owners).*

◆ **If insurance is not an option because of lack of insurability, pay expenses and taxes with cash assets in the estate.** This is the second most cost-efficient method. Use the cash in money-market, savings, and checking accounts to pay the bills of the estate. The reason I rank this approach below the use of life insurance is that it means the loss of the assets to the heirs. Consider typical estate expenses and taxes of $1,000,000 on a $2,500,000 taxable estate, which represents a 40 percent shrinkage ($1,000,000 ÷ $2,500,000). Those assets could have been used to provide income to the heirs or left to appreciate for future generations if the owner had provided life insurance of $1,000,000. The cost of life insurance is age dependent, so the premiums will vary greatly. A 50-year-old could buy permanent insurance for roughly $12,000 annually for a $1,000,000 policy, whereas a 70-year-old might pay three times that annual premium. However, the insurance is never as expensive as liquidating assets.

◆ **Sell assets, if necessary, to raise the cash to meet expenses and taxes.** Selling assets to raise money for taxes is an option, assuming the assets are liquid. There are disadvantages to this approach, however. First, the assets are lost to the heirs, as with the use of cash assets. Second, selling assets usually incurs an additional expense, such as a stock or bond commission, a real estate commission, or a CD penalty. Third, sale of the asset could result in a market loss. This occurs when stock, for example, has dropped in value but must be sold for liquidity. The executor does not always have the flexibility to wait for the best time to liquidate an asset (assuming one knew when that time would be). Fourth, the easiest assets to sell are often the best assets to retain. Families may be forced to sell blue-chip stocks because a business interest cannot be liquidated in time.

Again, life insurance will eliminate all of these disadvantages. If the estate owner is uninsurable, consider selling some of the assets when the time is right rather than waiting until they must be sold. This may mean when the stock market is at all-time highs or interest rates for long-term bonds are their lowest. Remember to consider the cost of capital gains taxes when making these decisions.

◆ **Borrow money to pay the expenses and taxes as a last resort.** Ms. Gillan, heir to the Hill County ranch mentioned earlier, chose the mortgage route. In 1991, Ms. Gillan and her husband Bart borrowed from the Federal Land Bank to pay off the taxes. However, by that time, the original $1.7 million tax bill had generated an additional $840,000 in interest expense. And that is the primary disadvantage of borrowing—the cost of the interest.

◆ **Check to see if the estate qualifies for a reduced interest rate.** If you must borrow, check to see if part or all of the tax bill qualifies for special installment-payment treatment under Section 6166 of the IRC. If a closely held business interest of the decedent exceeds 35 percent of the adjusted gross estate and the decedent owned a large enough share of the business to meet the IRS's guidelines (all of a sole proprietorship, or 20 percent of a partnership or corporation with 15 or fewer other owners), the estate could apply for a 2 percent interest rate on that portion of the tax bill attributable to the first $1,000,000 in valuation of the business interest. However, the IRS will have a lien on your property. Ask your accountant if you qualify. The provisions are complex and demand strict adherence to the guidelines.

Mr. Rich is 70 years old and a widower. His assets are primarily real estate, which he wants to keep in his family. His financial planner has advised him that his estate-tax bill will be $1,000,000. He wants to continue to own and enjoy the land. He has asked what would be the comparative costs of the four methods of paying this $1,000,000 tax bill. He asked his advisers to assume his death will be no more than 15 years from today. He also asked them to assume he could borrow the $1,000,000 for 10 years at 8 percent interest. The expenses of liquidation assume real estate commissions and closing costs of 10 percent (see TABLE 1.4, below).

If you can afford the premiums—and not everyone can—the life insurance has the lowest cost over 15 years, the approximate life expectancy of Mr. Rich. Some types of policies, such as universal or variable life, have the potential of accumulating sufficient cash value reserves to make further premiums beyond 15 years unnecessary. The estate owner must be insurable, and that requires evidence of insurability, usually by a physical exam.

If you are suspicious of using life insurance, try to look at the premiums as advanced funding of the tax. No one likes paying life insurance premiums, but intelligent estate owners know a good buy when they see it. As you see in TABLE 1.4 below, $546,825 is better than $1,000,000—if you qualify and can pay the premium.

1.4	ESTATE TAX ALTERNATIVES		
METHODS	SINGLE PAYMENT	ANNUAL PAYMENT	TOTAL PAYMENTS
Insurance		$36,455	$546,825
Cash	$1,000,000	$0	$1,000,000
Liquidate	$1,100,000	$0	$1,100,000
Borrow		$145,593	$1,455,931

Your **attorney** should be involved in any estate-planning recommendations raised by financial planners or life insurance agents.

Use your **planner/life insurance agent** to estimate taxes and expenses from a hypothetical probate and to fund the total due using life insurance. However, keep your attorney involved in the process.

SEE ALSO

- **Problem 2:** *The Estate-Tax Bite.*
- **Problem 10:** *Improper Beneficiaries and Owners* to see how improper ownership of life insurance used to pay estate taxes can actually increase taxes.
- **Problem 12:** *Excessive Expenses and Delays at Death* to find out how to avoid the unnecessary.

PROBLEM 4

WHAT TO SELL, WHAT TO KEEP

Estate owners usually decide what to own and how to own it in response to their lifetime wants and needs. Death, however, has a way of restructuring priorities and relationships, especially for the heirs. Estate planning is about reconciling needs before and after death.

WHEN JOE ROBBIE, the founder of the Miami Dolphins, died in January 1990, Dan Paul, attorney for Robbie's wife, worried that part of the team might have to be sold to pay estate taxes, then estimated to exceed $26 million. In fact, Robbie's heirs were forced to sell the entire team and half of Joe Robbie Stadium just to pay the $47 million tax bill within the required nine months after his death.

Joe Robbie's children, Tim, Janet, and Dan, were appointed by their father to serve as trustees of the estate. They ultimately benefited from Mr. Robbie's business acumen. However, his estate planning cost them a bundle. It's likely that the biggest beneficiary was Wayne Huizenga—a south Florida businessman known for his creations, Waste Management and Blockbuster Video—who was able to take advantage of the executor's dilemma by coming up with the cash to buy the Dolphins. Huizenga positioned himself for this outcome by buying 15 percent of the team and 50 percent of the stadium just after Joe Robbie's death. As part of the deal, he bought the right to match any other offers for the team before it was sold. He exercised that right. One man's misfortune became another man's fortune.

The story is instructive not just because of the magnitude of the tax, although that is certainly staggering. It points out the dilemma facing so many executors or trustees—greater demands for cash, valuable but troublesome assets, and heirs with diverse objectives. This dilemma is as likely to surface with a $1 million estate as a $100 million estate. The larger ones are just more interesting to read about.

Closely held businesses and real estate trigger most of an executor's asset-selection problems. There is probably no favorable solution for illiquid real estate other than a forced sale or a mortgage. Part 3 shows you the techniques for planning the succession of ownership in a business, and solving the liquidity need at the same time.

A different set of challenges faces the executor torn between the needs of different classes of heirs with conflicting objectives. The executor is often placed in the unenviable position of having to select assets for distribution to the spouse and children without guidelines from the decedent. For example, how would the executor decide who should receive a cherished but unsalable vacation home in an estate where there are barely sufficient assets to provide an adequate income to the surviving spouse?

These types of questions often create friction among family members and sometimes even litigation. Often the executor is forced to decide how to distribute stocks and bonds of varying quality. An aging parent may be content with a portfolio of bonds for income purposes and some stock for growth. The surviving spouse may share the penchant for safety and income. However, the children may prefer a portfolio of technology stocks. These problems can arise when trusts are created without including clear directives to the trustees regarding the trustor's priorities.

SOLUTIONS

◆ **Tell your executor exactly what you intend.** Spell out your preferences in the will or a separate document that can be authenticated as yours. For example, if your surviving spouse's needs are to be considered first, then say so.

◆ **Give your executor and trustee broad authority.** Give your executor the power to make decisions about investments and distribution issues you did not anticipate or about which you were unwilling to decide. This often arises when there are income needs of survivors but the assets are not income producing. If you have created a *trust,* a legal entity to manage money or assets, the person empowered to carry out your intentions is called a *trustee.*

◆ **Choose an executor you believe will follow the dictates of your will and trusts.** Bernard "Bud" D'Avella, a business and estate-planning attorney with the law firm of Hannoch & Weissman in Roseland, New Jersey, tends to favor friends and advisers as executors and trustees because they are more personal, more likely to know what the decedent cared about, and more willing to interpret the documents in a manner consistent with their perception of what the decedent would want.

◆ **Discuss your estate plan with your family now.** This gives your heirs the opportunity to make plans of their own and to ask your motivation in making certain bequests. An honest sharing of the plan should help thwart disagreements after your death.

◆ **Specify who is to receive special assets.** If you have assets you want to pass to specific heirs or be retained in the family, you must make provisions in your will or trust. Personal property, such as rings and other jewelry, automobiles, antiques, and paintings should be identified and itemized if you want them to pass to a specific person.

CASE STUDY

Under the terms of Mr. Welloff's will, his second wife, Mrs. Welloff, is entitled to receive half of Mr. Welloff's assets, which are comprised of equal amounts of income-producing bonds, and real estate in the form of a home he purchased prior to their marriage. Mrs. Welloff lives in the home, but is without a source of income except her Social Security and the interest from the bonds. The children want the bonds, because they live in different sections of the country and don't want to be bothered with the house. What should the executor do?

Mr. Welloff has left his executor and his family in a no-win situation. The executor can't make the decision without one party suffering. It would have been better if Mr. Welloff had left specific instructions for his executor as to the actual division of his assets. Had he reviewed his plan before his death, he might even have provided greater assets, such as through life insurance.

Keep your estate plan current. Make sure to review your plan at least annually and whenever there is a change in your family circumstances, as spelled out in the "Solutions" section of *Problem 1*. Many of the problems in estates are caused by outdated wills. Also, federal tax laws and state laws governing estates change from time to time. Your attorney should be aware of these changes, and reviewing the will with the attorney should keep your documents current.

Put yourself in your executor's shoes. The best way to anticipate problems you are leaving for your executor is to assume you have one month to live and review your situation from that perspective.

RECOMMENDED ADVISERS

Let your **planner** update your hypothetical probate each year as part of the review process. This will keep you abreast of law changes and identify trouble spots, and shouldn't cost too much.

Have your **attorney** review your plan annually.

SEE ALSO

◆ **Problem 1:** *Lack of a Current Estate Plan* to review the circumstances that should trigger a will update.

◆ **Problem 3:** *Insufficient Cash in the Estate* for a list of the problems that generate liquidity troubles.

PROBLEM 5

EXCESSIVE JOINT OWNERSHIP WITH SPOUSES

The estate-tax marital deduction makes it possible to delay estate taxes. Instead of imposing a tax at the death of each spouse, Congress introduced the marital deduction in order to effectively defer the tax bite until the second spouse dies. The deferral, however, could result in a larger tax bill at that second death. An alternative is to use trusts to maximize both the marital deduction and the unified credit, discussed in *Problem 2*.

THE RATIONALE FOR the marital deduction is both sound and straightforward. Congress believed that the imposition of the estate tax should not interfere with the ability of a husband or wife to accumulate adequate assets to care for themselves.

The deferral is not automatic. The transfer must qualify; that is, assets must pass outright to the surviving spouse or in trust for the surviving spouse with sufficient rights to either the income or assets to satisfy the IRS that the spouse enjoys the use of the assets. These are legal requirements to be satisfied by your attorney when drafting your will and trust.

One of the ways to ensure the passage of an asset to your spouse is to own it as *joint tenants with right of survivorship*. This is how most married couples own their homes. At the death of one joint owner, the property automatically passes to the survivor, by operation of law; the property does not go through *probate*, the legal process for the marshaling and distribution of assets after an individual's death.

Many estate owners, especially with long-standing marriages, own almost all of their assets as joint tenants with right of survivorship. While this shows great confidence in the relationship, it often increases the estate-tax bill at the death of the surviving spouse.

CASE STUDY

Walter and Sharon Kontent, husband and wife, have a net worth of $1,700,000, comprised of a $500,000 home and a $1,200,000 stock portfolio. Everything is jointly owned with rights of survivorship. Walter died in 1998. All of the assets pass automatically to Sharon. No probate, no hassle, no estate tax, no unified credit. Wait! No unified credit? Remember the discussion in *Problem 2,* that every estate owner was entitled to pass $625,000 of assets in 1998 ($1,000,000 in 2006) tax free because of the unified tax credit *(see* TABLE 1.5, *at right).*

When Walter died, his survivor received all of the assets by operation of law, and the full $1,700,000 qualified for the marital deduction. There was no need to apply the unified tax credit because all of the assets

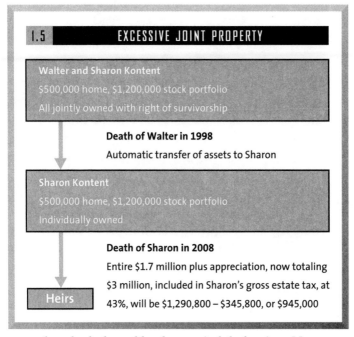

1.5   EXCESSIVE JOINT PROPERTY

Walter and Sharon Kontent
$500,000 home, $1,200,000 stock portfolio
All jointly owned with right of survivorship

Death of Walter in 1998
Automatic transfer of assets to Sharon

Sharon Kontent
$500,000 home, $1,200,000 stock portfolio
Individually owned

Death of Sharon in 2008
Entire $1.7 million plus appreciation, now totaling
$3 million, included in Sharon's gross estate tax, at
43%, will be $1,290,800 – $345,800, or $945,000

Heirs

were already sheltered by the marital deduction. Note, there is no dollar limit on the marital deduction.

So far, so good. Now assume that over the next 10 years, the $1,700,000 that Sharon inherited by virtue of the jointly owned property appreciates to $3,000,000, at which point she dies without having remarried. If we ignore expenses for the moment, the tentative tax at Sharon's death will be $1,290,800, or about 43 percent of the $3,000,000. By the year 2007, Sharon's unified credit will have escalated to $345,800 (sheltering $1,000,000 of assets); *(see Table 1.2)*. The tax bill will be $945,000 ($1,290,880 – $345,800).

In effect, Walter's unified credit of $192,800 was wasted, because the marital deduction reduced the taxable estate to zero. With a taxable estate of zero, there is no tentative tax to apply the credit against. And, because Sharon received the entire $1,700,000, the entire $3,000,000 is included in her estate for tax purposes.

What could Walter and Sharon have done differently?

SOLUTIONS

◆ **Keep assets equal to the unified credit out of the surviving spouse's hands.** Strictly from a tax standpoint, the perfectly planned estate would pass an amount equal to the assets sheltered by the maximum unified credit into a unified-credit trust ($625,000 in 1998, increasing to $1,000,000 in 2006 and thereafter). The income from that trust would be available for the surviving spouse during his or her lifetime. All the assets in excess of that unified-credit dollar amount would pass directly into a separate marital trust for the spouse. At the second spouse's death, the assets in the unified-credit trust could then pass to the children or other intended heirs. This would effectively remove these assets in the unified-credit trust from the estate of the second to die. Such a trust is also called a *bypass trust.*

What is the rationale for keeping $625,000 outside the provisions of the marital deduction in the Kontent estate plan? If, when Walter died, all of the property was not in their joint names, Walter could have availed himself of the unified credit and passed $625,000 into a unified-credit or bypass trust for Sharon's benefit during her lifetime. The remaining $1,075,000 could have passed to Sharon outright or under a *marital deduction trust.* Even if all of the appreciation of the $1,100,000 is in Sharon's assets, she will only have $2,400,000 in her estate at her death. This is obviously approximately $625,000 less than under the joint-ownership scenario. Follow the graphical depiction of the difference.

As **TABLE 1.6**, *at right,* illustrates, the tax now due at Sharon's subsequent death is $631,000. Under the "inherit-it-all" scenario, her tax was $945,000. The savings to the heirs is $314,000. Would a $314,000 savings be worth 5 to 10 hours of your time and an attorney's fee of $2,000 to $5,000? If you don't think so, you should check with your children. Maybe they'll pay the fees, since otherwise they are the ultimate losers.

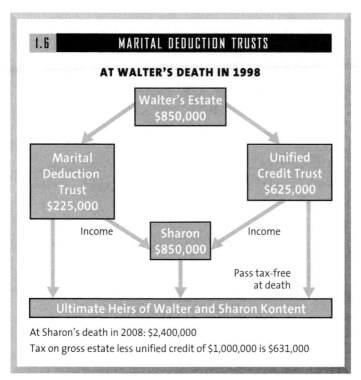

1.6   MARITAL DEDUCTION TRUSTS

AT WALTER'S DEATH IN 1998

Walter's Estate
$850,000

Marital Deduction Trust $225,000

Unified Credit Trust $625,000

Income

Sharon $850,000

Income

Pass tax-free at death

Ultimate Heirs of Walter and Sharon Kontent

At Sharon's death in 2008: $2,400,000

Tax on gross estate less unified credit of $1,000,000 is $631,000

You should know that maximizing the marital deduction doesn't motivate everyone. When Robert Magness, the founder of TCI, the telecommunications giant in Colorado, died recently with a net worth in excess of $1 billion, some experts were surprised to learn that his second wife, Sharon, had been left only $20 million and several properties outright. Although she was also the income beneficiary of a trust valued at $15 million, the bulk of the estate passed to his sons, Gary and Tim. He could have deferred the tax at his death until Sharon's death. What could he have been thinking about? He was probably thinking about Professor Freeland's advice in *Problem 2*. The tax tail did not wag Mr. Magness's dog. He distributed the assets the way he wanted, and let taxes take a back seat to his intentions.

◆ **Design current wills to conform to the Taxpayer Relief Act of 1997.** Have your will specify that the amount to pass into trust is to be the maximum allowed under the unified-credit provisions existing at the time of your death. This will maximize the deduction to conform to the increased credit as it rises from $625,000 to $1,000,000. These subtle phrasings are the very reason you need an attorney drafting your wills and trusts. Don't write your own will with a kit from the bookstore or from some paralegal over the Internet. You've worked too hard to risk botching the document.

◆ **Use trusts in the marital-deduction planning.** What makes the marital-deduction planning work? The availability of trusts. More than likely, you feel comfortable that the assets you have in your estate are sufficient to generate an income for your surviving spouse, but maybe not so comfortable that you'd be willing to give away between $625,000 and $1,000,000 (the unified-credit amount) until after your spouse's death. That is the rationale for the nonmarital, unified-credit trust. The surviving spouse can enjoy the income from the trust during his or her lifetime.

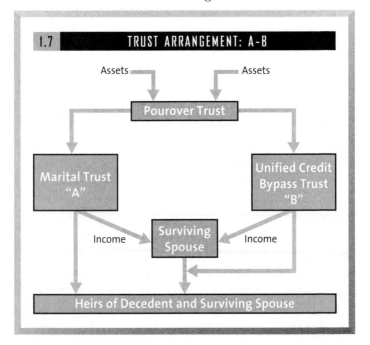

1.7 TRUST ARRANGEMENT: A-B

Assets ---→ ←--- Assets

Pourover Trust

Marital Trust "A"

Unified Credit Bypass Trust "B"

Surviving Spouse

Income ←   → Income

Heirs of Decedent and Surviving Spouse

There are two marital-deduction trust alternatives that can provide income to your surviving spouse and still reduce estate taxes by utilizing both the marital deduction and the unified credit: 1) the power-of-appointment type of trust, and 2) the QTIP trust. Attorneys and planners call these *A-B trusts* and *A-B-Q trusts*. The letters are just symbols for the trusts. Look at the illustration of the A-B trust, TABLE 1.7, *at left*.

In both the A-B and A-B-Q trusts, the will and trust documents provide that all your assets first pass into a *pourover trust*. This trust can collect all manner of assets, such as life insurance proceeds, inheritances, and retirement-plan monies. The trust is like a collection basket for all the decedent's assets until they are to be distributed. The pourover trust then apportions the assets into the "A" marital trust and the "B" unified-credit or bypass trust. The assets that "bypass" the surviving spouse's estate are equal to the unified credit ($625,000 in 1998, etc.; *see Table 1.3*). Everything else passes into the A trust for the spouse, who receives the income for life and a limited power to take some of the trust principal each year: $5,000 or 5 percent of the trust principal.

◆ **Break joint tenancies with your spouse if the marital deduction is overutilized.** If you have sufficient assets to incur the estate tax and if you want to minimize taxes, it is important that not all of your assets be jointly held. Some of the assets need to be individually owned so that they can pass to the nonmarital bypass or unified-credit trust.

◆ **Use the A-B trust for maximum control to the surviving spouse.** The A-B trust arrangement can allow the surviving spouse to dispose of the assets at his or her death as desired. This includes passing the assets to the children, the church, or any other beneficiary the spouse selects, including a new spouse. If you feel this much power is not desirable, then you could opt for the Q trust (*see* TABLE 1.8, *on the following page*).

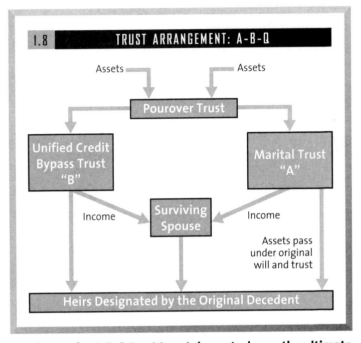

1.8   TRUST ARRANGEMENT: A-B-Q

Assets — [Assets

Pourover Trust

Unified Credit Bypass Trust "B"

Marital Trust "A"

Surviving Spouse

Income   Income

Assets pass under original will and trust

Heirs Designated by the Original Decedent

◆ **Use the A-B-Q trust to retain control over the ultimate beneficiaries of the trust.** The Q trust gets its label from the abbreviation "QTIP," which has nothing to do with cotton swabs on sticks. QTIP stands for qualified terminable interest property. Under a QTIP trust, the income from the trust is paid to the surviving spouse during his or her lifetime. If your spouse needs more money, you can provide for a power of invasion, which allows the income beneficiary to take some of the principal, subject to limits you determine in the document. However, you decide who the ultimate beneficiaries will be. You could, however, allow your surviving spouse to apportion the assets among the beneficiaries you have selected.

◆ **Consult an attorney if you live in a community-property state.** In Arizona, California, Idaho, Louisiana, Nevada, New Mexico, Texas, Washington, and Wisconsin, assets acquired during a marriage are presumed to have been acquired equally, so that half of the value of each asset is included in each spouse's estate for tax purposes. If you live in these states, find an attorney who specializes in estate planning.

◆ **Remember, your intentions first, tax considerations second.** With all the discussion about minimizing taxes at both deaths, it is easy to forget that the primary purpose of financial and estate planning is not to minimize taxes, it is to enjoy your accumulated wealth during your lifetime and to pass it to those you love at your death. If you can accomplish that and save taxes too, all the better.

◆ **Realistically assess the money-management skills of your heirs.** Many people are poor money managers. If your heirs are not financially savvy or responsible, consider a trust for wealth-preservation purposes. Few financial losses are as tragic as watching hard-earned assets being wasted by well-intentioned but incompetent heirs. A money manager of trust assets can avoid this tragedy with your money, as outlined in *Problem 29*.

◆ **If trusts make sense for you, do your homework.** In selecting a trustee, one alternative is someone you know and trust already, such as a relative with investment experience. If no such person appeals to you, consider an institutional trust department, such as a local bank or trust company. Interview the potential trust officers. Find out about their experience and the institution's investment track record, as well as their fee structure. This information is available from them if you ask for it. Remember, there are more alternatives than exist in your own hometown. Many stock-brokerage firms have trust departments, as do some insurance companies. Put yourself in your heirs' shoes by understanding that rapport with the trust officers is helpful for inexperienced heirs. Choose trust officers you believe they can work with.

RECOMMENDED ADVISERS

You should use an **attorney** to help you decide whether to employ one of the trust arrangements to maximize the use of the unified credit, and to draft wills and trusts to implement any changes in joint ownership.

A **planner** can show you tax ramifications of different ownership scenarios.

SEE ALSO

◆ **Problem 29:** *Professional Money Management* for help in finding and selecting people to help manage your money, during your lifetime and after your death.

PROBLEM 6

INSUFFICIENT INCOME FOR THE HEIRS

Part of your estate planning should consider the income-producing potential of your assets. If your wealth is not of a type that can generate income for your survivors, you need to plan for conversion of the assets before your death.

NET WORTH TRANSLATES to income only to the extent that your assets are income producing. A $2 million home may make its occupants feel wealthy, but if they have no source of income they won't feel well-off for long. This false sense of wealth and security can be easy to maintain as long as the primary wage earner is alive. However, at that person's death, a shortage of income can wreak havoc on an estate.

There are two primary circumstances in which people with valuable assets leave their beneficiaries with too little income. The first is the problem of non-income-producing assets.

CASE STUDY

Dr. I. M. Rich, widowed with six children, lives in a home valued at $1,000,000, has a medical practice valued at $500,000, a summer home at the beach valued at $500,000, and another piece of investment real estate valued at $2,000,000 on her financial statement. That piece is held in a partnership with seven other doctors who have no intention of selling any of the property for years to come.

On paper (including the paper her estate tax return is printed on), Dr. Rich is worth $4,000,000. The estate taxes associated with these assets will be approximately $1,500,000, depending on the expenses and other deductions from the estate. Where is Dr. Rich's executor going to raise the cash to pay the taxes and provide enough income to feed, educate, and care for her children? If the executor can't sell the $2,000,000 real estate investment, Dr. Rich will have to sell the practice and both homes just to pay the IRS, and even then, will only have $500,000 remaining to provide income.

How much income will $500,000 provide? The answer depends on how that money is invested, of course. However, for planning purposes, you should use a conservative assumption for the interest rate: say 6 percent. Why be conservative? Interest rates fluctuate. (We have a solution for that, too. You should spread your fixed-income investments over multiple maturities to avoid being caught in a very low interest rate environment with all of your money maturing at the same time.)

As you can imagine, Dr. Rich didn't accumulate her real estate assets on a $30,000 income ($500,000 x 6 percent). The executor is going to have to dramatically reduce the children's standard of living, or start using the principal of $500,000 as well as the interest. This will ultimately exhaust the entire $500,000, depending on how much income the children actually consume.

The pressure on the purse of the survivors can be increased by estate taxes, as in the case of Dr. Rich, or because of the lack of liquidity of a closely held business or farm.

CASE STUDY

Mr. Loner owned a very popular restaurant when he fell over dead one Saturday during the busiest hour of the evening. He loved the business. You could see it in his devotion to details, from the decor to the layout of the seafood platter. His hand was in every aspect of the restaurant; he was the only one who knew the business from kitchen to cash register.

The fact that he had sold or borrowed against everything else he owned to open the restaurant made his wife very unhappy. His death reconfirmed every fear she had felt along the way. No one even knew where the business did its banking. The Loners' only source of income had been what he pulled out of the register, usually in cash and poorly accounted for.

Mrs. Loner found out the hard way why the restaurant business is the most difficult business in the world, as she tried unsuccessfully to keep the doors open while she searched for a buyer. The bank finally forced her to give up the assets of the business to avoid bankruptcy. The only asset she escaped with, for all of Mr. Loner's efforts, were autographed pictures of celebrities once pampered by her husband. The untimely death of a sole proprietor often creates such casualties.

The second situation where substantial assets do not always equate to sufficient income is where the surviving spouse and/or children live beyond their means.

Death of a spouse or partner invariably changes one's *style* of living, and frequently the *standard* of living. Too often, the survivor has not been involved in the family's finances and investments. This is especially true of women in their 50s, 60s, and 70s. Preceding the baby boomers into late middle age and retirement, these women are far more likely to outlive their husbands. Premature death of a husband often catches the wife hopelessly unprepared to deal with either household or Treasury bills. Even the wealthy hate to plan for their premature death.

Paradoxically, the U.S. Trust Company survey found that the most prevalent value associated with being wealthy by those who were considered wealthy was the ability to give their children advantages that they did not have growing up. Being able to live comfortably was second. There are some steps you can take toward both these goals, attaining them more completely than someone who has more money than you do.

SOLUTIONS

◆ **Do an analysis of the capital needs of your heirs at your death.** Professional insurance agents have computer programs that will perform a capital needs analysis (CNA). It will quantify the cash requirements of your estate and survivors, and then reduce those cash and income requirements by the amount of capital and income you already possess. The difference can be made up by purchasing insurance or repositioning your assets into vehicles that generate greater income. The CNA computer programs likewise consider the impact of inflation and the time cost of money.

SAMPLE CAPITAL-NEEDS ANALYSIS

Juan Day owns a coffee shop worth $500,000 according to his accountant. However, Juan is worried because a national coffee franchise just opened an outlet across the street. He personally cosigned $250,000 in loans to the business for equipment and working capital. At 52, Juan and his wife Soma had hoped to begin putting money aside for retirement. He once thought they would sell the business in another 10 years to help fund their retirement. Now he realizes that if he dies, Soma would be fortunate to sell the business for enough to pay off the $250,000 in loans. He no longer believes Soma could continue the business if he died.

They have three children almost in college and expect to fund their tuition from his earnings from the business. He is concerned about what will happen if he dies prematurely. Juan told his planner he would want to have sufficient cash on hand to pay final expenses of $10,000, pay outstanding bills of $15,000, pay off his mortgage of $150,000, and provide $40,000 for each of the three children for college education expenses. He would like Soma to receive $74,200 annually—the cash they currently take home from the coffee shop. He has a $6,000 income from a pension plan in the military. In addition to the business, the Days have $175,000 in investments, a $65,000 IRA and $50,000 of life insurance.

Juan and Soma's financial planner presented them with the following CNA from the computer.

Capital-Needs Analysis

SURVIVOR'S CASH NEEDS	
Final expenses	$10,000
Children's education	$120,000
Bills and debts	$15,000
Home mortgage	$150,000
Total Cash Needed	$295,000

SURVIVOR'S INCOME NEEDS	
Income needed	$74,200
Minus existing income	$6,000
Net income needed	$68,200
Capital Necessary to Produce Income	$797,574

AVAILABLE CAPITAL	
Investments, savings	$175,000
Retirement assets	$65,000
Liquidation of business interest	$0
Life insurance proceeds	$50,000
Net Capital	$290,000

SUMMARY

Required for cash needs	$295,000
Required for income needs	$797,574
Total required capital	$1,092,574
Less available capital	$290,000
NET CAPITAL NEEDED	$802,574

Juan is shocked by the shortfall, but he realizes he was the source of the information his planner used and that the objectives were reasonable. His planner shows Juan several alternatives to funding the shortfall.

There are three ways to fund the difference between what you want to provide at your death and what you have:

1 *Create more assets.* This is a desirable goal, but one that will take time.

2 *Reduce your objectives.* This means a reduction in living standards for your heirs, but it may be your only choice.

3 *Buy life insurance.* This is the usual approach to bridging the gap between what you have and want to have, especially if you are still building your estate. If the difference is temporary or the need less than 15 years, buy *term insurance,* which is strictly indemnification against premature death. If the need for insurance is permanent or will last longer than 15 years, buy permanent insurance, such as whole life, universal life, or variable life.

◆ **Find a real professional life underwriter—one with the designations and experience in the business.** There is one recognized professional designation in the life insurance field—CLU (chartered life underwriter). The designation is life- and health-insurance oriented. A CFP (certified financial planner) or a ChFC (chartered financial consultant) may also have some insurance experience, although the training is more financial-planning oriented.

◆ **Become money-wise before you have to.** Don't allow either yourself or your spouse to monopolize the finances and investments. "Having it all in your head" is a great disservice to your partner and your children. If you are already "stuck" with the total responsibility for the finances and investments—whether by divorce, death, or inheritance—get help.

◆ **Find a financial planner to help with your budgeting, financial planning, and investing.** Read *Problem 26* and the book *Smart Questions to Ask Your Financial Advisers,* by Lynn Brenner. Concentrate on finding the most qualified individual or firm, and not on the form of compensation. There are great commissioned planners and inexperienced fee planners, and vice versa.

◆ **Plan for the disposition of family farms and closely held businesses now,** before death starts the clock ticking on an impossible timetable likely to result in a forced sale or refinancing. Tony Hendricks of Marion County, Oregon, learned about those pressures years ago. His parents died within several years of each other in the 1970s. Each death triggered an estate tax of $150,000. The IRS gave Hendricks 15 years to pay off the tax bill, at $22,000 a year. However, this was an onerous payment for an 1,100-acre, family-run farm. A bad crop in 1982 forced Hendricks to sell 105 acres in a bank foreclosure.

When farms and businesses are run by one spouse without the other, rarely can the surviving spouse step into the decedent's shoes. If it was that easy to run your family business, there would be so many people doing it that the competition would bury you before the IRS did.

RECOMMENDED ADVISERS

 Have your **attorney** draft documents that will best implement the plans to provide the necessary income for your heirs.

Use your **planner** to provide a CNA and a financial plan.

SEE ALSO

◆ **Problems 18–25** found in Part 3, "Business Succession Problems." They deal with the strategies for trading the value of an illiquid business for cash or a stream of income.

PROBLEM 7

"TAXFLATION" AND RAPIDLY APPRECIATING ASSETS

Inflation is reputed to be the worst economic evil in America. The mere thought of this monetary virus sends chills down the spine of aging adults and fiscal watchdogs. And, to be sure, inflation can erode your purchasing power. It has companions, though, whose presence can bring even more havoc to your life and your estate: "taxflation" and rapidly appreciating assets.

WHAT IS *TAXFLATION?* Donald F. Cady, author of an annual reference book for estate and financial planners entitled *Field Guide to Estate Planning, Business Planning, and Employee Benefits,* uses the term to describe the combined impact of "increased living standards, inflation, and progressive taxation."

Most Americans increase their standard of living with each increase in income. Some increase the standard beyond their income. Bigger homes, bigger cars, expensive jewelry, and vacation homes are the most conspicuous examples.

Inflation is the rise in the cost of goods and services over time. On January 1, 1998, the U.S. Postal Service charged $.32 to deliver a first-class letter. In 1976, it cost $.13. The price for the same service has almost tripled in two decades. According to the *Chase Investment Performance Digest,* since 1970, inflation has averaged approximately 5.5 percent. Just because inflation has been low for the last three years, one shouldn't assume it will always be low. The price of a loaf of bread, an orange, automobile, and a house are all subject to the eroding power of inflation.

Inflation is most damaging to older Americans living on fixed incomes. Rising prices are especially painful for this group because they frequently are not in a position to earn additional income to supplement their Social Security, pensions, and savings. Many corporate retirement plans were "defined-benefit plans," until the popularity of 401(k) plans became apparent in the late 1980s. A *defined-benefit plan* is a type of pension plan that promises to pay the employee a fixed percentage of salary for the employee's lifetime. A retiree who had earned a salary of $50,000 and was entitled to a 50 percent pension benefit would receive $25,000 a year. No provision was made to increase the benefit to keep up with the inflationary rises in the prices of groceries or utilities.

CASE STUDY

Mr. Pride retired as a manager in 1975 when he turned 65. He felt secure with his defined-pension benefit of $1,000 a month. However, by 1998 that same $1,000 was worth less than $350 in purchasing power, because of inflation.

To be sure, Social Security benefits are indexed annually to increase with the general rise in the rate of inflation. In July 1980, benefits increased 14.3 percent; in July of the following year, 11.2 percent. However, in recent years, the adjustments have been in the 2 to 3 percent range annually.

If you are a late baby boomer, the entire discussion of Social Security may become academic (unless you are supporting your parents). By the time you reach retirement age, there will probably be some type of reduction, such as restricting eligibility for Social Secu-

1.9	INCOME TAX TABLE 1998				
	SINGLE TAXPAYER			JOINT RETURN	
TAXABLE INCOME TAX INCOME	TAX ON BASE	% ON EXCESS		TAX ON BASE	% ON EXCESS
$20,600	$3,090	15		$3,090	15
$24,650	$3,698	28		$3,698	15
$41,200	$8,332	28		$6,180	28
$85,350	$21,462	31		$18,542	28
$99,600	$25,880	31		$22,532	31
$124,650	$33,645	36		$30,298	31
$151,750	$43,401	36		$38,699	36
$271,050	$86,349	39.6		$81,647	39.6

rity benefits to senior citizens with assets or income above a specified threshold. You should assume that if you are in a position to worry about wealth preservation, you will probably not qualify for Social Security retirement income and therefore cannot look in that direction for any help because of indexing.

Progressive taxation is more insidious. Some commentators call it *tax bracket creep,* the tendency to pay higher marginal income or estate taxes as your income or assets increase. The principle was easy to see in the tax tables. In *Problem 2, Table 1.2,* you saw that the marginal estate-tax rate ran from 18 percent to 55 percent. As you know, the marginal income tax rate likewise goes up as your income increases (*see* TABLE 1.9, *above*).

Despite some changes in the Taxpayer Relief Act of 1997 aimed at helping lower-bracket taxpayers, tax bracket creep is still with us. The more money individuals, estates, and corporations earn, the higher percentage they pay in taxes.

Rapidly appreciating assets compound the problem of taxflation.

CASE STUDY

Mr. Trees owns orange groves in southern California. By Midwestern standards, it would be considered a small grove. However, the price of land in California is considerably higher than in Iowa. His entire estate is valued at $2.625 million, primarily because of the groves. He doesn't consider himself to be wealthy. In fact, his annual income averages only $75,000. However, real estate values—and taxes right behind them—are beginning to increase again.

The tax on his $2 million taxable estate in 1998 (after applying the $625,000 unified credit) would be $780,800. If Trees's groves appreciate at the rate of 6 percent each year, his estate will grow from $2.6 million to $4.6 million in 10 years, to $8.34 million in 20 years, and to $15 million in 30 years. The increase in the unified estate and gift-tax credit from $625,000 to $1 million over the next decade won't help very much.

The 1998 tax shrinkage in Trees's estate would be 30 percent ($780,800 ÷ $2 million). In 10 years, the tax on $3.6 million ($4.6 million − $1 million tax credit) will be $1,620,800. This represents a 35 percent shrinkage. The tax on $14 million in 10 years is $6.79 million, or a 45 percent shrinkage. That increase from 30 percent to 45 percent is taxflation on rapidly appreciating assets.

What if the source of one's wealth is not gradually appreciating real estate but stock in a publicly traded company, such as Microsoft, Intel, or Cisco Systems? Silicon Valley has spawned an entire generation of millionaires, and it is not the only place to do so. An Omaha, Nebraska, guru has done the same for his stockholders: Warren Buffett of Berkshire Hathaway. On a split-adjusted basis, a share of Intel could have been purchased for 10 percent of its current price only five years ago. Berkshire Hathaway has appreciated from a price of $1,000 a share to over $65,000 a share in 30 years.

The explosion in the value of specific stocks reflects (although it does not mirror) the increase in the value of the stock market as a whole. Many middle-class families have been lifted into the ranks of the wealthy on the tidal rises of the market. (As Warren Buffett has commented, while the tide is in, everyone in the water rises with it. However, when the tide goes out, as it will with a major stock market correction, you find out who's been swimming naked.)

Is this a warning to wade out of the market? No! The only purpose in mentioning rapidly appreciating or depreciating assets is to understand their impact on your plans to be financially secure and tax efficient.

SOLUTION

◆ **Make realistic allowances for inflation in your estate and financial planning.** If your income is standing still, you are losing ground. Build inflation into the CNA recommended in *Problem 6.*

What is a reasonable assumed rate of inflation? The inflation rate since 1970 has been close to 5.5 percent. Inflation in the 1990s has been under 3 percent. I use 3 percent with my clients unless they believe the rate is too low. You can always increase the percentage assumptions during subsequent annual reviews; at least you'll have a line for inflation in your calculations.

How do you factor in inflation if you don't have access to a computer-generated CNA?

CASE STUDY

Mrs. Johnson has expenses of $4,000 per month. She has some flexibility in managing her investments and in making withdrawals to pay her bills, but she is worried about inflation. She wants to know the actual dollar impact of a 3 percent inflation rate.

A 3 percent inflation rate assumes that the cost of goods and services will increase by that percentage uniformly each year. Therefore, what costs $4,000 this year will cost $4,120 next year ($4,000 x 1.03). Admittedly, 3 percent is an approximation. Realistically, not every expense of Mrs. Johnson's will increase at the same rate. For example, if she has a fixed-rate mortgage, the monthly payment will not increase at all. Her property taxes and medical expenses, though, might go up faster than inflation. In Year 2, Mrs. Johnson's expenses will grow to $4,243.60 ($4,120 x 1.03). In 24 years, Mrs. Johnson's $4,000 a month in income will buy half of what it purchases today. If Mrs. Johnson had considered the erosion caused by inflation in her financial planning well before retirement, she would have found ways either to increase her reserves, such as working a bit longer before retiring, or her expenses, such as less-expensive housing.

Project your inflation-adjusted income needs for more than your life expectancy. If you are a healthy female of 65—late middle age according to Gail Sheehy in her book *New Passages: Mapping Your Life Across Time*—your life expectancy is approaching 20 years. Be conservative and project your income needs for at least your life expectancy. Look at TABLE 1.10, *at right*. This life insurance table, "The Commissioners' 1980 Standard Ordinary Mortality Table," is used by many life insurance companies to set rates.

Start giving now to your children and grandchildren if you have more assets than you will need. Consider your income needs for today and in the future, factoring in inflation. You can make annual gifts of up to $10,000 per recipient, without incurring a tax liability. If you are married, your spouse can join in the gift and increase the limit to $20,000 per recipient.

This means that a wealthy widower with a $4,000,000 estate, four children, and six grandchildren could gift $100,000 each year to his offspring ($10,000 x 10 offspring). That helps the *donor* (person making the gift) by preventing that $100,000 from increasing the size of his estate and fostering taxfla-

1.10	1980 MORTALITY TABLE	
AGE	MALE FUTURE LIFETIME	FEMALE FUTURE LIFETIME
0	70.83 years	75.83 years
50	25.36 years	29.53 years
60	17.51 years	21.25 years
65	14.04 years	17.32 years
70	10.96 years	13.67 years
75	8.31 years	10.32 years
80	6.18 years	7.48 years
85	4.46 years	5.18 years
90	3.18 years	3.45 years

NOTE: The 1980 Table is one of many actuarial tables used by insurance companies to set insurance premiums. The tables are not updated regularly.

tion. The donees benefit by receiving money tax free while the donor is still alive to see it used or invested for such things as vacations and secondary-school and college tuition.

What else could the widower do?

Gift the unified-credit exemption amount. He could take advantage of the unified tax credit during his lifetime. The gift(s) would remove the $625,000— as adjusted annually under the 1997 tax laws—from the taxable estate; but equally important, it would also remove any further appreciation on that amount from the estate.

Using the approach recommended in *Problem 6,* what would be the economics of the transfer of the stock in a rapidly growing technology company appreciating at an average rate of 24 percent a year?

Use the "Rule of 72" to estimate the time it takes to double your assets. The rule states that you divide 72 by the rate of growth, and the answer is the time it takes to double your assets. For example, if a company's stock is expected to grow by 24 percent, its value should double every three years. This means $600,000 of stock in this company would be worth $1.2 million in three years, $2.4 million in six years, and $4.8 million in nine years. While a straight line of 24 percent appreciation never happens, such an average is quite possible.

Understand the power of compound interest to hike your taxes along with your assets. What if the growth rate after taxes is 12 percent? The same Rule of 72 requires that you divide 72 by 12 percent. The result, six, is the number of years it will take to double your assets. Thus, $600,000 in a good-growth mutual fund with a total return of 12 percent (after taxes, for dividends and capital gains distributions) could grow to $1,200,000 in 6 years, and $2,400,000 in 12 years. That appreciation could be taking place in a child or grandchild's estate, possibly deferring taxes for almost a century. (The estate tax might even be repealed by then.)

The push-pull of inflation and taxflation makes it imperative that you plan. You are under constant attack from taxflation throughout your entire financial life.

RECOMMENDED ADVISER

Use your **planner** to calculate the impact of inflation on all your plans.

SEE ALSO

◆ **Problem 2:** *The Estate-Tax Bite* for strategies to prevent the shrinkage caused by the estate and gift tax.
◆ **Problem 15:** *Living Too Long and Long-Term Care.*
◆ **Problem 16:** *Outliving Your Income.*
◆ **Problem 28:** *Finding the Best Investment Vehicles* for help in making the investment choices that best perpetuate your income.

WHAT'S IT WORTH: VALUATION PROBLEMS WITH THE IRS

The starting point for the calculation of the estate and gift tax is the inclusion into the gross estate of all of the assets the decedent owned. The value selected by the executor will have a dramatic impact on the taxes due. If you understand the problems inherent in assigning value to certain assets, you can plan your estate intelligently.

AS A GENERAL RULE, assets are to be included in the gross estate at fair market value. The date of the valuation is to be either the day of the decedent's death or a date six months after death, called the *alternate valuation date.* The executor may elect the alternate valuation date if doing so helps lower the value of the estate and the consequent tax.

If there is an established market for an asset, the market price is the place to start. The most accessible markets are the stock exchanges for public companies: the New York Stock Exchange (NYSE) and The American Stock Exchange (AMEX). Stocks listed and actively traded on these exchanges have readily available values at the opening and closing of each day on which they trade. Open-ended mutual funds similarly have readily available daily values, because the fund management must revalue their shares each day that the fund shares can be traded. Bonds, likewise, are frequently valued daily. The *Wall Street Journal* publishes these prices Monday through Friday. If you need the price of a stock on any given day years in the past, most stock-brokerage firms can provide this information upon request.

Assets that are not actively traded are harder to value. They might include corporation or partnership interests, farms, ranches, other real estate, antiques, fine art, craft work, and precious jewelry.

To get an idea how much valuation matters, look at the estate's expected marginal tax rate *(see Table 1.2)*. For taxable estates of $3 million, each extra $1.00 of value means $.55 in taxes. A $10,000 difference in valuation for a painting can mean $5,500 in taxes either saved or spent. The stakes go straight up for bigger items, such as real estate and business interests: a difference of $250,000 between the executor's appraisal on the estate tax return and the IRS's opinion could result in an extra $137,500 in taxes.

Even worse, disagreements often lead to litigation, which drives up legal and accounting fees and delays the closing of the estate. The executors of the estate of Edward A. Tully, a paving contractor whose case was heard in 1978, fought with the IRS for nearly 14 years over the value of a share of stock in Tully's company. The executors valued Tully's business at $100 per share. The IRS said the business was worth $344 a share. That's a big difference, especially at a potential tax rate of 55 percent for each share. The court ultimately found the value to be $165 a share.

Tully's heirs probably felt better about their outcome than Robert A. Goodall's executors, who fought the IRS for 11½ years, and lost. The executor valued a share of Goodall's electrical-parts business at $7.44 a share. The IRS claimed a per share value of $10.30. The court agreed with the IRS. People who were close to the case still speculate whether Goodall rolled over in his grave. *Problem 18* in this book shows you how to avoid posthumous valuation squabbles with the IRS by using business continuation agreements.

What factors should you consider when valuing an interest in a closely held business? The IRS itemized the factors in a ruling back in 1959:

> (a) The nature of the business and the history of the enterprise from its inception.

(b) The economic outlook in general and the condition and outlook of the specific industry.

(c) The book value of the stock and the financial condition of the business. *Book value* is the net worth—assets minus liabilities.

(d) The *earning capacity* of the company, that is, how much profit the company earns.

(e) The *dividend-paying capacity*, that is, the extent to which the company can pay out the profits to the stockholders.

(f) Whether or not the enterprise has goodwill or other intangible value. *Goodwill* is the value attributable to the reputation and market position of the company.

(g) The price of the stock in sales to nonfamily members, and the size of the block of stock to be valued.

(h) The market price of stocks of corporations in the same or a similar line of business having their stocks actively traded on an exchange or over the counter.

Blocks of stock that represent a controlling interest in a business may be worth more. Minority blocks can often be discounted to reflect the lack of control. Executors for the renowned sculptor Alexander Calder were able to apply the "block theory" to reduce the value of his artwork in his estate for tax purposes.

Real estate is susceptible to similar ambiguities in the determination of fair market value. The *IRS Valuation Guide* specifies three basic ways to value realty: the market-data or comparable-sales approach, the capitalization of income approach, and the reproduction-cost approach. The first alternative, *market data,* compares the sales price of comparable pieces of property close to the date of the decedent's death. Business properties usually use the *capitalization of income* approach, whereby the net income from the rental property is converted via a reasonable interest rate into a fair overall market value. For example, a commercial building with a net income of $100,000 per year would be worth $1,666,667 if capitalized at 6 percent ($100,000 ÷ 0.06). The *reproduction-cost* approach looks at the cost of replacing a building on a property. Again, with each of these methods there is latitude in assigning a value to property, depending on interest rates assumed or comparables selected. Some types of assets, such as mineral rights and forest lands, have rules or guidelines of their own.

Valuing significant assets that have no ready market is hardest for an executor when the estate owner has neglected to address the question of valuation before death.

SOLUTIONS

◆ **Make a list of your property most likely to pose valuation problems.** Include antiques, heirlooms, fine art, valuable craft work, expensive jewelry, rare books, and other collectibles.

If the items pose a threat of estate-tax challenges, have each valuable asset appraised by a professional appraiser with estate experience. Take photographs of the assets, keep the appraisals and photographs in a safe-deposit box, and notify your executor of the existence of the appraisals.

This is an important exercise, for at least three reasons. First, having real current values will help your planners identify assets that are available for gifts, sales, and techniques that can freeze the value of an asset in your estate. Second, valuable assets, should be itemized for insurance purposes. Many policies require a special additional policy or policy rider for coverage of rare and valuable assets, such as paintings, books, and jewels. Third, totaling up the value of these items often prompts you to reconsider the security of your home, office, or other place(s) such valuables are kept.

◆ **Enter into business continuation agreements.** Business continuation agreements (BCAs), commonly referred to as buy-sell agreements, can fix the value of closely held businesses for federal estate-tax purposes *(see Part 3, "Business Succession Problems").*

◆ **Take advantage of special-valuation provisions for "special-use" real estate.** Your executor may identify certain real estate used in a family farm or business as available for a special-valuation rule. A provision of the tax law allows your executor to value the qualifying property at its current use rather than its "highest and best use." For example, if your family farm happens to lie in the midst of expensive development acreage, its value as a potential subdivision would give it a much higher value than its appraised value as a farm. The subdivision might be its "highest and best use." However, the law allows the executor to ignore its higher valuation and use its current-use valuation.

The law has limits. The most the executor can subtract from the gross estate is $750,000. The property must actually be in use as a farm or in the family business; the property must be worth at least 50 percent of the decedent's gross estate; it must pass to a *qualified heir* (usually immediate family or descendants of the decedent or the surviving spouse); and it must have been a farm or used in the business for five of the prior eight years.

◆ **Hire an appraiser to value your business and real estate.** This continues the theme you will find throughout this book. Hire professionals to do critical work on your estate. Try to save money where you can, but not by doing it yourself—this is not like painting a bedroom or changing the oil in your car. There is considerably more at stake, as the IRS valuation cases demonstrate. Even if you win, as the executor did in the 1974 Sundquist case discussed below, you could still run up attorneys' and accountants' fees and the costs of delaying closing the estate, such as the expenses of your executor and bank and brokerage accounts. In *Sundquist et al. v. the United States* the executor placed a value of $270 per share on the stock of Sundquist's cold-storage business. The IRS, upon auditing the estate tax return, refused the valuation and placed a value of $500 a share. The court ultimately sided with the executor—seven years and nine months after the death of the business owner. An appraisal completed before Sundquist's death might have been accepted by the IRS and avoided the dispute.

◆ **Plan for discounts for lack of marketability and lack of control.** Most estate and financial planners find it easier to plan while the business owner is alive. This remark is more than just a facetious one. Tax attorneys and planners often do considerable planning after the owner's death, called *postmortem planning*.

This seems to be what happened in the estate of Bob Magness, the billionaire founder of TCI Cable mentioned in *Problem 5*. The estate reached an agreement to sell 32 million shares of TCI stock in a deal valued at $529 million, in part to raise enough cash to pay an estimated $500 million in taxes. The initial reaction of many estate planners was that Mr. Magness dropped the ball, leaving the problems to his heirs and executor. After studying the stock sale to Merrill Lynch and Lehman Brothers, the experts are now willing to admit that selling the stock in this fashion probably enabled the estate to take significant discounts in the value of the stock. The discounts included reductions because the stock could not have been sold without depressing the market price, reductions because the block could not have been sold *at* the market price, and a reduction because of Securities and Exchange Commission (SEC) restrictions on the salability of insider stock. Evelyn Kapassakis, top planner at the accounting firm Coopers & Lybrand, stated that discounts can cut the size of an estate by 30 to 50 percent. That could result in a $275 million tax—down considerably from the more than $500 million originally projected.

If you are the owner of a sizable minority interest in a business, sit down with your planners now to plan for the most advantageous disposition of your interest, including a strategy for pegging the value for estate-tax purposes.

◆ **As an executor, take advantage of the alternate valuation date.** In another example of postmortem tax planning, an executor can elect to value the estate six months after the date of death. This option allows executors to lower the tax bill if the value of the assets have fallen during the six months after death.

RECOMMENDED ADVISERS

Your **accountant** should be involved in valuing your assets, including building a case for low-to-reasonable values.

Your **attorney** is necessary for the drafting and implementation of documents, such as business continuation agreements, wills, and trusts.

Let your **planner** run hypothetical probates at varying valuations for your holdings. This will bring home the need to anticipate the problem areas and solve them your way, not the IRS way.

SEE ALSO

◆ **Problem 2:** *The Estate-Tax Bite* to counteract shrinkage attributable to taxes.

◆ **Problem 18:** *Business Continuation and the Closely Held Corporation* to see how valuation issues affect business buyouts.

◆ **Problem 46:** *Business Disposition Problems* to understand the impact of valuation issues in superwealthy estates.

GENERATION-SKIPPING DILEMMAS

Congress enacted the generation-skipping transfer tax in order to discourage the wealthy from reducing estate taxes by passing over generations with their assets. Without such a tax, families would be rewarded with lower tax bills if they left assets directly or in trust for their grandchildren and great-grandchildren, bypassing their own children. Even with the tax, however, there is still sufficient motivation to consider a limited generation-skipping transfer.

A *GENERATION-SKIPPING TRANSFER* (GST) is a gift or transfer at death to anyone considered two or more generations below that of the estate owner or transferor. The most common example is a transfer from a grandparent to a grandchild while the transferor's children are still living. A person two or more generations below is called a *skip person.*

The GSTT (generation-skipping transfer tax) is imposed on top of the normal estate or gift tax. The maximum 55 percent tax rate is used to calculate the tax. In effect, the GSTT makes up for the tax that would have been collectible at the first-generation-recipient's death.

Each taxpayer is allowed an exemption of $1 million, applicable to lifetime gifts and death transfers combined. Even with the exemption, the GSTT can be onerous.

CASE STUDY

Mr. Graham Pah is a widowed and retired executive from General Electric. In his 40 years with GE, he amassed a significant position in the company's stock. Since his retirement a decade ago, the rising price of the stock has increased his estate to $6.5 million, of which $6 million is the GE stock. He has three children, all wealthy themselves. His children have given him five grandchildren. In his rush to try to save the extra estate tax when his children would pass the stock to his grandchildren, Mr. Pah has rewritten his will to leave only his $500,000 Nantucket house to his children, and the stock equally to the grandchildren. Any problems at Graham Pah's death? Only if you consider estate shrinkage of 92 percent a problem.

The bequest to the grandchildren is a GST. It will trigger a GSTT. The tax is calculated by first finding an "exclusion ratio." This is how the GSTT gives credit to the $1 million exemption. The total bequest to the skip persons is $6 million. The ratio is created with the $1 million exemption being the numerator and the total skip transfer being the denominator: ($1 million ÷ $6 million), or one-sixth. This exclusion of one-sixth means that five-sixths or 83.3 percent of the transfer is to be included as a GST. This 83.3 percent is multiplied against the 55 percent maximum tax rate to yield a tax rate of 45.815 percent. This 45.815 percent is multiplied by the $6 million transfer. The resulting tax is $2,748,900. This will be levied on top of his estate tax on the $6.5 million estate. If the estate tax was $3,215,800, the total taxes are $5,964,700. This is a shrinkage of 91.76 percent. So much for amateur planning.

What if Mr. Pah had left $1 million for the grandchildren and $5.5 million for their parents? If the parents live for another 27 years and allow the $5.5 million to accumulate, everyone is better served. At 8 percent, the $5.5 million will be worth $44 million. After a tax of 55 percent, the grandchildren inherit roughly $24 million. Their $1 million would be worth $8 million. On the other hand, if they had invested the $535,300 remaining after taxes in the GSTT scenario at the same 8 percent rate, they would have $4,282,400.

Which is better, $4.2 million or $24 million? Most people opt for the $24 million, but only if they take the time to think it through.

SOLUTIONS

◆ **Do not attempt to draft generation-skipping documents without an attorney.** The rules for satisfying the requirements are complex. The financial penalties for inadvertently triggering the GSTT are severe. Use an attorney who specializes in estate planning. Start looking in the Yellow Pages under "Specialties," check with your state's bar association for a listing of estate-planning specialists, and get referrals from friends.

◆ **Use generation-skipping transfers to the extent of $1,000,000 only.** This is the limit before the GSTT kicks in. An attorney can draft the proper language in the dispositive document to ensure that $1,000,000 is the maximum GST, unless the laws change and the limits are liberalized, in which case you still will need the lawyer to update your documents.

◆ **Use generation-skipping trusts rather than generation-skipping transfers for situations where you want the income from these assets passed to the skipped generation.** Whether you want to provide income for the first generation or just protect the beneficiaries from the trials of modern life such as divorce and bankruptcy, a trust can satisfy that desire to insulate the funds. The trust could distribute income to the child for the child's lifetime and then pass to the grandchildren, or the trust could continue for both generations. The trust could pay education expenses for the beneficiaries or help them start new businesses. Ask your attorney to explain all your alternatives in detail.

◆ **Make sure both grandparents use the GST.** This increases the amount of the exemption to $2 million ($1 million per grandparent). Look at the graphical depiction of the generation-skipping trust created by the first grandparent to die in TABLE 1.11, *at right*. It pays income to the surviving grandparent for life, then passes to the grandchildren. The second grandparent also passes $1 million to the grandchildren at death.

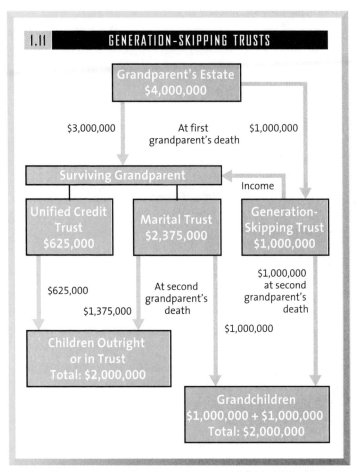

1.11   GENERATION-SKIPPING TRUSTS

Grandparent's Estate
$4,000,000

$3,000,000   At first grandparent's death $1,000,000

Surviving Grandparent

Income

Unified Credit Trust $625,000

Marital Trust $2,375,000

Generation-Skipping Trust $1,000,000

$625,000   At second grandparent's death $1,000,000 at second grandparent's death

$1,375,000 $1,000,000

Children Outright or in Trust Total: $2,000,000

Grandchildren $1,000,000 + $1,000,000 Total: $2,000,000

Combine the GST gift with annual $10,000 gifts. Augmenting the $1 million exemption with annual gifts helps reduce the size of the grandparent's estate without incurring the gift tax. It is critical that a tax adviser be included in the planning for these gifts.

You must use an **attorney** to safely plan to take advantage of the GST exemption. The rules are too complex and the cost of mistakes too high to attempt the transfers on your own.

Involve your **tax accountant** to track the aggregate transfers and the annual $10,000 gifts per donee. Make sure you keep copies of these records from year to year, in case you change accountants.

SEE ALSO

◆ **Problem 10:** *Improper Beneficiaries and Owners* to learn how irrevocable life insurance trusts can be combined with GST trusts to preserve assets.

PROBLEM 10

IMPROPER BENEFICIARIES AND OWNERS

Life insurance and retirement plans were designed to provide an economic benefit. Designating the wrong beneficiary can significantly reduce that benefit. In the case of a life insurance policy, having the wrong owner can be just as bad.

"IMPROPERLY ARRANGED LIFE INSURANCE" is Number 2 on Stephan R. Leimberg's list, "The 10 Most Common Estate-Planning Mistakes." Professor Leimberg, prolific author and lecturer in law in the Masters in Taxation program at Temple University School of Law, says that this is one of the "problems that can cost you and your family tens of thousands of dollars and unbelievable heartache."

The first place to look for an "improper arrangement" is the beneficiary designations. In *Problem 1*, you read about the "funnel of probate." Life insurance policies can pass outside the funnel if you name beneficiaries other than your estate. Some people name their estate for lack of a better idea of who should receive the proceeds. This automatically subjects the proceeds to probate, which means that they are vulnerable to claims by the creditors of the insured. It also puts the entire policy proceeds into the insured's estate for federal estate-tax purposes.

A named beneficiary receives an income tax–free check, often a significant check, for the proceeds shortly after the claim has been filed. That's great. However, if the beneficiary is not in a position to handle the money responsibly, you may have undone much of the good you sought to do by having the insurance in the first place. There are many reasons why a beneficiary should not receive a large sum of money at one time: the beneficiary may be too immature and irresponsible; the beneficiary may be incapacitated due to injury or illness; the beneficiary may no longer be a desired recipient, such as an ex-spouse; or the beneficiary may be deceased.

A *contingent beneficiary* receives the proceeds in the event the primary beneficiary cannot. Contingent beneficiaries, like primary beneficiaries, need to be capable of receiving the proceeds and handling them. Many policy owners fail to name contingent beneficiaries. This can result in the policy proceeds passing to the estate and being decimated by the claims of creditors, probate expenses, and estate taxes.

Improper beneficiaries can also plague business life insurance. A *key-employee life insurance plan* is a policy owned by a corporation insuring the life of an employee who makes a financial difference to the business. The policy should be payable to the corporation or to a creditor to secure a loan. If the policy is payable to anyone else, the IRS could argue that the proceeds were not received tax free, as life insurance is normally. The IRS could also argue that the proceeds are a dividend, increasing the tax penalty. Dividends are taxed at the corporate level and again when an individual receives it.

Improper ownership of an insurance policy can increase estate taxes. Remember that the gross estate of the decedent includes all assets that an individual owns or has an ownership interest in, to the extent of that interest. For a life insurance policy, the ownership interests are called *incidents of ownership,* and they include actual ownership of the policy, the right to withdraw cash from the policy, and the right to name the beneficiaries.

CASE STUDY

Mr. Wellington "Well" Covert was a divorced business owner with a net worth of $3 million, mostly in his awning business. After his divorce, he purchased a $1 million policy and named his three adult children as primary beneficiaries. No contingent beneficiaries were named, despite the fact that each of his children has children. Two days before Well Covert's death, his eldest child died in an automobile accident. Any problems after Covert's death? Yes, serious problems.

To begin with, unless Covert named his children as primary beneficiaries *per stirpes,* only the two surviving children share in the $1 million death benefit. *Per stirpes* means that each share follows the natural line of descendants. Therefore, any children who predecease the insured would automatically be replaced by their children in the lineup for benefits.

The second problem is that the entire $1 million death benefit is included in Covert's estate, adding to the existing $3 million. At 55 percent, the policy would actually create an extra $550,000 in taxes. This happens because Covert owned the policy and had the incidents of ownership mentioned above. He could have made other arrangements that would have kept the proceeds out of his estate, as you will learn in the "Solutions" section.

Another common trap is the "gift" scenario. If the owner of a policy insuring someone else names a third party as the beneficiary, the owner is making a gift of the proceeds. The gift becomes a taxable gift when the insured dies and the proceeds are paid. It is too late at that time for anyone to change the beneficiary designation.

The final area of improper beneficiary designations

involves retirement plans, especially IRAs. You have a right to name a beneficiary on your IRA. By naming someone other than your estate, you can enable the accumulated monies to bypass the probate funnel explained in *Problem 1*. The tax laws potentially grant an even larger break if the surviving spouse is the named beneficiary. In that case, he or she may elect to continue the IRA in effect as though it were their own. Nonspousal beneficiaries must take the full sum within five years, all taxed as ordinary income. Most IRA owners will want to name their spouse as beneficiary, even though a large IRA may result in the overqualification of the marital deduction, the condition explained in *Problem 5*.

CASE STUDY

Emily Loyal, an executive for a large corporate employer, has recently left the company, taking with her a $1 million 401(k) plan balance. She opted to roll it over into a self-directed IRA. She and her husband have $1 million worth of assets in addition to her IRA: a $500,000 home and $500,000 in jointly held mutual funds. At her death, everything will pass automatically to Mr. Loyal, including his right to continue her IRA. However, at his subsequent death, the entire $2 million will be included in his gross estate for estate-tax purposes. This is a case where they probably should have put $600,000 into a bypass trust for Mr. Loyal, thereby reducing the estate tax at his death. Again, refer to *Problem 5*.

SOLUTIONS

◆ **Make a list of all of your life insurance policies and IRAs.** These are the vehicles that lend themselves to "improper arrangements." List the owner, primary beneficiary, and contingent beneficiary for each, along with the death benefit of the life insurance policies and the accumulated value of each IRA. Make certain your preferred beneficiaries are the ones you've named.

If you have too many IRAs spread out among different institutions, consider consolidating them into one self-directed IRA. This allows you to manage many investments in one account.

◆ **Avoid naming your estate as beneficiary.** In the vast majority of situations, a named beneficiary is preferable. This will avoid probate and the claims of creditors.

◆ **Make certain each primary beneficiary is the one you want and is capable of handling the proceeds.** If he or she is not, call your life insurance underwriter and request the right forms to make the changes. If the intended beneficiary is incapable, see an attorney about creating a trust as the beneficiary. The trust could invest the money, handle the disbursements, and protect the proceeds from misuse. You can have multiple primary beneficiaries.

◆ **Use the *per stirpes* designation.** If you name your children as beneficiaries and you want their children to inherit their share if your children die before you do, name the children as beneficiaries *per stirpes*. The life insurance companies will usually give you a form with examples of the language they prefer.

◆ **Name contingent beneficiaries on all life insurance policies and IRAs.** Sometimes the primary beneficiary cannot receive the proceeds. Often, policy owners forget to name a new primary beneficiary when their spouse dies. Proceeds will automatically pass by default to a contingent beneficiary, but if none is listed, the proceeds will end up in the estate.

◆ **Do not use corporate-owned life insurance to benefit anyone other than the business, the business owners, or a creditor.** One of the great benefits of life insurance is that the proceeds are receivable income tax free. However, if a corporation uses insurance to enrich another party, the corporation could lose its income tax–free advantage.

◆ **Keep life insurance out of your estate for estate-tax purposes.** You accomplish this by removing all your incidents of ownership in the policy, such as the right to change the owner and beneficiary of the policy, the right to borrow the cash value, the right to assign the policy to another, the right to surrender the policy, and the right to pledge the policy as collateral for a loan.

◆ **Avoid the *transfer-for-value rule*.** The rule, created in the tax laws, imposes penalties on certain transfers of ownership of life insurance policies. If you run afoul of the rule, the entire proceeds of the policy may be subject to income tax. Transfer-for-value penalties exist in the tax laws to discourage the transfer of the policy in exchange for some economic benefit. Do not transfer a policy's ownership rights without checking with a professional.

◆ **Adopt an irrevocable life insurance trust (ILIT).** An ILIT can keep the proceeds out of your estate for tax purposes. It can also make loans or sell assets to the estate at death, aiding the liquidity of the estate. This trust vehicle can also govern investment management, provide income for the family or other heirs, protect the privacy of your wealth, avoid the expenses and delays of probate, and take advantage of the gift-tax laws.

Here's how it works. You contribute the premiums to the trust. The beneficiaries, your heirs, must have a right to demand the value of the gifts to the trust each year for, say, 30 to 45 days. If they do not exercise these rights to withdraw the funds—and they should be told why they shouldn't—then the trustee can use the gifted funds to pay the premium on a policy insuring the grantor of the funds. An ideal amount to contribute to this trust is a maximum of $10,000 per beneficiary, to the extent needed to buy the desired amount of life insurance. Remember, you may gift $10,000 per donee each year, tax free. The tax laws allow you to consider each beneficiary of the trust as

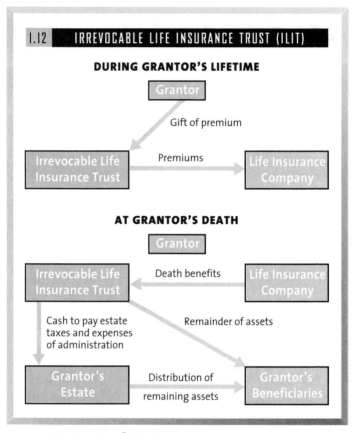

1.12   IRREVOCABLE LIFE INSURANCE TRUST (ILIT)

DURING GRANTOR'S LIFETIME

Grantor

Gift of premium

Irrevocable Life Insurance Trust → Premiums → Life Insurance Company

AT GRANTOR'S DEATH

Grantor

Irrevocable Life Insurance Trust ← Death benefits ← Life Insurance Company

Cash to pay estate taxes and expenses of administration

Remainder of assets

Grantor's Estate → Distribution of remaining assets → Grantor's Beneficiaries

entitled to the $10,000 free gift. If you had five children, you could gift $50,000 annually to the trust to be used to pay life insurance premiums. Upon your death, the policy pays its death benefit to the ILIT, which in turn pays out benefits to the beneficiaries, or to the estate to pay taxes or any other need.

The mechanics of the ILIT are shown in TABLE 1.12, *above.*

The ILIT is rapidly becoming a vehicle of choice for wealthy estate owners seeking to provide liquidity for the settlement of their estate and safety for their heirs, all without increasing the tax bill due at death. It provides the necessary liquidity that the owner's estate needs, without increasing the size of the estate to do it.

Your **attorney** will draft ILIT documents and counsel your beneficiaries on the advantages of not using the annual gifts during your lifetime.

Your **life insurance agent** will help you arrange beneficiary designations to accomplish your desired scheme of distribution.

SEE ALSO

◆ **Problem 5:** *Excessive Joint Ownership with Spouses* to review the problems of overqualification of the marital deduction.

PROBLEM 11

FUNDING RETIREMENT PLANS

Retirement plans continue to serve as tremendous vehicles for accumulating significant wealth. The 1997 tax law removed an excise tax that was one of the few remaining impediments to amassing unlimited fortunes through these plans. However, now there are several more choices to make in deciding how to best take advantage of these tax-deferred retirement vehicles.

MARTIN NISSENBAUM, of the accounting firm Ernst & Young in New York City, offered his read on the 1997 tax law: "Life is about to get a whole lot simpler for wealthy people, and even some middle-income people, who have watched their retirement savings rocket thanks to the extended bull market." One of the primary reasons Nissenbaum felt this way was the repeal of the confiscatory 15 percent excise tax on "excess distributions."

Prior law sought to penalize retirement-plan withdrawals greater than $160,000 in any given year. That same penalty also attached to lump-sum withdrawals of $800,000 or more (as adjusted for inflation under the law). By combining income taxes, estate taxes, generation-skipping taxes, and excess-distribution taxes, it was possible to lose 90 percent of one's retirement fund account just to taxes.

The 1997 law permits you to accumulate an unlimited amount in pension, profit-sharing, 401(k), and IRA plans, and the excise tax on distributions is repealed. The next questions any respectable cynic would ask is, where's the catch? Why has Congress done such an about-face? The answer probably lies in the fact that the excise tax was a lousy idea from the beginning. In the 1980s, many economists believed that the greatest threat to our economic well-being was the low savings rates of Americans. Increased contributions to IRAs and 401(k) plans indeed helped alleviate that problem. A decade later it began to look ridiculous to penalize the people who saved most successfully. It took Congress a while to realize that the superwealthy were not the only ones accumulating such large sums in their retirement accounts. A little math will put this into perspective.

First, life expectancies have improved. A male age 65 today is expected to live to 83, his female counterpart to 85. (For comparison, when Social Security was enacted as a safety net in the 1930s, male life expectancy was three years lower than the normal retirement age of 65.) Second, baby boomers are savers. No one would have guessed that Americans, renowned for their excessive materialism in the 1980s, would have become so savings and investment oriented.

Compound interest, which is interest on principal and on accumulated interest, builds up mightily inside a retirement plan where it is not being taxed. Many successful people still don't appreciate how powerfully that works over time.

EXAMPLES

Suppose you have $10,000 to set aside in an account and the institution offers a long-term rate of 7 percent:

$10,000 principal x 0.07 interest rate = $700 interest

CHART BY MYRA KLOCKENBRINK

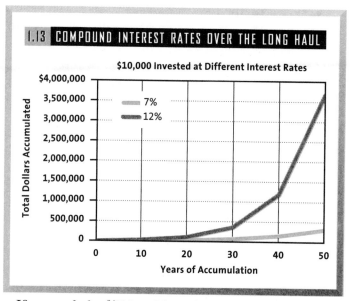

1.13 COMPOUND INTEREST RATES OVER THE LONG HAUL

$10,000 Invested at Different Interest Rates

7%
12%

If you took the $700 and bought clothes, you would have nothing to reinvest. If you left it with the account and it was added to your $10,000 principal earning 7 percent, it compounds. Next year:

$10,700 x 0.07 = $749 interest
$10,700 +$749 = $11,449

The magic of compound interest works slowly at first, but it becomes dramatic at the end of the accumulation period. Look at the graphical depiction in TABLE 1.13, *above.*

You can see that the amount of money in the account jumps up geometrically with both time and rate of return. Increasing either factor yields tremendous growth in your savings at retirement. It is not uncommon for people today to accumulate well in excess of $1 million in their IRA. This is often a result of a direct rollover of a pension, profit-sharing, or 401(k) plan account upon termination from an employer.

The removal of the 15 percent excise tax makes it

even more imperative that you consider and maximize these advantages of tax-deferred investing. However, having a bloated 401(k) or IRA will bring other challenges. One of the more common problems is the inheritance of a jumbo IRA by the surviving spouse.

Among the great benefits of an IRA is the ability to name your spouse as the beneficiary. This enables the surviving spouse to elect to continue the decedent's IRA as though it was his or her own, and to delay the income tax on withdrawals by deferring distributions until the survivor needs the income, or age 70½, whichever is earliest.

The potential problem is that naming a spouse as beneficiary qualifies the asset for the marital deduction. If most of the decedent's other assets are similarly structured to pass to the spouse, you have the situation addressed in *Problem 5*, overqualification of the marital deduction.

In the wake of the tax-law changes, what strategies should you use for accumulating wealth inside or outside of the *qualified plans*, that is, plans recognized by the IRS as qualifying for special tax treatment? Dollars *inside* these retirement plans grow tax deferred, but they usually come *out* taxable. Would you be better off accumulating assets outside the plans where you can pay taxes as you accumulate and take advantage of capital gains rates for withdrawals? To answer that question, you'll need to ask a few others. Will the plan contributions be tax deductible? What are the relative tax brackets before and after retirement? It is not always an accurate assumption that you will be in a lower tax bracket after you retire. How long will retirement last? Finally, what types of assets are being used to fund the retirement plans?

SOLUTIONS

◆ **Maximize tax-deductible contributions to all company retirement plans and make sure they stay well invested.**

You know you have a tax benefit today. You may not have a tax benefit tomorrow. Congress passes major new tax legislation at least once a decade.

◆ **Continue to fund retirement plans up to your actual retirement, even if that happens past age 65.** You may make tax-deductible contributions to 401(k)s, 403(b)s, simplified employee pensions (SEPs), and SIMPLE plans, depending on whether you can determine your own retirement plan, until actual retirement or at age 70½. Look at TABLE 1.14, *on the following two pages.* Self-employed individuals usually have greater flexibility than traditional employees in being able to determine when they choose to call it quits.

What about the incentive effect of the new IRA rules? According to John H. Gardner, senior manager in the Washington, D.C., office of KPMG Peat Marwick, "The real benefit of the tax bill for people who qualify is that there are now a bunch of options that will point people in the direction of saving for retirement and starting early." The new IRA Plus, alternatively called the Roth IRA (for the Senate Finance Committee chairman who championed the bill), allows taxpayers to set aside $2,000 each year *without* a current income tax deduction. However, the funds will accumulate tax deferred and can be withdrawn tax free as long as they are used for retirement, education, or a first home purchase.

◆ **Use the traditional IRA to set aside $2,000 and take a tax deduction in that year.** The funds accumulate tax deferred, but are taxed as ordinary income when withdrawn. The new law also allows taxpayers to convert existing IRAs to the Roth IRA. Whether you should convert or not is discussed later in this section.

◆ **Make regular, maximum, early contributions to the Roth IRA plan or the traditional IRA.** What makes the Roth IRA attractive is the tax-free income at retirement. That is not an option under any other qualified retirement plan. Steven Norwitz, from the mutual-fund com-

1.14	RETIREMENT PLAN ALTERNATIVES

TYPE OF PLAN	MAXIMUM EMPLOYEE-PARTICIPATION RULES
SEP (Simplified Employee Pension)	**Employer must include:** * Employees 21 years old * Compensation at least $400 * Employed 3 of last 5 years
SIMPLE (Savings Incentive Match Plan for Employees)	**Employer must include:** * Compensation $5,000 in any 2 prior years * Current-year compensation $5,000
401(k)	**Employer must include:** * Employees 21 years old * 1,000 hours of service current year
PROFIT SHARING	**Employer must include:** * Employees 21 years old * Employed 2 years (unless vesting schedule, then 1 year)
MONEY-PURCHASE PENSION	**Same as profit sharing**
DEFINED-BENEFIT PENSION	**Same as profit sharing**

Note: Vesting refers to the right of the employee to take the accumulated plan benefits. Employees with two years' eligibility vest immediately.

pany T. Rowe Price Associates, believes that people "come out significantly ahead with the new IRA." He believes that the tax-free treatment in the future outweighs the current tax deduction to the old IRA. Not everyone agrees with this conclusion. Some planners believe the tax bracket of the individual drives the decision. If you know you are going to be in a much lower bracket in retirement, you may be better off with the current deduction—in other words, the old IRA

MAXIMUM EMPLOYER CONTRIBUTION	TIPS
* Lesser of 15% of annual compensation or $30,000	Excellent for small company where owner wants to reward employees; low administration expenses
* $6,000 deferral per employee per year * Minimum contribution required of employer	Perfect for self-employed with spouse in the small business or company; low costs
* Lesser of 25% of annual compensation or $30,000 * Maximum limit on employee tax deferral is $9,500	Incentive plan to encourage employees to fund own retirement; administration is expensive
* Lesser of 15% of annual compensation or $30,000 * Contributions discretionary with the employer	Greatest flexibility to make contributions; age-weighted plans can favor older employees
* Lesser of 25% of annual compensation or $30,000	Can combine with a profit sharing to permit 25% of which 15% is discretionary
* 100% of highest compensation average over 3 years, not to exceed $120,000	Good choice if owner is older and highly paid and has few employees

(see TABLE 1.15, on the following two pages).

◆ **Convert your old IRA to the new Roth IRA only after consulting your tax adviser.** All the experts agree that the advisability of converting your existing IRA to the Roth IRA is more difficult to judge than where to make new contributions. The primary reason is the tax treatment at conversion. The old IRA is treated as all taxable income in the year of conversion, though payment of the taxable amount can be spread out over

1.15   IRA ALTERNATIVES

CHARACTERISTICS	TRADITIONAL IRA
Contribution limits	$2,000/year to the extent of earnings
Tax deductibility of contribution	Yes, if earnings below limits on AGI.* No deduction if single taxpayer with AGI of $40,000 in 1998, married with $60,000; limits increase over next 10 years
Tax-deferred growth	Yes
Tax-free retirement income	No
Penalty-free withdrawals before 59 ½	Yes, for qualified education expenses or up to $10,000 for first-time home buyers
Contribution age limit	70 ½
Required minimum distribution	Yes, starting at 70 ½

*AGI=Adjusted Gross Income.

four years if you convert in 1998. Stephen Corrick, tax partner in the Washington, D.C., office of Arthur Andersen, feels the conversion can be a "pretty neat opportunity." The net effect, according to Corrick, is that "you pay today for the opportunity never to have to pay tax in the future on the appreciation."

William Brennan, a Washington-based tax and financial adviser, states the alternate view, "[The government is] asking them to pay a current tax now, for a theoretical future benefit." He is less excited about the prospects for the future than Corrick.

The rules for conversion include a cap on income—$100,000 of AGI—in order to qualify in a given year. Ask your tax adviser if conversion makes sense, especially if your income will be close to the maximum $100,000 AGI conversion limit. If you are

ROTH IRA	COMMENTS
$2,000/year to the extent of earnings and if AGI less than $95,000 for singles and $150,000 for marrieds	Roth IRA not a choice for high earners
No	The tax deductibility is the trade-off for the tax-free income at retirement under Roth
Yes	
Yes	
Yes, if the funds are untouched for 5 years; earlier can trigger taxable income	New liberalized rules waive 10% penalty for limited withdrawals for education/home
None	Roth IRA offers great opportunity for employees over 70 $\frac{1}{2}$
None	

unsure your income will be less than $100,000 in 1998, wait until late in the year to convert.

◆ **When you leave an employer's retirement plan, keep your retirement plan intact or roll your existing retirement-account balance to a self-directed IRA.** The compound-interest story in *Table 1.13* should convince you that no amount is too small to retain or roll over. An amount of $10,000 set aside in a good-growth mutual fund at 9 percent for 30 years can grow to more than $500,000. Inside your self-directed IRA, there is no tax until distributed at retirement, or 70½, when distributions must begin. Remember to make sure it is a tax-free rollover. Don't take receipt of the money yourself. Request that the check be sent payable to the IRA custodian on your behalf.

1.16   INVESTMENT PYRAMID

HIGH RISK

Aggressive Growth
(speculative & volatile
stocks, funds, commodities)

Growth
(growth stocks and
growth mutual funds)

Growth & Income
(blue-chip and utility stocks and
growth & income mutual funds)

Income
(certificates of deposit, bonds, CMOs,
and fixed-rate single premium annuities)

Cash or Cash Equivalents
(savings accounts, money market funds,
cash on hand)

LOW RISK

◆ **Balance investments inside and outside your retirement accounts.** One of the keys to successful investing is *asset allocation,* which is the distribution of your assets over several of the available investment classes. These classes are cash or cash equivalents, income assets, growth and income assets, growth assets, and aggressive-growth assets. Use the investment pyramid *(*TABLE 1.16, *above)* to classify your holdings.

◆ **The percentage of your assets allocable to the various classes should depend on factors such as your risk tolerance, age, objectives, and resources.** The higher up the pyramid, the more risk you assume. You need a balance. The proper allocation for your situation and risk tolerance should be determined by your financial planner.

◆ **Weigh the benefits of the spousal right to continue an IRA against the overqualified marital deduction.** If you are more concerned with your spouse's ability to continue your IRA during his or her lifetime than with the estate tax on that IRA after both of you are deceased, find alternative ways to pay the estate tax at the second death. Consider the ILIT diagrammed in *Table 1.12* or the use of survivorship life insurance discussed in the next solution.

◆ **Buy survivorship life insurance to pay the tax at the second death.** This type of permanent life insurance covers both you and your spouse in one policy. Unlike traditional policies insuring each of you, this single policy insures both of you and pays a benefit only at the second death. The premium is considerably lower than that of a policy or policies paying at the first death. Remember, it is imperative that the policy be owned by someone other than the insured to keep the proceeds out of the decedent's estate for tax purposes. Consult your life insurance agent.

RECOMMENDED ADVISERS

 See your **tax adviser** for directions on how to play the new IRA alternatives, traditional or Roth. If you own your own business, review the need for tax-qualified retirement plans.

 Ask your **life insurance underwriter** about survivorship life insurance to offset taxes on a deliberately overfunded marital deduction.

SEE ALSO

◆ **Problem 5:** *Excessive Joint Ownership with Spouses* to get a jump on the estate-tax problems associated with too much joint property.

◆ **Problem 10:** *Improper Beneficiaries and Owners* to spot life insurance arrangements that don't consider the tax ramifications of ownership and beneficiary designations.

EXCESSIVE EXPENSES AND DELAYS AT DEATH

Sometimes the greatest frustrations caused by the death of a relative or friend occur because of the probate process. Without proper estate planning in place, the person responsible for winding down the decedent's affairs can experience a lifetime's worth of bureaucratic aggravations in a few months. The heirs can experience the same frustration waiting for the distribution of the estate and watching the shrinkage due to unnecessary expenses.

ONE WAY TO get people to take estate planning seriously would be to require everyone to serve "executor duty." It would entail a mandatory service as an executor of an estate, just like jury duty. Very few would emerge from the experience without wanting to plan their own asset disposition—unless, of course, they just had a mean streak. The executor's job is often difficult, time consuming, and fraught with liability. And the pay usually stinks.

This discussion adds to the information given about the probate process in *Problem 1*. The process requires the gathering of all the assets of the decedent; the payment of debts, taxes, and expenses of the decedent and the estate; and then the distribution of the remaining assets to the rightful heirs according to the will or the laws of intestate succession. Each step is complicated and time consuming.

Before the process can begin, a court must determine where the decedent was domiciled, that is, where he or she intended to make a permanent home. Once that determination is made, the will is filed in the decedent's home-county court, often called *surrogate's court*. The will names an executor. If there is no will or if a will is declared *invalid* (for example, because of inadequate signatures or witnesses), the court will appoint a personal representative, called the *administrator,* to carry out the duties outlined above.

The court will issue an authorization to the person handling the estate. For an estate where there was a will, the court issues "letters testamentary" to the executor. For an estate with no will, "letters of administration" are issued to the administrator. These "letters" actually pass title to the decedent's assets to the personal representative for the period of the administration of the estate, and before they are distributed to the heirs.

The first responsibility is to gather the assets of the decedent. How does the executor find out what the assets are and where they are located? Well-organized people have a list of assets and liabilities in a home office or safe-deposit box. What about the rest of us? You can imagine the difficulties with decedents who kept poor records. The process involves interviewing family members and digging through files, boxes and drawers, old bank statements, tax returns, and correspondence.

The executor should hire a capable estate attorney; estate laws can be complex and the executor has a responsibility to collect and protect the decedent's assets.

The asset-gathering process includes opening the safe-deposit boxes; filing claims for life insurance proceeds; applying for government entitlements, such as Social Security and Veterans Administration (VA) death benefits; filing claims for pension, profit-sharing, and 401(k) benefits; and freezing securities, bank accounts, and IRAs. This can be a daunting task if the decedent had dozens of mutual-fund accounts, numerous brokerage relationships, pensions from several prior employers, relationships with different banks, and real estate in more than one state.

If the decedent was an owner of a closely held business, the executor must decide whether the business should be continued or liquidated to best safeguard the assets. A sole proprietorship or partnership terminates automatically at the death of an owner. However, a buy-sell agreement can authorize the continuation of a business, overriding the automatic termination. Naturally, any cessation in the operation of a business can be detrimental to the bottom line, which brings us to one of the many negatives of serving as executor: *personal liability for negligence.* Nowhere in the process does this exposure loom larger than when there is a closely held business interest, especially without business continuation agreements (BCAs). If you are a business owner, read Part 3. You need to address the problem of succession.

During probate, the executor must protect the assets of the decedent. This requires investing monies until they can be distributed, insuring assets that are subject to theft and fire, and valuing assets such as art and antiques fairly if they are to be sold. Courts hold executors personally liable for negligence. Holding monies in non-interest-bearing accounts could trigger court action. Continuing a business without court authorization could generate liability as well. Significant foreseeable stock market losses are another threat.

The process of paying debts, taxes, and expenses begins with advertising the death of the decedent and calling for claims of creditors. Debts include all of the household bills, credit cards, bank loans, personal loans, and even back taxes. Taxes include the decedent's federal and state income taxes, federal and state estate and inheritance taxes, property and intangible taxes, and possibly foreign taxes as well. Expenses of the estate can include attorneys' fees, accountants' fees, bank and brokerage fees, real estate and brokerage commissions, appraisers' fees, and funeral costs.

The final step is the distribution of the assets to the rightful heirs, after which the executor submits a final accounting to the court. If the court finds the accounting satisfactory, it will issue a *release,* enabling the executor to close out the estate. The distribution process can be complicated by litigation with creditors or the IRS, or even cobusiness owners. There could also be delays finding heirs and beneficiaries.

SOLUTIONS

◆ **Choose your domicile clearly before death.** Many wealthy people own property in several states. For example, if you spend half a year in Florida, four months in Connecticut, and two months traveling each year, consider taking the necessary steps to choose Florida as your domicile. In addition to Florida's having no current personal income tax, you might find your surviving spouse prefers to settle in the South. Make a clear choice of domicile now so that you can avoid problems for your personal representative later.

◆ **Keep a current will.** As discussed in *Problem 1,* review your will, and if applicable, your trusts, at least annually.

◆ **Get organized.** Put together a book of all your financial matters. Most insurance and brokerage firms have such a binder, often called a "personal organizer." List all your assets, major liabilities, banking relationships, and advisers. Tell your executor and/or spouse where the book is located.

◆ **Name a responsible executor.** This is a tough job. Make sure the person selected is both willing and able. Choosing a great person does no good if they won't accept the job after your death. Don't surprise your friends, thinking their selection is an honor. Get their permission in advance.

◆ **Give the executor broad authority and specific instructions.** Don't hamstring your executor by making him or her more vulnerable to negligence than already possible under the law. If your estate is complex, consider a *corporate fiduciary,* such as a bank or trust company to serve as executor.

◆ **If you have special assets, make sure to specify your intentions with regard to those assets.** For example, if you want to leave a rare painting or your mother's ring to a daughter, spell it out in your will.

◆ **Settle business succession questions now.** If you own part or all of a business, enter into BCAs today. Apply the solutions found in *Problems 18 through 20.*

◆ **Avoid the funnel of probate.** Take advantage of beneficiary designations for insurance, retirement benefits, brokerage accounts, and CDs; joint ownership with right of survivorship; and BCAs to bypass the funnel of probate. Do so in conjunction with a planner to ensure you are not complicating other estate objectives, such as a properly funded marital deduction.

◆ **Execute a revocable living trust.** A living trust is not a tax-advantaged trust, but by transferring all your property into the trust you minimize the amount that has to go through probate. The trust also makes the settlement of your estate private. Probate is a public process. The trust is controlled by you, changeable by you, and revocable by you. Some states have tried to make probate easier; therefore, some attorneys recommend wills and going through probate over living trusts. They argue that it is less expensive to go through probate compared to the expense of drafting the living trust. Ask your attorney for an opinion and for cost estimates each way.

RECOMMENDED ADVISER

Use your **attorney** to draft the documents necessary to minimize the expenses and delays associated with settling an estate.

SEE ALSO

◆ **Problem 1:** *Lack of a Current Estate Plan.*
◆ **Problem 3:** *Insufficient Cash in the Estate.*
◆ **Part 3:** *Business Succession Problems.*

HEIRS WITH SPECIAL NEEDS

We all consider our families to be special, but there are situations that call for extra preparations. Usually, these concern individuals who do not have the physical resources or the mental capabilities to meet their needs without direct intervention. Heirs with special needs, in all likelihood, will have those needs met only if some special plans are made for them.

DISABLED AND AGED family members come to mind first. However, the list extends to children with learning disorders and those considered geniuses, parents who are young yet dependent, children of deceased siblings, and others. The solution often lies in recognizing a present or future dependency sitting under your roof or just outside your door.

Many Americans today face the challenge of being part of a *sandwich generation*—parents with both dependent children and dependent parents. More adult children are living with their parents than ever before. One-third of unmarried men between 25 and 34 years of age live at home. Sons and daughters at home can be expensive.

The number of aging parents living with their children is also on the rise. Our parents are living longer than they once assumed they would. Young adults in the 1930s hoped they would live into their 60s. At that time, the life expectancy was around 62. A baby girl born in America in 1997 has a one-in-three chance of living to age 100. That will mean the extra burden of funding a 35-year retirement, and a greater likelihood of needing long-term medical care. Baby boomers, and the generation reaching 65 right before them, will often have the added responsibilities of subsidizing their parents' later years.

The expense of sheltering and protecting parents is generally highest if they are *not* living under your roof, however. Many parents prefer their own homes or apartments. Yet, when their lives extend into their late 80s and 90s, being truly independent becomes difficult. Long-term care is discussed in detail in *Problem 15*.

In the event of your untimely death (it is always untimely when you are the subject), how will your parents or your spouse's parents be affected? They may not be dependent upon you now, but are they likely to be in the future?

Children or family members with physical and mental disabilities present a different challenge. In past decades, we might have assumed that the government would help—maybe even shouldering full financial responsibility if need be. Anyone making that assumption today is subjecting their family to the whims of congressional budget cutters. You are wiser to presume that the full responsibility is yours. However, what kinds of plans are necessary to meet it?

The chance of your becoming disabled poses a double-edged dilemma: lack of income *and* extra expenses. If you haven't already addressed this possibility, you should insure yourself against a long-term disability, at least during your high-earning years. However, what if the disability strikes someone else in your family? For example, what if a child with marginal earning capacity becomes disabled? To the extent they cannot work meaningfully enough to provide for themselves, how much responsibility are you willing to assume? And what happens if you are no longer there to provide the attention or the money?

As you learned in *Problem 1*, if you do not have a will, the state of your domicile will draw one for you. However, it will not be able to evaluate the extraordinary needs of a spouse or child or parent. Totally disabled dependents are often easier to plan for than partially functional adults. You are the one in the best position to judge the extent to which family members will always need support.

SOLUTIONS

◆ **Make provisions for special needs of family members in your will.** This could involve the use of trusts to provide the necessary money management as well as guardianship in the event of your early death. If you fail to indicate the guardian you want in your will, the court will appoint one. It may not be a person you would have chosen.

A trust could even function during your lifetime. By setting aside monies today, a bank or trust company could manage the funds and pay out income as you directed.

◆ **Factor special needs into your life insurance planning.** If you have a child with a disability that will require lifelong support, make sure you own enough life insurance to pay for it. This should be built into the capital-needs analysis (CNA) performed by your life insurance agent or financial planner, as recommended in *Problem 6.* If you believe your parents may depend on you financially, build their needs into your life insurance plans.

◆ **Involve other family members in your planning.** Would other family members pick up the burden if you are not able? Make sure they are willing—don't assume they are, especially if you are trying to make certain a family member is not institutionalized, such as a parent with Alzheimer's disease or a child with mental challenges. Sometimes the estate owner's presence may be enough to intimidate or shame others into helping. Remove that presence though, and the support network can fold.

◆ **Use an attorney to create a special-needs trust.** While your financial planner can assist with the funding, only your attorney can create the legal documents, such as a will and trust, most appropriate to implement the ongoing support vehicles you will need. Lincoln D. Cathers, a planner with PLAN, Planned Lifetime Assistance Network, in Glen Falls, New York, recommends a supplemental-needs trust (SNT) when parents are caring for disabled children. These trusts are recognized in most states as effective vehicles to provide for the ongoing personal needs of the disabled beneficiary, without jeopardizing eligibility for government benefits such as Medicaid and Social Security income.

RECOMMENDED ADVISERS

 Use your **attorney** to draft the will and trust best suited to ensure ongoing protection and care for family members with special needs.

 Ask your **financial planner** for a CNA based on providing long-term or lifelong support for the individual in need. Discuss the long-term funding needs of the special family member, separate from the other financial objectives you have.

SEE ALSO

◆ **Problem 6:** *Insufficient Income for the Heirs* to review how you can plan for the income needs of your family, including dependent parents and adult children.

PROBLEM 14

GIFTS WITH RETAINED INCOME

One of the most common vehicles for reducing the size of your estate is the grantor-retained trust. It is useful when you want to reduce your estate without giving up the income that its assets can generate.

THE INTERNAL REVENUE CODE (IRC) has created specific rules for trusts that allow the estate owner to gift the asset while retaining income, known generically as *grantor trusts*. The donor creates a trust to receive the assets and pay an income back to the grantor for a specified number of years, or during the grantor's lifetime. At the end of that term, the trust transfers the assets to named noncharitable beneficiaries. If the grantor lives for the number of years specified in the grant of the gift, the asset is no longer in the donor's estate for federal estate-tax purposes. The value of the gift will be well below the market value of the asset because it is reduced (discounted) to reflect the fact that the donee will not receive the property from the trust until some time in the future. The farther into the future, the lower the gift-tax value.

There are three types of grantor trusts commonly used today:

1 Grantor-Retained-Annuity Trust (GRAT). The GRAT is a trust created with property transferred by the grantor for a fixed number of years, during which time the grantor receives a fixed amount of income, usually defined as a percentage of the assets at the time of the gift, say 5 or 6 percent. At the end of the specified time period, the assets pass to the beneficiaries named by the grantor. These are not charitable beneficiaries; gifts to charities use different trust vehicles *(see Problems 41 and 42).*

GRATs are especially useful when you are trying to bring the value of your estate below the combined unified credits of the owners. For example, a couple with a combined gross estate of $2,000,000 could transfer sufficient assets into the GRAT to reduce the estate to the current unified-credit limit of $1,250,000. *(See Table 1.3 to review how a couple's unified credit will increase to $2,000,000 by 2006 under the new tax laws.)*

2 Grantor-Retained Unitrust (GRUT). With a GRUT, the grantor's income is based on the annual revaluation of the trust assets, though it, too, is specified as a fixed percentage for a fixed term of years. For example, an income based on 6 percent of the trust principal each year will increase as the trust assets appreciate, or decrease if the assets decrease in any year. With the average long-term appreciation of common stocks, GRUT incomes have risen significantly over time.

3 Grantor-Retained-Income Trust (GRIT). The GRIT is

now used primarily for gifts consisting of personal property, such as valuable art and antiques or a personal residence. When your residence is used, the GRIT usually is a qualified personal residence trust (QPRT). You can only include one residence in the trust, but you may include fractional shares in the residence. The grantor must reside in the home and use the home solely as a private residence. A QPRT is not intended to be an income vehicle.

CASE STUDY

Grandmother Holmes, an 80-year-old widow with an estate whose value is well over the $625,000 unified credit limit in 1998, wants to eliminate as much tax as she can, but does not want to move out of her home sooner than she has to. Her health is poor but she refuses to sell her home in order to go into a nursing home at this time. Her tax adviser recommended a QPRT for her $400,000 home that she owns mortgage free.

The accountant said she could put the residence into a QPRT for five years and gift $163,780 immediately out of her estate. The accountant arrived at the figure using the grantor's age, actuarial tables in the IRC regulations, and the grantor's needs. The value of the *retained interest,* that is, her ability to live in the home for five years, would be valued at $236,220 ($400,000 – $163,780). If she died during the five years, only the $236,220 would be included in her estate. If she survives the five-year period, the entire property escapes estate taxation.

If the property appreciated only 3 percent each year, the house would be worth $463,710 in five years. By removing the complete asset from her estate, the potential estate-tax savings is $110,974 ($463,710 – $163,780 = $299,930 x 0.37 = $110,974). Grandma gets to stay in the house for at least another five years, and the asset will pass to her children as she had intended, only without an estate tax.

Arthur Kolecter has owned a significant fine-art collection for most of his adult life. However, his tax advisers have convinced him that his death will likely force his executor to sell some of his finest pieces to pay the estate tax. He has heard that owning paintings in a GRIT could help reduce the tax bill without his having to give up the enjoyment of the masterpieces. He has a rare modern sculpture valued by the market at $1 million.

Art wants to keep the sculpture in his private collection for 15 years, then let it pass to his grandchildren. By transferring the work into a GRIT, Art is able to make a gift of over $250,000 to his grandchildren, thereby reducing the value of the asset for estate-tax purposes by 25 percent ($1 million x 0.25). If he survives the 15 years, the trust transfers the sculpture to the grandchildren tax free, and the $1 million is completely removed from his estate for tax purposes.

If the artwork appreciates at only 3 percent each year, its value will grow to $1,557,967 in 15 years. Being in the 55 percent estate-tax bracket, the potential estate-tax savings is approximately $850,000 ($1,557,967 x 0.55 = $856,881.85).

Ms. Lotta Land is a 70-year-old with significant real estate holdings producing barely enough income for her to live on in her retirement. She realizes that the estate tax at her death will be staggering, but she has a difficult time parting with any assets that are income producing. Her accountant has told her that she should consider transferring one of her $1 million apartments into an income-producing trust. She asked what the advantages would be.

The accountant suggested a GRAT with a level payout of 6 percent, or $60,000 on her $1 million asset. She agreed as long as the trust continued for at least 25

years. With these parameters, Ms. Land's gift-tax value
of $607,636 would just about match her unified credit
of $625,000. The value of her retained-income inter-
est would be $392,364. She would be reducing her tax-
able estate to zero at the end of the 25 years. Clearly,
one can plan one's gifts to meet the available credit.

CASE STUDY

Mr. Grant Ore owns an interest in a $1,000,000 parcel
of real estate believed to have gold in an old mine. He
wants to get rid of the property, but not the income
that he receives from the lease of the land to a
prospecting company, currently generating 6 percent
of the value of the land, or $60,000, annually. The
lease also provides that the lease income payment is to
increase annually at a rate of 3.5 percent. What are the
potential advantages of the trust to Mr. Ore?

If the property appreciates at 7 percent a year, what
is the value of the gift into a grantor-retained trust for
Mr. Ore? According to the tax tables, the value of
Grant Ore's gift is $483,760. He will receive $60,000
this year, $60,580 next year, and by the end of the 10th
year his income will be up to approximately $65,000.
Mr. Ore can live out his life on the land yet escape the
potentially high taxes on the property in the future,
particularly if the lessees strike it rich and the property
appreciates quickly. All of that appreciation would be
out of Ore's estate.

There are literally thousands of alternatives to
choose from when contemplating grantor trusts. The
requirements though are burdensome and complex.

SOLUTIONS

◆ **Ask your tax adviser about the advantages of creating
grantor trusts.** The grantor-retained trusts are essentially tax-planning vehicles. They must be created with
great attention to detail and legal requirements in
order to steer clear of confrontations with the IRS.

The property must be placed in an *irrevocable trust,* which means you as the grantor cannot change your mind after the property is transferred. The assets should be appraised so that you can substantiate the property's value for purposes of calculating the amount of both the gift and the retained-income interest. The payout of the income must be mandatory, not discretionary. Neither the grantor nor his or her spouse should serve as trustee, especially after the retained-income interest expires.

An attorney will usually charge less than $2,500 for a grantor trust, but check before the drafting begins. You can often save attorneys' and accountants' fees if you allow a knowledgeable financial planner to make hypothetical calculations for you in advance of your meetings with the fee-based professionals.

◆ **Explore the use of a QPRT.** This is an outstanding vehicle for removing an expensive residence from an estate, while preserving the owner's right to continue living in the house. The attorney should execute a lease that permits the grantor to lease the house if the original term of the trust expires. This fair market value–lease will enable the owner to stay indefinitely. Note that if the property ever ceases being used as a personal residence, the law requires the trust be terminated and the assets distributed to the resident, except that the assets could be converted into an annuity trust. It is important that the attorney provide for such a contingency.

◆ **Consider the use of grantor trusts if you are single with a substantial taxable estate.** Because single taxpayers have no marital deduction to soften the estate-tax blow, grantor-retained trusts can decrease the size of the estate today without taking away all of the income attributable to the assets. As a rule, gift the assets most likely to appreciate the greatest in the future.

◆ **Consider the use of grantor-retained trusts when your estate exceeds the combined unified credits for you and**

your spouse. In 1998, the combined credits are worth $1,250,000. Within 10 years, the combined credits will equal $2,000,000. However, the credits in 10 years will be applied against the value of your estate at that time. If your assets appreciate at 7.5 percent, your estate will be worth twice what it is worth today. Creating a GRAT or GRUT could reduce the current estate value, perhaps down to the $1,200,000 million level, and remove future appreciation from the estate altogether.

RECOMMENDED ADVISERS

 Consult your **tax accountant** before initiating steps to create grantor trusts. He or she can help substantiate values of assets and identify the ones most suitable for gifting.

 Use an **estate-planning attorney** with experience in creating grantor trusts to satisfy the stringent rules in the IRC.

SEE ALSO

◆ **Problem 2:** *The Estate-Tax Bite* to assess how significant the shrinkage can be.

PART

2

Longevity
PROBLEMS

THIS PART EXAMINES the mixed blessings of aging. Many planning problems arise because we are living too long—not in a Kevorkian sense, but in a financial sense. Americans are living longer just as a huge bubble in the population—the baby boomers—is nearing middle age. The implications? Longer lives require more funds for normal retirement needs, medical expenses, and assisted-living care.

Longevity is wonderful, but it makes greater demands on your investments. Inflation will have decades to erode your wealth, not just a few years. Living longer requires us to revise our perception of retirement and nursing homes, because so many more of us will live there. Higher medical costs push us to consider new insurance alternatives, such as long-term-care insurance, which is expensive.

The new paradigm for your later years puts

pressures not only on your investments but also on strategies for retiring from your business, if you have one of your own. Often, retirement money will be needed for two generations of seniors—you and your parents. If it is a priority to leave some of your estate to your children or your charities, planning assumes new levels of importance.

Part 2 teaches you how to finance long-term health care needs, how to calculate long-term income needs, and how to provide for yourself in your final days.

PROBLEM 15

LIVING TOO LONG
AND LONG-TERM CARE

Americans are living longer. At the same time, families are more mobile and less likely to be living near and able to care for aging parents. The combination of longer lives and less dependence on one's children puts pressure on the financing of retirement and professional assistance in old age. Increasingly, aging Americans are turning to new, assisted-living alternatives, and they are able to fund them with long-term-care insurance.

LONGER LIVES—GOOD NEWS or bad? Gail Sheehy, in her book *New Passages: Mapping Your Life across Time,* points out that "two-thirds of the total gains in life expectancy accomplished since the human species emerged have been made in this century alone." She documents this shift with sobering statistics. "A woman who reaches age 50 today—and remains free of cancer and heart disease—can expect to see her 92nd birthday." She also states that "a girl born in the United States today has a one-in-three chance of living to 100." The implications for trying to fund a retirement that spans 35 to 40 years are immense.

Jeff Sadler, author of *The Long-Term-Care Handbook,* adds to the statistical evidence of increased aging, "Since 1900, the percentage of all Americans over 65 has more than tripled." His research leads him to predict that "the most rapid increase is expected from 2010 to 2030 when the last of the baby boom generation reaches age 65." In fact, he projects there will be 15.3 million people over age 85 by the year 2050.

According to the June 30, 1997, cover story for *Newsweek* magazine, "How to Live to 100," the 100-plus age group is the "fastest-growing segment of the population," currently 61,000 strong and projected to hit 214,000 in the year 2020. By way of comparison, in 1940 only 3,700 Americans were age 100 or older.

Among the economic difficulties caused by these longer lives, the likelihood of needing long-term nursing care heads the list for most Americans. Adequacy of your retirement funds is the subject of *Problem 16.* The focus of *Problem 17* is protection against disability and incompetence occasioned by old age or disease.

What is the long-term-care threat all about? According to Sadler's *The Long-Term-Care Handbook,* a 65-year-old has a 43 percent chance of spending some time in a nursing home. The national investment firm Edward Jones, in St. Louis, tells its customers that one in four Americans will spend more than 90 days in a nursing home, and that the average stay is approximately three years. The average expense of nursing-home care is currently $38,000 a year. Northwestern National Life Insurance Company commissioned a study in 1992 of the effect that medical expenses would have on future retirement income. One of their findings was that the typical retired married couple in the early 21st century will deplete their assets within four years if just one adult needs home-health care.

The Northwestern National study found that 60 percent of Americans were concerned about their security in retirement because of health care costs. If this worries you, what should you do about it? Understand the types of long-term care you may need and how they can be financed.

The insurance industry has responded to the threat of expensive assisted living by offering long-term-care insurance. This insurance was designed to protect assets against the expenses of confinement in a nursing home or similar facility. There are four levels of nursing-home care: skilled, intermediate, custodial, and in home.

1 **Skilled care** is 24-hour supervision and assistance, provided by licensed professionals, such as registered nurses and physicians, and under the direct supervision of a licensed physician. It is medically necessary, usually involves a treatment plan, and is recuperative in nature. Less than 1 percent of all confinements involve skilled care and yet, they are the only ones covered by Medicare.

2 **Intermediate care** is likewise medically necessary and recuperative in nature, but the assistance can be

provided by registered nurses, licensed practical nurses, or nurses' aides. Only 4.5 percent of the cases involve intermediate care, and these are not covered by Medicare insurance. Consequently, these expenses are usually paid for out of pocket by the patient.

3 Custodial care can be provided by professionals or nonprofessionals and is usually not medically necessary. It involves assisting the patient with the activities of daily living (referred to as ADLs): bathing, mobility, eating, toileting, continence, and dressing. Almost 95 percent of all long-term care is custodial. Most insurance does *not* cover custodial care.

4 In-home care is usually performed by skilled professionals in your own home. It is recuperative and short term. Many people prefer to remain in their own homes for recuperation, but insurance coverage for treatment outside of medical facilities is usually very limited.

Medicare covers skilled care only. In the other three situations, you are on your own. However, insuring against these long-term needs is not the right answer for everyone.

SOLUTIONS

◆ **Buy long-term-care insurance for yourself only if you need it and can afford it.** The National Association of Insurance Commissioners (NAIC) requires insurance agents to provide buyers with the booklet *A Shopper's Guide to Long-Term-Care Insurance.* The booklet states, "Not everyone should buy a long-term-care policy. For some, a long-term-care policy is an affordable and attractive form of insurance. For others, the cost is too great, or the benefits they can afford are insufficient. You should not buy a long-term-care policy if it will cause a financial hardship and make you forego other, more pressing financial needs." That's a good rule of thumb, but for people concerned with preserving wealth, the premiums, while often hefty, usually will not create a financial hardship. What about the other side of the coin, though? At some point, you should avoid the premium expense and forgo the coverage because you have sufficient assets to cover the costs of long-term care yourself.

Where is that point?

◆ **Find out the cost of nursing homes in your area.** There is a significant difference in the quality and cost of long-term care throughout the country. Long-term care means more than just nursing-home services. According to Jeff Sadler, while there were 1.5 million Americans in nursing homes in 1993, there were 12 million receiving long-term-care services. Nevertheless, nursing-home expenses are a good place to begin your inquiry. Look in the Yellow Pages under "Retirement" and "Health Care" and call a few facilities to find out the range of daily rates in your area. In many communities, a good-quality nursing home costs $150 a day. This equates to $54,750 a year. The daily-rate figure is the starting point for your analysis.

◆ **Consider how likely it is that both you and your spouse will need long-term care.** If you are married, there is a strong probability—one in four—that one of you will. There is also the possibility that both of you will. Will your projected retirement income cover two households? Even if only one of you is placed in long-term care while the other stays home, you will have two households to support. Living on a retirement income of $75,000 a year, for example, could pose a problem for a married couple in a city where the annual cost of custodial care is $60,000. Their income will support the spouse in the care facility *or* the spouse at home, but not both. They will eventually begin exhausting their principal.

The guideline, then, is to buy insurance if you will not have the income to fund long-term care for each member of the immediate family. If you will have a retirement income of $150,000 a year, you most likely have enough to support the two households and therefore do not need long-term-care insurance.

◆ **Buy long-term-care insurance for parents if their incapacity will fall to you.** If you are the expected resource for parents likely to need long-term care, consider purchasing the insurance for them—you'll be protecting your own wealth along with theirs. Ask other family members to join in paying the premium.

Buy long-term-care insurance from sizable, quality insurance companies; the financial stability of the company is very important. Consult the NAIC *Shopper's Guide,* available from anyone who sells this type of policy, for the numbers of private companies that rate insurers as to financial strength. The oldest and most respected is A. M. Best Company. Because you will most likely need the coverage well into the future, you want to make certain your insurance company will be there. You want companies that are rated highly for creditworthiness and financial solvency. Insist on doing business with companies rated "A" or better.

If you buy insurance, buy only what you need. If the cost of care in your area is $150 a day and you have sufficient income to fund most of it, buy just what is necessary to make up the difference. There is no reason to buy the entire $150 daily benefit. And if you have sufficient cash reserves to pay for the first three months of care, select an *elimination period*—the time that you must satisfy out of your own resources before coverage is effective—that lasts 90 or 100 days. This is similar to a deductible and will reduce your premium. Under most policies, the coverage can be protected against inflation by purchasing a rider.

◆ **Place a higher emphasis on lifetime coverage than on a high monthly benefit.** The best way to decide on choosing insurance benefits is to take the "Big-Mistake Test." Ask yourself, for example, which would be the bigger mistake: to have full coverage for an insufficient length of time, or not quite sufficient coverage for the longer term. Suppose the premium is so high that full coverage for a lifetime benefit is unaffordable. Where do you compromise—on the daily benefit amount or the length of time the benefits will last? Some salespeople prefer to sell the higher benefit for a shorter time frame, such as three years. However, the policy is called long term for a reason. The period of time in a nursing home could easily be 7 or 10 years. In other words, the bigger mistake is to buy coverage that won't stay with you for the longer term. If necessary, try to reduce premiums by using higher elimination periods (such as 100 days) and fewer frills (such as inflation protection), but aim for a lifetime benefit.

If you buy insurance, look for key provisions:

— If affordable, buy lifetime benefits. When insurance runs out, your assets are next.

— Buy a benefit level consistent with the area's rates, reduced by the contribution you can make from your resources.

— Select as long an elimination period as you can afford, based on your cash reserves: 90 or 100 days is preferable.

— Make sure custodial care is covered and that the coverage begins when several, not all, ADLs are impaired. Some policies begin coverage when only two of the six ADLs are impaired.

— Make certain *cognitive impairment* is covered. This includes Alzheimer's and similar diseases that take away your ability to function mentally.

— Avoid policies that require prior hospitalization.

— Avoid policies that require a doctor's certification of medical necessity. Custodial care, the level of care required in 95 percent of all cases, is not medically necessary. There is often not a single, specific sickness or injury necessitating care. A policy requiring certification will not pay benefits unless a doctor says the confinement is medically necessary.

— Buy an inflation rider if available and affordable.

Most quality policies offer options to add inflation protection. For the last few years, inflation has been relatively low by historical standards, but that situation could easily change.

— Only buy policies with *guaranteed renewable* premiums. This means your coverage cannot be canceled or the premium raised on your individual policy if you have a claim; the insurance company can cancel your coverage only for fraud or failure to pay the premium. And it can only raise premiums for the entire class of policies sold in your state.

◆ **Consider retirement communities with long-term-care capabilities.** Living to age 90 or 100 can put an unforeseen burden on the wallet and the family. Awareness of this possibility has made continuing-care retirement communities (CCRCs) very popular, especially where they offer medical and long-term-care facilities on the premises. Some of the better communities are full and have waiting lists. If you are within three years of needing to "downsize," don't wait until you are ready to move to look into a CCRC. Look now in case a waiting period is required. Make sure the community cannot cancel your contract for any reason, such as poor health.

◆ **Don't try to circumvent the rules for Medicare and Medicaid by transferring assets out of your name.** Medicaid is a welfare program for people with low incomes. If you are wealthy today, you shouldn't even be considering transferring assets for yourself or your spouse. You should seek other than Medicare or Medicaid means for aiding your parents as well. Consult an attorney before transferring any of your assets or your parents' assets. There are criminal penalties for fraudulent transfers.

RECOMMENDED ADVISERS

Use an **attorney** for any arrangements for long-term-care assistance that involve the transfer of assets.

Consult a professional **life insurance underwriter** for long-term-care insurance from a quality company and with liberal benefits.

SEE ALSO

◆ **Problem 16:** *Outliving Your Income* on having enough income-producing assets to live comfortably through an elongated retirement.

◆ **Problem 17:** *Mental Incapacity and Life Support* to see how the insurance you own can be coupled with the documents you have to ensure a smooth transition from living to death.

PROBLEM 16

OUTLIVING YOUR INCOME

Increasing longevity and persistent inflation combine to pose the greatest financial threat facing retirees—outliving their income. Planning for retirement today requires a longer outlook than ever before, because you are setting the foundation for a future that could easily span 40 years. Inflation erodes wealth insidiously, undetected until it is almost too late. You must be reasonable in your expectations and conservative in your lifestyle.

WHEN THE SOCIAL SECURITY ACT passed in 1935, the intention was to create a safety net for older workers in this country. The normal retirement age was 65. However, the life expectancy for a male worker in 1935 was only 62. If the system were being implemented anew today, the normal retirement age would be well beyond age 70. Benefits would logically start only at about age 75. Yet, Americans no longer consider Social Security a safety net, they believe it to be an entitlement for having paid Social Security taxes during their working years. Workers even talk about "getting back what they paid in."

One might assume that if you are considered

wealthy, adequacy of retirement income is not going to be a major concern. However, "wealthy" often means having a sizable net worth, not necessarily a high income. Such has been the plight of the farmer for years—high net worth because of the real estate value of the farm, but relatively cashless.

If we are going to live for 40 or more years in retirement, we had better understand the dynamics of keeping enough principal to make it over the long haul. Ideally, you would have enough to provide a never-ending stream of income.

CASE STUDY

Ms. Forever, with $1 million in bonds yielding 7 percent, will have an annual income of $70,000 every year. Assuming the bonds had long-term maturities—say 30 years—Ms. Forever could feel confident that this 7 percent income would remain stable at least that long. And if she could live on $70,000, her principal of $1 million would remain intact. Unfortunately, that's only half the story because she must also contend with inflation. If inflation is 3 percent, then her $70,000 will only have the purchasing power of $67,900 the second year ($70,000 x 0.97 = $67,900) and $65,863 the third year. Is that so bad?

If we invoke the Rule of 72 in Ms. Forever's planning, we find that the $70,000 will have half the purchasing power in 24 years:

72 ÷ Interest rate = Years to double
72 ÷ 3 = 24

If Ms. Forever is 60 when the income commences, she will, in effect, have $35,000 worth of annual purchasing power at age 84. If she lives to 108, her yearly $70,000 will have the purchasing power of $17,500 today.

The natural response to Ms. Forever's dilemma is to systematically reduce the principal to receive addi-

2.1	MS. FOREVER'S DILEMMA		
YEAR	INVESTMENT ACCOUNT VALUE	INVESTMENT ACCOUNT EARNINGS AT 7 PERCENT INFLATION	WITHDRAWAL OF ADJUSTED INCOME
1	$1,000,000	$70,000	$72,100
2	997,900	69,853	74,263
3	993,490	69,544	76,491
4	986,543	69,058	78,786
5	976,816	68,377	81,149
10	876,490	61,354	94,074
15	657,169	46,002	109,058
20	258,431	18,090	126,428
22	30,380	2,127	134,127

tional interest income. But by how much? By the rate of inflation. In Ms. Forever's case, she could increase her income by 3 percent each year. Therefore, an income of $70,000 this year would need to be $72,100 next year and $74,263 the year after:

$70,000 x 1.03 = $72,100
$72,100 x 1.03 = $74,263

The obvious risk is that the person will live so long that the principal will actually disappear. How long will that take in Ms. Forever's case? Look at TABLE 2.1, *above.*

Ms. Forever's income and principal runs out in 23 years. For a 60-year-old woman, that is just about her life expectancy. Not a very pleasant prospect once she is aware of how fast the funds will disappear.

The problem becomes more severe when the retiree withdraws more than the funds earn.

CASE STUDY

Mr. Spensit, a 65-year-old widower, sold his pharmacy to a national chain for well over a million dollars in cash. After being tied to the business for years, he now travels extensively, favoring cruises and tours with other singles his own age. He maintains his home worth $350,000 and his personal property, but his only other assets are in the bond portfolio he established with the $1 million net after taxes from the sale of his business. The portfolio yield is 7 percent a year. He starts taking out $100,000 a year in income (increasing his withdrawals by 3 percent each year to keep up with 3 percent inflation). How long can Spensit's money last? See TABLE 2.2, *below*.

Poor Mr. Spensit's lifestyle will catch up with him sooner than he thinks. His life expectancy carries him into his early 80s. Unfortunately, his spending habits will carry him into the poorhouse in his late 70s. His $1 million will be gone in 14 years.

The challenge is to adopt a standard of living that matches your income and assets. This means balancing investment results and withdrawals. The best allocation of investments is one that gives you a measure of safety combined with returns that keep you ahead of inflation. There is a tendency for many people in and near retirement to be too conservative with their investments, rely-

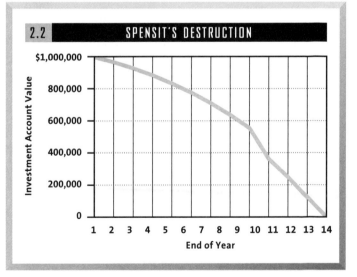

2.2   **SPENSIT'S DESTRUCTION**

Investment Account Value vs *End of Year*

ing entirely on fixed-income investments such as bonds.

Bonds appeal to risk-averse investors because of their safety of principal: a $10,000 U.S. government bond paying 5.5 percent provides $550 income a year, without worry about safety of the $10,000. Unfortunately, with inflation, the "real rate of return" is somewhat less than 5.5 percent. To find the real rate, you must subtract inflation. If inflation is 3.5 percent, the real rate of return on that bond is 2 percent. On the other hand, if a common stock with a 2.5 percent dividend also appreciates in its share value at 8 percent annually, its total return is 10.5 percent and the real rate of return is 7 percent.

The historical returns of the various investment asset classes illustrate the reason for investing a portion of your assets in *equities,* that is, common stocks and mutual funds that own stocks. *Chase Investment Performance Digest* reports that the long-term rate of return on stocks is significantly better than the return on bonds (*see* TABLE 2.3, *on the following two pages*).

Many retirees, especially those old enough to remember the depression years from 1929 into the early 1930s, still cling to their preoccupation with safety. They create a portfolio of certificates of deposit (CDs) or government bonds and sit back believing their assets are safe forever, only to find they can no longer live on the interest alone, because of inflation.

SOLUTIONS

◆ **Determine your retirement income.** List all your income sources not including your investments, such as company pensions, Social Security, annuities, and gifts. Then list your income-producing assets and the current income from each. If the total is less than you need to live, figure out where you can cut back your expenses or improve your rate of return.

◆ **Trim your expenses.** Unless you are among the very wealthy, with say, $5,000,000 of income-producing

2.3 CHASE'S RETURNS OF DIFFERENT ASSET CLASSES

A comparison of average investment performance over time

ASSET CLASS	5 YEARS	10 YEARS
U.S. 3-month CD	4.55%	6.03%
U.S. 10-year Treasury Bond	6.60%	7.51%
Moody's BAA Corporate Bond	8.36%	9.35%
Standard & Poor's 500 Stock Index	15.20%	15.19%
Lipper Growth Mutual Funds	12.79%	13.48%

assets, watch what you spend. Do an annual budget. See where your money goes each month. Decide what you don't need and get rid of it. Some people fill their homes with magazines they never read. Stop the subscriptions and spend an afternoon a week in the library. Discontinue clubs you no longer frequent. Take advantage of seniors' discount programs. Ask for breaks on your automobile insurance premiums because of your age. (You probably don't need to go as far as Anne Scrieber, however. A retiree from the Internal Revenue Service [IRS] in the 1940s, she parlayed $5,000 into over $20 million by investing in common stocks, and in part by paring her expenses back so far that she even refused to buy a *Wall Street Journal* to track her portfolio.)

◆ **Get involved in your family finances while you and your spouse are alive.** If your mate or living companion does all the investing and bookkeeping, start to get involved. It is very painful for a recent widow or widower to try to learn about money after a lifetime of being cared for, especially during a period of bereavement. At a minimum, insist on being included in the investment decisions.

◆ **Create a balanced portfolio, based on your needs and resources, with the help of a financial planner.** Your investments need to last at least as long as you. If you have obligations of support, not just for yourself but

15 YEARS	20 YEARS	25 YEARS
7.09%	7.99%	7.53%
8.64%	9.01%	7.66%
10.68%	10.94%	9.38%
16.68%	14.42%	12.43%
14.58%	14.79%	11.99%

SOURCE: 1997 CHASE INVESTMENT PERFORMANCE DIGEST

also for a partner, the assets need to last at least as long as both of you. And if you want to leave something to your heirs, you must calculate your needs so as to never fall below the minimally acceptable inheritance level. A financial planner with good computer programs should be able to tell you how much money you will need to set aside. He or she can also show you how to achieve the desired investment results.

◆ **Factor inflation into your planning.** Whether you accommodate inflation by increasing your income each year or reducing your expenses, take it into account—at high enough numbers to be conservative. While current rates are less than 3 percent, the historical average since 1970 is 5.5 percent.

◆ **Be realistic in budgeting Social Security income.** If you are a generation ahead of baby boomers, born in 1945 or earlier, you can probably count on some retirement income from Social Security at age 65 (62 if you opt for early-retirement income). If you are a boomer or younger, plan your retirement needs without Social Security income. There is a strong likelihood that the changes required to save the Social Security system from bankruptcy will base benefits on a *means test,* that is, a test of your inability to provide an income for yourself. For planning purposes, it is simpler and safer to assume you will be precluded from receiving any Social Security income.

RECOMMENDED ADVISER

Use your **financial planner**'s capital-needs analysis (CNA) *(see Problem 6),* to determine your projected income needs for retirement.

SEE ALSO

♦ **Problem 7:** *Taxflation and Rapidly Appreciating Assets* to learn more about outfoxing inflation.

♦ **Problem 15:** *Living Too Long and Long-Term Care* to understand how to keep inflation from lowering your standard of living, and how to keep assisted-care costs from driving you into financial ruin.

PROBLEM 17

MENTAL INCAPACITY AND LIFE SUPPORT

Few issues are as emotionally charged as prolonging someone's existence on life-support devices. And few diseases are as feared as Alzheimer's because of the loss of one's mental faculties. As difficult as it is to imagine oneself in either circumstance, it is equally hard to appreciate in advance what they mean for the family and heirs of the victim. It is painful to see someone you love living at less than optimum levels, more so if they are in a coma or mentally incapacitated. It can also be a tremendous financial drain. You should prepare for these contingencies by adopting agreements that spell out how your affairs should be managed in your absence.

WHAT HAPPENS WHEN someone loses their capacity to care for themselves?

CASE STUDY

Ms. Mentis is a wealthy widow in her 70s. She has a portfolio of stocks and bonds worth $1,500,000, her own home at the beach, and a 10-year-old Cadillac with a current value of $2,500. Her income from the portfolio is $97,500 a year, paid out to her monthly by her broker. This has been more than sufficient, and she has been giving $10,000 a year to each of her two children and her two grandchildren to pay for college education expenses. Neither of her daughters lives close to Ms. Mentis, so she communicates with them primarily by phone. Her younger daughter, Faith, has noticed a certain "fogginess" during their conversations lately, but not enough to push a panic button. She has mentioned the tuition bills recently, but Ms. Mentis has not responded to Faith's hints. Her concern became alarm when she could not reach her mother on the phone. After a day's deliberation, Faith flew out to check on her mother.

Faith was not prepared for what she found. Her mother had allowed a family to move in with her, with a lease hastily scribbled on the back of a sheet of notebook paper. The terms all favored the tenant. Bills were stacked all over the house, although Ms. Mentis seemed to occupy only her own room, which was unkempt and dirty. The boarders were in possession of her checkbook and were cashing her checks from the brokerage firm. All the money in her accounts had been spent. The Cadillac was not at the house.

Faith's recourse is through the courts. However, the legal battle is likely to be a lengthy process. She must disrupt her life to try to salvage what is left of her mother's, before the unscrupulous tenants spend everything.

The scenario played out above is not farfetched. People lose their mental capacity, and not always slowly. People also lose the ability to care for themselves physically, through illness or accident. Life is much easier if someone in the family or a close circle of friends can step in and act for the person in need. This is the purpose of a power of attorney.

A *power of attorney* is a legal document that appoints another person, called the *attorney-in-fact,* to act on behalf of the *principal,* the person creating the document. The power may be all inclusive or narrow, and it usually lasts until canceled or until the principal is disabled or somehow incapacitated. A *durable power of attorney,* on the other hand, does not terminate at the disability or incapacity of the principal. On the contrary, it is written specifically for the event of incapacity.

The second issue addressed in this Problem is the cost of life-support measures designed to keep someone alive, even though there is no chance of recovery. You might have strong feelings about not wanting to be kept alive through life-sustaining measures and machines. However, the medical profession's duty is to keep you alive, regardless of cost. When the physician's and hospital's choice is life and your family's is a dignified death, the courts will often support the life-sustaining decision in the absence, from you, of a document to the contrary. That document is called a *living will* in most states.

SOLUTIONS

◆ **As part of your estate plan, execute a durable power of attorney.** This document enables the person or persons you designate to conduct your affairs when you are incapacitated. Be specific as to the extent of the power you wish to convey. It can be limited, such as to only permit the payment of bills. Or it can be very broad, i.e., to allow the complete handling of one's affairs.

◆ **Use a lawyer to draft the document.** Most states have adopted the "Durable Power of Attorney" section of the Uniform Probate Code (UPC). This is a federal statute recommended for states to adopt to allow uniformity in state laws. Those states that have not adopted it usually have their own statutes governing durable powers. The language required by these statutes is quite specific, though it may vary from state to state.

◆ **Appoint an attorney-in-fact who understands you, your needs, and your intentions.** For most of us, this narrows the list of potential attorneys-in-fact considerably. Yet, with the magnitude of the decisions and responsibilities of the attorney-in-fact, you will want someone close to you and your thinking at the helm. Family members are especially appropriate if they are close.

◆ **Decide whether you want a living will.** This is sometimes called a *health care directive* or a *health care surrogate form*—the name varies from state to state. The purpose is to appoint someone who can make the difficult decisions as to when to withhold or withdraw life-support systems. Many hospitals require this form before they will consider these issues. Use your lawyer. Most state laws require the document to be in writing and signed by two witnesses other than the attorney-in-fact. Frequently, it must also be notarized.

◆ **Give copies of the durable power and living will to family members, your lawyer, and your family doctor.** Do not wait until you are at the hospital's door. Discuss them with your family now. Make sure your family physician knows your intentions before he or she is called upon to make a judgment call.

◆ **If privacy is a major concern, consider incorporating the durable-powers provisions into a living trust.** By transferring title to your assets and the powers of attorney into the trust, you are assured of privacy in the decisions affecting your health and estate. Don't create a living trust just to avoid probate if probate isn't onerous.

RECOMMENDED ADVISER

Ask your **attorney** to draft both a durable power of attorney and, if you are opposed to the use of life-sustaining devices when there is no chance of recovery, a medical durable power of attorney (or whatever its title is in your state).

PART 3

Business
Succession
PROBLEMS

WNERS OF closely held businesses face special challenges when they want to retire or move on to other pursuits. Publicly traded companies enjoy a ready market for their stock. Closely held enterprises do not, primarily because they are owned by so few individuals or perhaps another company. Owners frequently wonder how they can exit the business, but rarely take action until it is too late. It is often difficult and sometimes impossible to find a buyer. Private companies also suffer because of the limitations imposed by the form of entity they have adopted: sole proprietorship, partnership, or one of the forms of incorporation. Business succession agreements overcome many of these challenges.

Death and disability are two events that can destroy a closely held enterprise whose owner failed to plan for these contingencies. Owners can, in most instances, make adequate preparations to dispose of their business interest in advance of either tragedy.

Owners selling closely held companies often fail to protect themselves against the subsequent failure of the business after their exit. New owners often run the venture into the ground. Sellers relying on installment payments find themselves forced to repossess the company after considerable damage has been done to the company's reputation and financial solvency.

Divorce also undoes many closely held businesses. There are measures that can minimize the negative impact of divorce on the source of the litigants' livelihood.

This Part helps the owners of closely held businesses deal with the threats to their wealth occasioned by their exit from the enterprise.

BUSINESS CONTINUATION AND THE CLOSELY HELD CORPORATION

What happens to the value of the stockholder's interest in the corporation when the stockholder-owner exits the business? The primary concern should be the well-being of the owner and the heirs, with the well-being of the business a very close second. Typically, there are three exit doors: retirement, death, and disability. One is welcomed, the other two are not. However, all three can be planned for.

ANY DECISION TO LEAVE a business is a "retirement," including selling and moving on to something else, hiring new management and reducing your role to passive ownership, or liquidating and collecting a "pension."

Inevitably the question arises, how can you walk away from the company in a way that converts the accumulation of money, invested and reinvested, and your sweat equity—long hours and hard work—into enough dollars to move on to the next phase of life?

The answer often hinges on the availability of successor-owners.

Business continuation can be an option if there are other owners or family members active in the business, or if there are competent key employees. However, successful continuation must be carefully orchestrated because the primary concern of the departing stockholder—you—is how to convert an illiquid corporate stock interest into cash.

If there are other stockholders, they are the likely first choice for successor ownership. However, most corporations don't have sufficient cash on hand to buy out the majority stockholder. And more often than not, the prospective owners' and/or the corporation's credit may not be strong enough to allow them to borrow enough to complete a cash buyout.

The more likely scenario is an installment purchase of the departing owner's stock. This may be acceptable to the retiring stockholder, even advantageous. From a time standpoint, the retiree receives the purchase price spread out over several years. And from a tax standpoint, there may be opportunities for preferential capital gains treatment over the same time period. However, what about the risks that the seller must assume? What security does the seller have that the buyers will live up to their promises to pay? Read *Problem 24* for a detailed discussion of installment sales.

Surprisingly, the risks are often greater if the installment purchasers are family members. What happens if the new owners are not successful in their efforts to continue the business? And how does the seller protect him or herself without threatening to rend the delicate fabric of the family? Internecine warfare among family members makes headlines when a public company goes through ownership challenges. However, smaller enterprises can generate just as much rancor.

Agreements between family members invite closer scrutiny than do contracts with outsiders. Internal Revenue Service (IRS) regulations penalize transactions that are not "bona fide business arrangements"—attempts by stockholders to pass the ownership of a business to family members for less than a fair price. Other provisions of the Internal Revenue Code (IRC), apply adverse tax consequences to corporate redemptions of stock if there are certain family ownership percentages. The rules are too complex for someone who isn't a tax professional; their mention is intended to warn against entering into agreements without good tax and legal counsel.

Retiring stockholders can look to loyal employees as potential buyers of the business. Most stockholder-owners fail to bring in capable key employees early enough to be ready to assume control when the owner wants out.

Getting the full value out of the business is difficult enough when there is time to plan the exit; it is magnified by the owner's death or disability. Either event removes a critical element from the planning process: time.

Total disability of a major stockholder creates a special challenge: the business is without a primary revenue producer at the same time that the owner needs not only a continuing income stream, but often extra income to meet expenses not covered by insurance. The family or other stockholders may be faced with the difficult decision as to whether to continue the business, and if so, how to do it without the primary stockholder's involvement.

Death exacerbates the problem of receiving full value for the majority-ownership interest. At death, without an agreement to the contrary, the stock passes to the estate. If the stock passes under the decedent's will, the executor has the responsibility of preserving the assets of the estate. If he or she believes the estate is better served by closing down the business and liquidating the assets, that is his or her responsibility, regardless of how it affects minority stockholders or loyal employees. If the stock passes to the decedent's spouse, the remaining stockholders and key employees may find themselves answerable to someone with no knowledge of the business. Or, the stock could pass into trust, with a corporate trustee or the family lawyer suddenly in charge. None of these are a bright prospect for the survivors. All are avoidable.

CASE STUDY

Ann Deavor and Sharon Itall own a successful antique gallery, as equal stockholders of a *Subchapter C* (a regular) corporation. Last year they turned down an offer to sell for $400,000, believing that the business was worth half again that amount. Besides, they wanted to keep working. Among the many keys to their success is their ability to work long hours with each other and to complement each other's strengths.

Their life insurance agent disturbed them by asking what would happen if either of them died or became disabled. Ann, a widow, was especially threatened by the thought. Sharon, who cares for her semi-invalid father, recognized the threat of disability. They asked what they should do. The agent recommended an insured *business continuation agreement (BCA)*. This is a contract that provides for the transfer of the stock ownership to a party who will continue to operate the business. They thought about it briefly, but deferred acting on the idea when sales activity exploded in anticipation of the Christmas season. Ann died of a heart attack just before the holidays ended.

Ann had a will drawn up after her husband's death. Unfortunately, it did not address her business interest. She left all her assets in trust for her minor children. The trust company serving as trustee is concerned because of the lack of liquidity in the trust. Ann owned the business and a nice home, but not much in the way of stocks, bonds, certificates of deposit (CDs), or life insurance. The trustee wants to liquidate the corporation, believing the sale of the antiques to be a quicker and easier approach than trying to sell or continue the business. Sharon is distraught because she wants to continue the business. Clearly the two stock owners, the trustee and Sharon, have competing objectives.

What could Ann and Sharon have done to prevent this unfortunate entanglement?

SOLUTIONS

◆ **Realistically assess the implications of your withdrawal from the business.** If you are the primary, or only, stockholder, do you have the quality of management in place to enable you to leave the corporation without having to sell your stock position? One of the advantages of doing business in the corporate form is the potential for the unlimited life of the enterprise. However, business structure alone will not guarantee success. You must create the environment that will give the new owners the optimal chance to succeed, especially if your future income depends on it.

◆ **Hire and train successor-owners long before your planned departure.** If your business is not the kind that can be easily sold for cash in the open market (and most can't), create your own market by setting up the key people in-house to be the purchasers. Don't assume you can bring in someone talented to take your place a few months before you depart. It takes time to find, recruit, and develop successor-managers who can become successor-owners.

◆ **Enter into a written BCA.** A written agreement, drafted by an attorney, is critical. By contracting with the ultimate purchaser, you create a guaranteed market for your business in the event of your death or disability. You also improve the likelihood of a market for your stock when you voluntarily retire. An agreement can avoid the problem of surviving stockholders ending up in business with a surviving spouse or the children's trustee. It can fix the price of the stock purchase stated in the agreement, either by a dollar amount or a formula. This agreed-upon sale price can peg the value of the stock for federal estate-tax purposes.

◆ **Consider stock-redemption agreements for complete buyouts if family members are not the purchasers of the stock.** A stock-redemption agreement, or an *entity agreement* as it is called generically, is entered into between the corporation and the stockholder(s). It obligates the decedent or the decedent's estate to sell the stock, and it obligates the corporation to buy the same stock interest *(see* TABLE 3.1, *at right)*.

When the stockholder dies, the redemption agreement returns the stock to the corporation. The estate, in turn, receives cash or promissory notes, or both. The remaining stockholders are in control of

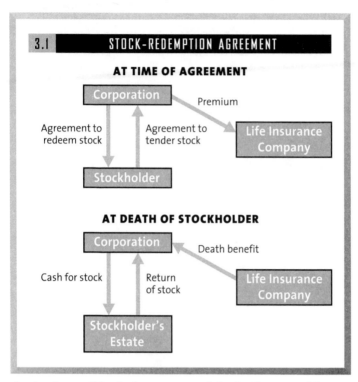

3.1 STOCK-REDEMPTION AGREEMENT

AT TIME OF AGREEMENT

Corporation

Premium

Agreement to redeem stock

Agreement to tender stock

Life Insurance Company

Stockholder

AT DEATH OF STOCKHOLDER

Corporation

Death benefit

Cash for stock

Return of stock

Life Insurance Company

Stockholder's Estate

the business. The heirs are out of the business and in receipt of the cash. The value of the stock owned by the remaining stockholders increases by the dollar amount of the redemption. However, their cost basis in the stock for income tax purposes remains the same.

EXAMPLE

If Ann and Sharon in the case study above had entered into a stock-redemption agreement before Ann's death, the result would have been much different, even with the provisions found in Ann's will. For example, assume such an agreement had an agreed-upon value of $600,000. And assume that the life insurance agent who pointed out their problem also sold life insurance to fund the agreement. The corporation would have purchased $300,000 policies on the lives of each of the two stockholders, payable to the corporation as beneficiary. The premiums paid by the business would not have been tax deductible, but the proceeds at Ann's death would be received by the corporation income tax free. Under the terms of the agreement, Ann's children's trustee would have been obligated to tender Ann's stock, and the corporation would have been obligated to buy the stock. The trust for Ann's children would have ended up with $300,000 in cash. Sharon would have ended up with 100 percent of the company's stock, at a cost of less than $1,000 per year for the premium on the policy covering Ann. If Sharon's original cost basis in her stock was $50,000, it would remain so after the redemption, meaning that she would have a gain on the sale of her stock for any amount above her $50,000 original cost basis. This means that if she then sold the business for $600,000, she would report a $550,000 gain on the sale.

Ann's estate would suffer no adverse income tax treatment because it would have received the stock at what is called a *stepped-up basis* at her death. The tax law permits the step up here because the value of the business was being included in Ann's gross estate for federal estate-tax purposes. Consequently, the heirs would receive a new cost basis equal to the fair market value of the stock at the date of death, which is, in fact, the value the executor uses for estate-tax purposes. (When there is a stock-redemption agreement, the executor will use the value established by the agreement.) In this case, the value was $300,000; therefore, this is the new cost basis to the estate. When the executor sold the stock under the agreement for the same $300,000 figure, there would have been no gain and no income tax due.

Insured stock redemptions in regular corporations can also trigger the alternative minimum tax. The receipt of the insurance proceeds can increase corporate earnings and profits enough to give rise to the tax. The specter of the alternative minimum tax and the lack of an increase in basis for the surviving stockholder is often enough to justify a cross-purchase agreement, explained in the next solution.

Use insured cross-purchase agreements to improve the tax position of the surviving stockholder. A *cross-purchase agreement* is a contract directly between the stockholders. It obligates the deceased stockholder's estate to sell to the surviving stockholder(s). The corporation is not directly a party to the agreement. Again, a written agreement can fix the price and the terms of the purchase. Insurance can provide the liquidity to fund the purchase obligation. Each stockholder owns insurance on the life of the other(s). If necessary, the corporation can "bonus" the stockholders the money to pay the premiums. At death, proceeds are received income tax free by the survivor, who then uses them to buy the stock from the decedent's estate.

Applying this alternative to the case above, Sharon would receive the $300,000 life insurance proceeds on Ann's life, tax free. She then buys Ann's stock from Ann's estate for $300,000. Sharon's basis in the corporate stock she purchases increases by that $300,000. If the original basis in her half of the corporation was $50,000, her new basis is $350,000. If she sells the business to a third party at some future date, the increase in basis of $300,000 could save her $60,000 in taxes under the new 20 percent capital gains rate ($300,000 x 20 percent).

Buy permanent insurance for permanent needs and term insurance for temporary needs. An example of a temporary need is one that is short term in nature, say 10 years or less. However, buy term insurance if the permanent premiums are too expensive for the corporation or stockholders to afford *(see* TABLE 3.2, *on the following page)*.

Insure buy-sell agreements against disability of the owners. Life insurance guarantees that the purchaser will have the cash to complete the purchase from the

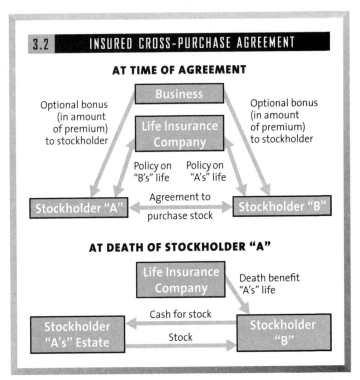

3.2   INSURED CROSS-PURCHASE AGREEMENT

AT TIME OF AGREEMENT

Business

Life Insurance Company

Optional bonus (in amount of premium) to stockholder

Optional bonus (in amount of premium) to stockholder

Policy on "B's" life   Policy on "A's" life

Stockholder "A"

Agreement to purchase stock

Stockholder "B"

AT DEATH OF STOCKHOLDER "A"

Life Insurance Company

Death benefit "A's" life

Cash for stock

Stock

Stockholder "A's" Estate

Stockholder "B"

decedent's trust or estate. If the owner doesn't die but is disabled, insurance is likewise available to provide the funds necessary to pay for the stock. Most agreements contemplate death but not long-term disability, despite the fact that disability is 2.9 times as likely as death for a 40-year-old, and 2.2 times as likely for a 50-year-old.

Disability policies can pay benefits in installments, in a lump sum, or, as is frequently preferable, as a combination of both. One concern shared by stockholders and insurance companies is the possibility that the disabled stockholder recovers after the buyout commences and wants to regain his or her stock interest. By requiring a waiting period of a year or two, the parties have adequate time to determine if recovery is a possibility before the buyout activates. The definition of disability in the redemption agreement or the cross-purchase agreement should mirror the definition in the policy. As with life insurance, disability insurance can be purchased by the corporation or by the stockholders, under either a redemption or cross-purchase agreement.

For maximum flexibility, adopt a "wait-and-see" buy-sell agreement. This approach gives the greatest flexibility to the parties to the agreement, the corporation, and the stockholders. The corporation has the first right to purchase the decedent's stock. The stock not purchased by the corporation may then be purchased by the surviving stockholders. If they do not purchase the remaining stock, the corporation must buy the remaining stock from the decedent's estate. This approach offers flexibility, but don't use it if you are trying to obligate the surviving stockholders because the wait-and-see agreement gives the surviving stockholders enough flexibility to say no to the purchase.

Build annual reviews or a formula for annual revaluation into the agreement. Review your agreement every year and whenever major shifts occur, such as changes in ownership, the company's level of debt, or its stock valuation. An outdated value can undo the binding nature of the valuation on the IRS. The more frequently the agreement requires a revaluation, the better an executor's argument in favor of the pegged value for estate-tax purposes.

RECOMMENDED ADVISERS

Use the corporation's **accountant** to help value the business. This valuation should serve as a starting point; from there negotiate the price with your fellow owners.

Have your **attorney** review the potential tax pitfalls and draft the agreement. Be sure to ask whether your situation calls for a stock-redemption or a cross-purchase agreement.

Insure your agreements against disability and death of the stockholders.

SEE ALSO

◆ **Problem 19:** *Partnerships and Quasi Partnerships* and
◆ **Problem 20:** *Death or Disability of the Sole Proprietor* to recognize the differences and similarities between continuation of a business as a corporation, partnership, or proprietorship.
◆ **Problem 22:** *The Family Business* to anticipate the binds that arise when family members own a business together.
◆ **Problem 23:** *The Family Farm* for similarities between ownership of family businesses and farms.
◆ **Problem 24:** *Relying on Income from the Sale of a Business* to ensure protection for the selling stockholder against unfinished buyouts.

PROBLEM 19

PARTNERSHIPS AND QUASI PARTNERSHIPS

What happens to a partner's ownership interest in a partnership when the partner exits the enterprise? A partnership is a form of doing business with very different characteristics from a corporation or a sole proprietorship. The specific differences dictate the best way to exit a partnership.

TAX LAWS TREAT the disposition of a partnership interest differently than they do the disposition of a corporate interest. When a partner exits the business, the departure could trigger an automatic dissolution of the partnership. Many partners are unaware of this "official" end to their business until the IRS—or if they're lucky, their accountant—starts to calculate tax bills based on the dissolution. In a *general partnership,* where each partner shares in the liability and the profits of the entity, each of the partners is liable for the debts of the partnership and the negligence or malpractice of the other partners.

CASE STUDY

Al Straight and Charles Edge entered into a partnership for the practice of psychiatry. Edge actually started the practice and brought the younger, less-seasoned Straight into his business as a 49 percent partner. Competition was fierce in the city and Edge seemed to have an opinion on how to get ahead at each juncture. Straight had some serious reservations about some of Edge's practices, but being the new guy on the block, he decided to keep his doubts to himself and tried to avoid confrontations. His mother told him to be thankful he had a job. He was shocked when he was sued for his partner's malpractice, not to mention physical-abuse charges brought by one of Edge's patients. After Edge's suicide, Straight was even more shocked to find out about the illegal drugs and about the company debt Edge had incurred to support his habit. When Straight called an old friend who was a lawyer, he was shocked when he was told, "Hire an entire law firm. You're liable and in deep trouble." Edge's death dissolved the partnership, but not Straight's liability.

The IRC says that if more than 50 percent of a partnership's capital and profits are sold in any 12-month period, then the partnership is automatically dissolved. However, the rules draw a distinction between a sale and a liquidation of the interest. For example, if Edge had actually agreed to sell his partnership interest to Straight at Edge's death, the partnership could have continued. A *liquidation* occurs when there are no plans for a continuation and death strikes a partner, and also when the parties just agree to end the company and liquidate the assets. A liquidation can also be planned to result in a recontribution of the assets to

3.3	COMPARISON OF BUSINESS TYPES	
CHARACTERISTICS	C CORPORATION	S CORPORATION
Description of owners	Stockholders	Stockholders
Number of owners	Unlimited	75 with spouses counted as 1
Liability of owners	Limited to personal actions	Limited to personal actions
Tax on profits	Tax at corporate level; if distributed, also taxed at stockholder level	Passed through to stockholder tax return
Tax on losses	Taken at corporate level	Same as tax on profits
Income splitting among owners	Not available	Not available

the partnership so as to restart the business without a taxable event. However, the recontribution is not automatic; you have to enter into an agreement that provides for the favorable tax treatment.

There are also potential income tax issues with certain assets of the partnership, called "hot assets"— usually unrealized receivables and substantially appreciated inventory items. These assets, if categorized by the IRS as "hot," could result in part of the purchase of the partnership interest being treated as ordinary income, rather than the more favorable capital gains income. Ordinary income is taxed as high as 39.6 percent, whereas capital assets held for 18 months and a day are taxed at a maximum rate of 20 percent.

Many people choose to conduct their businesses as partnerships because of the income tax laws. Profits can filter down to the partners' tax returns without a tax having been applied at the entity level, meaning there is no tax on the profits at the level of the business itself, just to the owners. However, two special types of corporations, Subchapter S corporations and

LIMITED-LIABILITY COMPANIES (LLC)	PARTNERSHIP
Members	Partners
Unlimited	Unlimited
Limited to personal actions	Personal actions are actions of partners unless limited partnership
Passed through to member tax return	Passed through to partners' tax returns
Same as tax on profits	Same as tax on profits
Available	Available

limited-liability companies (LLCs), have made it possible to gain many of the benefits of a partnership while enjoying the insulation of a corporation, increasingly advantageous in our litigious times. To understand the different forms of doing business, look at TABLE 3.3, *above.*

An *LLC,* then, is a form of doing business that seeks to insulate the members, as in a regular corporation, while preserving the tax treatment of a partnership; that is, the profits and losses are passed through to the members. That same tax treatment applies to a *Subchapter S corporation,* which is a corporation with a limited number of stockholders that is likewise taxed at the individual stockholder level and not at the corporate level.

Investors in an LLC are liable for the debts of the company only to the extent of their investment. In the case of a professional practice, such as a medical or legal practice, the participant can avoid being held liable for the acts of the other associates in the business. In a traditional partnership, there was no way to limit that liability. All states now allow LLCs or their equivalent, the limited-liability partnership (LLP). An *LLP* is the same thing as an LLC.

As in a partnership, Subchapter S and LLC losses and expenses can filter down to the individual's income tax return. However, with an LLC, there is the latitude to allocate both income and losses among the "members," unlike a regular or Subchapter S corporation, which requires passing the profits and losses strictly by percentage of ownership. Another advantage of the LLC is the ability to avoid the severe restrictions on the number and classes of stockholders under the IRS Subchapter S rules.

If you formed your LLC after December 31, 1996 and there are two or more owners, it will be taxed as a partnership, unless the owners choose to be taxed as a corporation. If there is only one owner, it will be taxed as a sole proprietorship. The presumption is that the owners prefer the more favorable tax benefits for themselves. In either case, there is no tax at the entity level. LLCs entered into prior to December 31, 1996 must satisfy tests that demonstrate that the business does not function as a corporation.

Partnerships, LLCs, LLPs, and Subchapter S corporations face the same exit challenges as any other business. Owners choose to retire or are forced to retire due to disability or death. They or their heirs are concerned about the ability to convert their investment into cash. The remaining owners want to retain control of their own business without interference by unwanted new owners or testamentary watchdogs. Buy-sell agreements accomplish these objectives.

SOLUTIONS

◆ **Use your accountant and attorney at the outset to help you choose the best form of doing business.** You'll need them both to explain the advantages of each form of business, as dictated by federal tax laws and your state's statutes. Often they can also create the entities more quickly and efficiently than you can because of their experience. Ask how much they charge to create the legal entity for you. It should be less than $1,000.

◆ **Enter into an insured buy-sell agreement.** Buy-sell agreements are important for partnerships, LLCs, and Subchapter S corporations. Cross-purchase agreements tend to be more advantageous taxwise, for partnerships particularly. This is primarily because of the increase in cost basis of the acquired interest by the surviving partner or stockholder, as discussed in *Problem 18.*

◆ **Consider joint life insurance policies to insure numerous partners.** When there are a large number of partners, such as in a law firm, a cross-purchase agreement with disability and life insurance could create a nightmare of paper. In a 30-partner firm with each partner owning life and disability insurance on the life of the other 29, the handling of 1,740 insurance policies would drive the firm's business manager bonkers.

Many insurance companies today issue a single policy insuring many lives. It pays a benefit at the death of each partner. This takes the cumbersomeness out of the insurance process, as in the case of numerous law partners or medical LLC members. Concerning individual or joint policies, there is no magic number, but you can make the decision by asking yourself just how many policies you'd want to handle if you were the business manager of your firm *(see* TABLE 3.4 *, on the following page).*

◆ **Consider shifting from a Subchapter S or partnership to a LLC or LLP.** If you have not explored the advantages of doing business under the new LLC or LLP provisions in your state, consult your attorney and accountant. The liability provisions of the new form of doing business are especially important for lawyers, physicians, accountants, psychologists, architects, and other practicing professionals. Owners in a LLC,

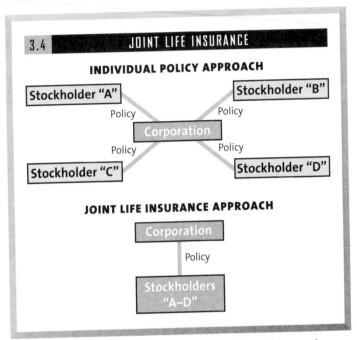

3.4   JOINT LIFE INSURANCE

INDIVIDUAL POLICY APPROACH

Stockholder "A"   Stockholder "B"

Policy   Policy

Corporation

Policy   Policy

Stockholder "C"   Stockholder "D"

JOINT LIFE INSURANCE APPROACH

Corporation

Policy

Stockholders "A–D"

called "members" in most states, function under an operating agreement. Typically, voting power reflects capital contributions. The agreement dictates how the company allocates both income and losses among the members.

RECOMMENDED ADVISERS

 Ask your **accountant** to recommend the best form of doing business for your industry and personal circumstances. Ask specifically about the application of the liability provisions of each entity.

 Have your **attorney** draft the documents of organization, such as the Articles of Incorporation, and buy-sell agreements between the entity and its owners or between the owners themselves.

 Insure your buy-sell agreements against the death and disability of owners, whether they are partners in a partnership, stockholders of an S corporation, or members of an LLC.

SEE ALSO

◆ **Problem 18:** *Business Continuation and the Closely Held Corporation* to understand the functioning of the typical corporation at the owner's exit.

PROBLEM 20

DEATH OR DISABILITY OF THE SOLE PROPRIETOR

The exit strategies of a sole proprietor are very different from those of a business with multiple owners. Most obvious is the lack of a co-owner to continue the operation of the business or buy out the departing owner's interest. By law, the death of a sole proprietor terminates the business. This places the personal representative (either an executor under a will or an administrator if there is no will) in the difficult position of having to choose between disposing the assets separately or selling the business intact, while lacking the express authority to continue the business operations in the interim.

IF A SOLE PROPRIETOR has time to plan, he or she can look in advance for a buyer of either the business or its assets. Typically, though, a sole proprietor waits until the last minute to think seriously about an exit strategy.

What if the sole proprietor doesn't have the time to recruit a new owner or find a buyer? When disability strikes or the owner dies prematurely, the value of the business is vulnerable to immediate and dramatic shrinkage. Almost by definition, the value of a sole proprietorship is largely indivisible from the sole proprietor's efforts, whether the business is an accounting practice or a jewelry store.

CASE STUDY

Mr. I. Shade, CPA, has built a valuable accounting practice in his town of 15,000 residents. He directs a staff of eight nonprofessionals and easily draws

$10,000 a month from his business. He considered a partnership once when the business was building so fast he could scarcely keep up, but he opted to restrict the number of clients instead. He has been able to set aside $12,500 into each of his four children's accounts for their education, but not much else. He thought he would worry about funding his retirement once they were out of school. He wanted his wife to forgo her career aspirations and raise the children. She did so happily, at least until he fell asleep behind the wheel after working late (as usual) during the tax season. His broken neck has left serious doubts as to whether he will ever return to work.

Mr. Shade and his family have gone from a comfortable, professional standard of living to financial crisis —overnight.

What happens to sole proprietorships such as I. Shade's in this situation? First of all, it's tax season. His clients must file their returns and pay their taxes. The staff stays late every night trying to keep up, but the clients with more complex problems must turn to other CPAs in the area. Their loyalty to Shade will not last forever, especially with the IRS lurking unsympathetically in the wings. Without the better clients, revenues shrink, and there are difficulties paying the staff's salaries, rent, and other overhead items. Gradually, the practice shrivels to nothing but bills for outdated tax-reference services and overdue leases.

Efforts to sell the practice fail when the potential buyers realize they could accomplish the same result by opening a business across the street from Shade's office. His clients will need to go somewhere. Why buy a cow when the milk's free?

The situation is not much better at home. Mr. Shade's efforts were the sole source of his family's income. Without his presence in the office and in front of clients, there is no income. By invading the four children's uniform gift to minors act (UGMAs), the Shades can pay some expenses attributable to the children's needs for a year or two, at best. The remainder of Shade's savings and investments won't carry them six months.

Would the situation have differed if Shade had died in the accident? Not much. Once the practitioner exits, his or her clients are fair game for every competitor in the vicinity.

If Shade had owned a bakery or a clothing store, there may have been more inventory or equipment the executor could have liquidated. However, who can say whether a bakery is an easier business to sell than an accounting practice?

What can you do differently from I. Shade to prevent this kind of tragedy from happening to you?

SOLUTIONS

◆ **Plan your voluntary exit well in advance of the time you want to retire from the business.** If yours is a personal-service business, you may need a year or longer to recruit a successor. You will need time to train the new associate and to evaluate his or her abilities and trustworthiness, especially if you are then going to sell the practice to him or her on an installment basis. Most sole proprietors opt to function alone for a reason. Admitting partners can be impossible for them. It will usually be difficult for them to work with less-experienced associates, even if it is just until both parties are comfortable with the buyout. Allow plenty of time and patience to work out the transition.

◆ **If your business is more product oriented, consider whether you would be better off selling the business, or just its assets, to another party.**

◆ **Protect yourself and your family with *disability-income insurance*.** This is insurance that replaces a portion of your income for a specified period of time, such as for

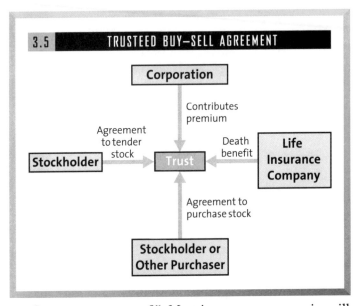

3.5 TRUSTEED BUY-SELL AGREEMENT

Corporation

Contributes premium

Agreement to tender stock

Death benefit

Life Insurance Company

Stockholder

Trust

Agreement to purchase stock

Stockholder or Other Purchaser

five years, or to age 65. Most insurance companies will allow you to purchase a policy guaranteeing a percentage of your income, not to exceed 50 to 70 percent. The premiums are not tax deductible, but the benefits are received income-tax free. Therefore, you don't need to replace 100 percent of your gross income, only your net after taxes.

◆ **Use the *elimination-period provision* to reduce premiums.** This is an option in the policy by which you specify the period of time that you must be disabled before benefits are payable. It is analogous to the deductible under your car insurance policy. When faced with a premium that is not affordable, opt for a longer elimination period and a lower monthly benefit, but keep the benefits payable for as long as possible. The rationale is that if you are disabled for life, you are better off with a reduced lifetime benefit than with a larger payout that stops entirely in several years.

◆ **Protect your family with life insurance.** Unlike multi-owner entities that have ready-made successors in interest, a sole proprietor's family may not realize any money from the winding down of the business. Some may even face liabilities in excess of the liquidation value of the assets. Personally owned life insurance guarantees your family an adequate income independent of a successful liquidation or transfer of the business.

◆ **Protect your business with business overhead insurance.** Sole proprietorships are especially vulnerable to severe drops in income in the event of the disability of the owner. Business overhead insurance provides the income to continue to pay the business bills during the owner's absence due to sickness or accident. The coverage is designed to pay the overhead for a limited period, such as 18 months or two years.

◆ **Look for a successor-owner in key employees or even competitors.** You can enter into buy-sell agreements with loyal employees, or even with your competitors. There is nothing to prevent the selection of successors who would buy your business only upon your death or disability. The agreements follow the same general guidelines for entity or cross-purchase agreements outlined in *Problems 18 and 19.* Or, you could enter into a *trusteed agreement (see* TABLE 3.5, *at left).*

The agreement is "trusteed" because it requires an individual or entity to act as a custodian, serve as an intermediary, and execute the transfer of the business, in return for the cash usually provided by a life or disability-income insurance policy. The ownership passes to the buyer upon receipt of the cash.

◆ **Update your will to give your executor the authority to continue or sell, as well as liquidate, the business or its assets.** This extra flexibility should make it easier to do what is best for your heirs. Without your authority, the executor will not likely try to do anything other than shut the business doors and liquidate the assets. This is because the executor is bound to protect the assets in the estate. If your family could continue the business and has shown some interest, give your executor the authority to transfer the business to them.

◆ **Don't confuse your family's interest in continuing the business with their ability to do so.** Just because a son or daughter, or even your spouse, has expressed an interest in the business, don't rely on this "interest" as the alternative to sound planning for your death, disability, or retirement, or as an excuse not to buy adequate life and disability insurance. If possible, involve any prospective successors in the day-to-day operation before assuming they can carry the load.

◆ **Realistically assess the value of your business.** A sole proprietorship is the most difficult business to sell. Choosing a value for the business is problematic because of the lack of a ready market, as well as the automatic dissolution at death. Don't overestimate the value of the business, especially in your estate planning. Your family shouldn't suffer because of your over-optimism. Have a professional appraise your business. He or she will likely point out the discount in its value due to the fact that it is a sole proprietorship without a ready buyer.

RECOMMENDED ADVISERS

 Ask your **accountant** to value your business and to recommend strategies for its disposition upon your exit.

 Use an **attorney** to draft any documents to substantiate the disposition of the business interest.

SEE ALSO

◆ **Problem 18:** *Business Continuation and the Closely Held Corporation* and **Problem 19:** *Partnerships and Quasi Partnerships* to understand the potential benefits of incorporation or a partnership as an alternative form of doing business.

THE LOSS OF A KEY EMPLOYEE

Most thriving businesses owe their success to having good people, usually in the form of talented management. These key employees are not always owners, but they are often every bit as valuable to the business. Smart owners make every effort to protect their business against losing key people to the competition, with either bonus packages, stock options, or similar incentives. However, they often overlook the monetary loss to the business brought about by the death or long-term disability of themselves or of these key employees.

THE DEATH OF a key employee creates a financial loss. The question is, how big? If the key employee is both the owner and the primary generator of new accounts, the loss will be reflected in lost sales. But how do you measure the lost opportunities? If the key employee is the originator of new products, how can you measure the lost creations? If the deceased is a successful litigator in a medium-sized law firm, how do you replace him or her in the middle of a case?

Many businesses could experience an immediate drop in revenues. Most are likely to incur significant expenses in trying to find a replacement, such as professional recruiter's fees, advertising, increased telephone bills, entertainment, and perhaps moving expenses and signing bonuses for the new person. The most vulnerable businesses are ones with the thinnest management structure—in other words, the typical closely held company.

What about the disability of a key employee? If an accident or sickness keeps the key person out for more than a year, at what point will you, as the owner, tell that valued employee that you've had to hire his or her replacement? Good business practice would dictate that you protect the business first, but that is not always an easy call. And if it's not an easy decision from the corporate point of view, how much more difficult will it be if there are no plans in place to continue the key employee's salary during the disability? Because of the obligation, moral or legal, to continue the disabled employee's income for some period, the expense of a disability could be greater than the expense of a death.

Putting a dollar value on such a person's contribution to the business is difficult. Donald F. Cady, attorney and chartered life underwriter (CLU), and the author of *The Field Guide to Estate Planning, Business Planning, and Employee Benefits,* says that "much like valuing a business, it is more art than science." A lot depends, he says, on the characteristics that make the person "key" to the enterprise; for example, "a sales manager who has substantial impact upon sales or a financial officer who has access to credit." Cady recommends several approaches to arriving at a number for that value:

1 **Contribution to profits.** Under this method, estimate the employee's impact on profits each year, then capitalize that contribution over the number of years it takes to find and train a replacement.

2 **Business-life value.** Under this approach, the estimated decrease in business earnings is multiplied by the years of work left in the key employee's career. That product is then discounted (reduced) using a reasonable interest rate.

3 **Multiple of salary.** Assuming salary to be a fair measure of a key employee's value to the business, multiply that salary times a factor of between 3 and 10, depending on just how valuable the employee is perceived to be.

4 **Discount of the business.** This approach discounts the entire value of the business by a percentage estimated to be the contribution of the key employee.

The problem of pegging a key employee's value becomes even more complex when the key employee is also a potential owner. In *Problem 20,* one recommendation was to consider the key employee as a prospect for a buy-sell agreement in the event of the death of the owner. What is the loss to the business if the key person dies before the owner, removing not only a key to its effective operation, but also a possible buyer?

And finally, what about the death of the key employee who also happens to be the owner? A buy-sell agreement with another key employee may be a great vehicle, but it may be underfunded if all the cash at the owner's death passes to the heirs under the agreement. After all, the surviving key employee will have the loss of the contributions from the owner, who was also a key employee. This could be especially onerous if the decedent was the primary business generator or the cosigner for all of the business debt. At the owner's death, any lender who was not asleep at the desk would demand immediate payment of outstanding loans.

SOLUTIONS

◆ **Buy key-employee life and disability insurance, with the business as premium payer and beneficiary.** One of the classic judgments of key-employee insurance came in a 1951 U.S. Court of Appeals 3rd Circuit case, *The Emeloid Co., Inc. v. Commissioner,* where Justice Joseph Staley Jr. wrote, "What corporate purpose could be more essential than key-man insurance? The business that insures its buildings and machinery and automobiles from every possible hazard can hardly be expected to exercise less care in protecting itself against the loss of two of its most vital assets—managerial skill and experience." The only thing that's changed since 1951 is that Staley would use the term "key person" today, and in fact, many companies are as likely to have key women as key men. Don't overlook that fact when protecting your corporation, and don't go by job titles alone.

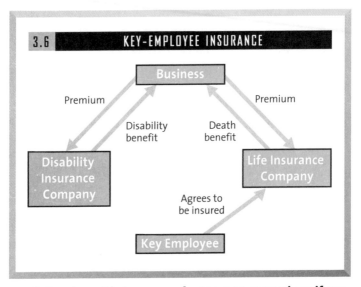

3.6　KEY-EMPLOYEE INSURANCE

Business

Premium　　　　　　　　　Premium

Disability　　　Death
benefit　　　　benefit

Disability Insurance Company

Life Insurance Company

Agrees to
be insured

Key Employee

◆ **Buy term life insurance for temporary needs or if per-manent insurance is called for but unaffordable.** This is not the venue to deconstruct the various types of life insurance. Read my 1996 book, *The Complete Idiot's Guide to Buying Insurance and Annuities,* or Janet Bam-ford's book published the same year, *Smarter Insurance Solutions.* Controversy usually revolves around whether to buy *term insurance,* which is strictly indemnification for a loss, or *permanent insurance,* which has a savings or investment element called *cash values* or *account values.* Term insurance is considerably less expensive in the short run.

Note that the premiums paid by the corporation, partnership, or proprietorship are *not* tax deductible. However, the proceeds received by the business are tax free. This advantage far outweighs the lack of a cur-rent tax deduction if the business ever collects.

◆ **Insure key employees for credit protection.** What hap-pens when a sole proprietor borrows $250,000 for the business, personally cosigns for the loan, and then becomes disabled? Put yourself in the position of this person's partner or co-owner. Enlightened lenders will require life insurance to guarantee repayment, yet they rarely think to require disability insurance for the same purpose. And rarely do business owners buy more life insurance than their bank requires (see TABLE 3.6, at left).

◆ **Use the loan appiication as an event that triggers your evaluation of the larger picture.** Key-employee insurance not only protects your credit ratings, it also provides the financial cushion necessary while you find the best replacement.

◆ **Coordinate key-employee insurance with buy-sell planning.** While these two needs are technically separate, key employees tend to be owners or those who are great prospects to be owners. Make sure the beneficiaries are properly arranged to have the right amount of funds on hand not only to fund the buyout, but also to indemnify the enterprise for the loss of a key employee.

RECOMMENDED ADVISERS

Ask your **accountant** to place a value on key employees using the various methods mentioned on pages 156–157, then pick the method and value that most closely approximates your perception of the key employee's worth to you and your business.

Buy insurance to protect the business against the death and disability of key employees. Find a professional **life insurance underwriter** you trust and ask for comparisons based on reasonable assumptions. Lynn Brenner's book, *Smart Questions to Ask Your Financial Advisers*, can help you get more out of the people whose advice you buy.

SEE ALSO

◆ **Problem 8:** *What's It Worth: Valuation Problems with the IRS* to understand asset valuation for estates and business continuations.

THE FAMILY BUSINESS

A family business, one owned or operated by more than one member of the same family, presents special challenges for owners and successors alike. Not all families function well together at home, much less at the office. Sibling rivalries, dictatorial parents, and differences between personalities intensify the problems found in any other enterprise. The more successful the family business, the more explicitly the owners should plan for transfer of the daily operation and control to the next generation.

THE MOST PRESSING problems facing family businesses frequently revolve around the day-to-day management of the firm. Usually the founder is the "chairman of the board," even in a neighborhood restaurant. In a mom-and-pop business with two people at the same generational level, the couple needs to learn how to function as a team, just as in a marriage. One overbearing spouse does more than just make the other intimidated and uncomfortable. He or she also makes it more difficult for the less-assertive spouse to prepare to run the business in the event of the overlord's death or disability. Spouses left in this situation are more vulnerable to being taken advantage of. They frequently hire or attract managers or new partners without knowing how to assess their skills or accomplishments, or how to structure a fair business arrangement.

When parents bring their children into the business, different problems arise. Good proprietors are not always good trainers. Even the best entrepreneurs need to learn how to delegate, and that often gets more difficult when there are familial bonds among the workers. Inevitably, children will one day think they can run the business better than Mom or Dad, just as younger managers and executives in public

companies do. It's a challenge to deal with the resulting anxieties or personal confrontations. It is easier to
tell an employee to move on than to ask a son or a
daughter to go work someplace else. It is also easier to
tell a nonfamily employee they are not as good as they
think they are, yet.

For those of us who had brothers or sisters growing
up, sibling conflicts were as much a part of family life
as summer vacations. However, most of us would question whether we could function effectively in business
with the same siblings we wrestled with as children.

In any organization, there needs to be leadership.
It is rare for even a partnership to function effectively
without a senior or managing partner. However, when
siblings get passed over for the top position, hostilities
can surface.

The situation can get even dicier when spouses of
children are brought into the business, even though
they may be just as qualified for the job as any outside
applicant. They could also be employees who marry
into the family after the employment relationship
develops. Or, they could be former in-laws who retain
an ownership interest after a divorce. Divorce has a
way of distorting emotions and can be crippling in a
small business. With approximately one in four marriages ending in divorce today, the chances are too
high not to consider the consequences in your planning. *Problem 25* specifically addresses divorce and
business interests.

What happens when death strikes your family business? Intrafamily lawsuits over inheritances are legion;
family businesses complicate these scenarios.

Disability creates even more tension because there
are ongoing management issues, driven by the extent
to which the disabled family member can participate
in the day-to-day business affairs. If adult children are
already hard pressed to care for retired, elderly parents, how does the plot thicken when the parents are

the child's employer? Or, what about the reverse case, where the adult son or daughter, active in the business, suffers a long-term disability?

Retiring from a business is frequently a problem for business owners because they have not set aside sufficient funds to retire, or because they want to "ease into" retirement, holding onto the reins while they decrease their contribution. Owners tend to regard this as their right, but it can lead to animosities in the family members left behind.

A set of subtle problems can arise out of the continuous and often rapid appreciation of the value of a family business in the owner's estate, even while multiple generations are involved as employees. Often the owner would consider making gifts of interests in the business, but is afraid of losing control. The estate-tax threat becomes the least of many evils and is therefore ignored.

SOLUTIONS

◆ **Plan for the disposition of family-owned business interests just as with any other enterprise.** Without a succession agreement, you can spend a major portion of your lifetime building an asset that the IRS and misdirected heirs can dismantle in months. It is a rare owner that doesn't feel strongly about the future of his or her business. Whenever family members are the potential successors, it is critical to lay out the business plan for new owners, also thereby frustrating the tax collector.

◆ **Insure your agreements and business debt against death and disability.** The importance of funding buy-sell agreements was presented in *Problems 18 and 19,* the importance of key-employee insurance in *Problem 21.* Family members need to be treated at least as well as nonfamily members in your business. Protect your family members, especially if they have worked alongside you to build the enterprise.

◆ **Use family limited partnerships to maintain operating control while reducing your estate.** A *family limited partnership* (FLP) provides for an orderly transfer of your company's assets to your children, and even to their children, while allowing you to retain control of the business until some future date. Until 1993, FLPs were regarded as untested, even risky. Today, thanks to Revenue Ruling 93-12, they are a widely accepted planning vehicle.

An FLP can be a general or limited partnership. The first type gives every partner a voice in the management of the business. It also makes each partner liable for the debts and other obligations of the business, including lawsuit judgments and taxes. The more common choice, a *limited partnership,* limits the exposure of limited or "junior" partners to their investment in the partnership. The general partners, usually the original owners, assume the liabilities and retain the operational control of the business.

In addition to control, there are several other possible advantages of the FLP:

1 *Estate-planning advantages.* Cynthia Coddington, vice president and director of financial planning at David L. Babson & Company, a Boston-based investment advisory firm, says, "When I deal with a wealthy client, I consider recommending a family limited partnership. They're not always appropriate, but when they are, they're great estate-planning tools." The popularity of FLPs is undoubtedly traceable to the ability they give a family to take significant discounts in the value of the assets transferred to the partnership. The discounts translate into estate- and gift-tax reductions. As Bill Brennan, CPA, of Washington, D.C., puts it, "Transfers within a family limited partnership usually claim a double discount. The discounts for lack of control and for lack of marketability can add up to significant tax savings." The partnership agreement restricts a limited partner's ability to transfer an interest

---

3.7   **FAMILY LIMITED PARTNERSHIP**

Parents
Gift of limited-partnership interests

| Children |

Create partnership by contributing assets   Partnership transfers both general and limited partnership interests

| Partnership |

Control	Vests in parents because they retain the general-partnership interest until their death or voluntary retirement
Income	Can be retained in the partnership or allocated among general and limited partners, as the general partner decides
Liability	General partners assume liabilities of the partnership
Disposition of shares	Restricted by agreement, usually to family

---

beyond certain parties, such as other family members. This makes the interest less valuable. It also ensures the interest will stay in the family. Discounts of up to 30 percent are not unusual. The FLP can also make it easier to transfer the partnership interests at the death of the estate owner, without threat of liquidation of the partnership's assets (see TABLE 3.7, *above*).

2 *Family retention of assets.* Restrictions on the transferability of the partnership's interests will prevent a portion of the business falling into nonfamily hands, whether by sale, gift, or divorce decree. Parents can also maintain general-partnership shares while placing

most of the value in limited-partnership shares. They can then pass the limited shares under the $10,000 annual gift-tax exemptions each year to each beneficiary. For example, a husband and wife could gift limited-partnership shares worth $200,000 each year if they each gifted $10,000 to a total of 10 children and grandchildren. By retaining the general-partnership shares, parents continue to control the operation of the business.

When combined with the valuation discounts, the gifts can reduce the estate quite quickly.

3 *Creditor protection.* The FLP vehicle can afford some measure of asset protection, especially if the primary owner is in a business highly vulnerable to litigation, such as manufacturing or handling environmentally sensitive materials. Personal assets can be transferred into the FLP. This shield is not without problems of its own, though.

Always use an attorney in deciding whether and how to implement an FLP. As you can imagine, the IRS is going to vigorously attack FLPs that attempt to go too far in claiming discounts.

◆ **Take advantage of the new $1,300,000 exemption for closely held businesses staying in the family.** The Taxpayer Relief Act of 1997 increased the personal exemption from $600,000 to $1,300,000 for the owner of a closely held business interest, if certain conditions are met both before and after the death of the estate owner. These conditions are stringent enough to discourage Ross Nager, a Houston partner in Arthur Andersen and the national director of that firm's Center for Family Business. According to Nager, "The details of this [law] make [the exemption] unavailable to the majority of business owners." The family members who inherit the business must take an active part in the business. The business interest of the decedent must account for at least 50 percent of the estate. Additionally, the 50 percent family ownership applies to one family. If two families are involved, the percentage increases to 70 percent, and to 90 percent for three families.

If the successor-owners sell the business within 10 years following the estate owner's death, there is a recapture of the taxes saved because of the $1,300,000 exemption. There are no provisions that make exceptions for hardships. In short, while the new tax laws have created the increased exemption, be realistic about using it for your business.

◆ **Use life insurance to ensure the heirs are not put in a position of having to sell the business during the 10-year period.** Key-employee insurance could meet this need appropriately, assuming the proceeds were not payable to the business thereby potentially increasing its value at death. On the other hand, life insurance proceeds could possibly be used to increase the value of the business sufficiently to meet the new 50 percent requirements.

RECOMMENDED ADVISERS

 Your **accountant** needs to be consulted for tax questions and business valuation in order to plan for FLPs or to take advantage of the new exemption.

 Only an **attorney** experienced in tax matters should offer advice about or draft these documents.

 Insure key employees and buy-sell agreements for their full value to ensure the heirs will have sufficient funds to continue the family business.

SEE ALSO

◆ **Problem 3:** *Insufficient Cash in the Estate.*

THE FAMILY FARM

The family-owned farm has long been a cherished piece of the American landscape—except to the IRS. The Taxpayer Relief Act of 1997 extends a token hand of relief in the estate-tax area, but just as with the increased exemption for family businesses discussed in *Problem 22*, the conditions for its use are stringent. For many family farms and ranches, the lack of liquidity of the enterprise, especially at the death of the owner, makes planning imperative if the farm is to be retained for future generations.

ACCORDING TO SENATOR Richard G. Lugar, in his testimony to the Senate Finance Committee in April 1997, 95 percent of farms and ranches are either sole proprietorships or family partnerships. The vast majority face the threat of federal estate taxes because the real property alone makes the value of the assets greater than the personal exemption. In fact, the U.S. Department of Agriculture (USDA) says that farmers are 6 times more likely to face estate taxes than other Americans. Commercial farming operations, which produce some 85 percent of the nation's agricultural products, are 15 times more likely to pay estate taxes.

If you are one of this nation's agricultural pioneers, you know that the plight of the family farmer is about more than estate taxes. It is about commercial competition, backbreaking work, escalating real estate values, and the choice of a lifestyle. The average farmer in this country is approaching 60 years of age. The USDA estimates that in the 10-year period bracketed by 1992 and 2002, more than 500,000 farmers will retire. Only half of these retirees will be replaced by other farmers. As many as 100,000 of these retirees will have to address the estate-tax issue in the next 20 years.

One of the challenges for farmers is inflation. Keith Collins, chief economist of the USDA, points out that the value of an average acre of farmland has increased from $158 to $890 in the last 30 years. According to Collins, more than 75 percent of that increase is attributable to inflation, and it is inflation that is driving the value of more and more farms into estate-taxable territory. Price inflation is especially difficult for farmers, because their standard of living is not increasing with their taxable estate.

Farmers traditionally pour everything they earn back into the business of farming. Agriculture is a labor- and capital-intensive business. Farmers who amass significant wealth frequently do so on the basis of their land values. Pension plans and individual retirement accounts (IRAs) are rare on the family farm, despite their popularity in every other workplace in America.

The problems inherent in farming are intensified in the family farm. We all have an image of family members carrying out their respective chores and living a clean, healthy existence. Why, then, are so few retiring farmers being succeeded by their families? Economics is part of the reason, and some of the techniques discussed in the "Solutions" section will address these issues.

If increasing values tend to lie at the center of the controversy over farms and taxes, then threat of disputes with the IRS are a part of the problem. Knowing your local politicians does not always help. Washington State Representative Larry Sowa is embroiled in a court case with the IRS over the value of timberland in his mother's estate. The IRS claims the land is worth twice what Sowa's executor declared on her estate tax return. The tax attorney for the estate, Jeff Thede of Portland, Oregon, expressed the heart of the dispute for all taxpayers: "The service's in-house appraisers tend to come up with higher values, but I guess their motivation is different than ours."

The Sowa case revolves around a provision of the IRC that allows family farms and businesses to value land on the basis of its current use rather than its highest and best use. The Sowa family is claiming a valuation based on the land as timberland. The IRS could claim that the property should be valued at its highest and best use, which usually is for development. This has long been a bone of contention in Florida and California, where orange groves abutting cities such as Los Angeles and Orlando could have land values varying by several hundred percent, depending on whether they are classified for agricultural use or commercial use, such as future apartments.

The Sowas aren't the only Oregon family feeling the IRS's bite. Tony Hendricks, mentioned in *Problem 6,* struggled with a $150,000 estate-tax bill on the family's 1,100-acre farm when his father died in 1975. Two years later in 1977 when his mother died, the IRS was back, demanding another $150,000. Because of tax law provisions giving business owners a chance to pay the tax in installments at a low-interest rate, Mr. Hendricks was able to spread the tax payment over 15 years, at $22,000 a year. However, after a bad crop, Hendricks fell behind on the payments and lost 105 of his acres to a bank foreclosure. As Hendricks put it, "It just took all our cash. It was a bad time."

What can you do to ward off the "bad times"? Probably nothing, but there are plenty of tips to minimize their impact.

SOLUTIONS

◆ **Consider an FLP.** An FLP often makes sense for all the reasons given in the *Problem 22* discussion of family businesses. After all, that's what a family farm is. The FLP vehicle eases the transfer of ownership of the underlying assets in the enterprise, while keeping control of the operations in the hands of the estate owners. Flexibility in control is especially helpful in families where some of the offspring are still on the farm and others have scattered to chase other dreams. The

FLP estate-tax discounts for lack of marketability and a minority share should help accomplish the objectives more quickly.

◆ **Use a knowledgeable attorney.** If your town lacks the tax talent, go elsewhere. Don't try to save money by letting your local lawyer create an FLP. How can you find out if your local attorney has estate-planning experience? Call the bar association in your state. In some states, attorneys are required to be members. Bar associations have led the movement toward certification of specialties such as taxation and estate planning.

◆ **Take advantage of the new estate-tax exemption of $1.3 million.** If your farm has been operated by the family for five out of the past eight years and is expected to continue to be so in five out of the next eight years, you may be eligible. As discussed in *Problem 22*, the estate-tax break doesn't provide much relief, but it is better than nothing from Congress. Review the requirements from *Problem 22* and check with your tax adviser about the advantages and disadvantages.

◆ **Take advantage of the installment-tax provisions of the IRC.** If you can't avoid estate taxes, pay them on the installment plan. The requirements for qualifying are stringent. If the business interest exceeds 35 percent of the value of your estate and certain ownership tests are met, you can defer the tax on the first $1 million of business assets. The law allows you to pay interest only at 4 percent for the first 5 years. The loan is then amortized over the next 10 years. For the business value in excess of the $1 million special-rate amount, the interest rate on the installments is 3 percent over the short-term federal rate of 4 percent.

◆ **Buy insurance to pay estate taxes and ensure the continuation of the farm.** Life insurance premiums now will almost always be lower than the tax principal payments and any interest charged on an installment loan to spread out those payments. If you are choosing to perpetuate the farm rather than cash out when you retire, insurance can pay the taxes and expenses, leaving your heirs in a better position to carry on. Refer to *Problem 3* for other ways to pay your estate taxes.

◆ **Have a family meeting.** One of the benefits of an FLP is the requirement that there be a family meeting to discuss the business. Your family members may sit down together for most meals, but there is often less meat in the conversation than on the table. Start communicating your vision for the farm by setting aside time for a formal business meeting, at least quarterly.

◆ **Try meeting with a written agenda.** Share the business's financial statements with your family, just as you would for a manufacturing company or a retail store. Invite suggestions on how the business might be more profitable. Assign projects to family members based on their interests and talents. For example, if a child is especially interested in computers, ask him or her to check out ways to computerize the farm's operations. Any training you encourage now will make junior family members more capable of taking over from you later.

RECOMMENDED ADVISERS

Use your **accountant** to value your business and to explain the advantages of the FLP.

Use an **attorney** knowledgeable in tax law to create the documents necessary for a succession plan, including the partnership papers for an FLP.

Provide **life insurance** to pay estate taxes rather than relying on installments or exemptions that tie the hands of your heirs by restricting their subsequent sale of the farm.

SEE ALSO

◆ **Problem 22:** *The Family Business* to understand the problems inherent in any business run by more than one member of the same family, and to understand the advantages of doing business as an FLP.

RELYING ON INCOME FROM
THE SALE OF A BUSINESS

Business owners often rely on an installment sale of their business—that is, a sale over time—as a major source of cash to reinvest in their next venture or for retirement income. The installment sale has some significant advantages, but requires the seller to assume a great deal of risk. It is important to structure the sale to maximize the affordability and tax benefits, while minimizing the possibility of a default. This can be done by securing the transaction with the business assets, at a minimum, and if possible with the additional personal assets of the buyer.

AN *INSTALLMENT SALE* is the sale of an asset in which at least part of the purchase price is received by the seller in more than one tax year. An installment sale often allows the buyer to make a purchase not affordable otherwise because of a shortage of cash. From the seller's perspective, it can spell the difference between selling and not selling the business. Additionally, the tax on appreciated assets is deferred until installments are received, by which time the seller may be in a lower tax bracket.

Unfortunately, there are no guarantees that the new owners will have the same success as the retiring owner. If the continuation of the installment payments depends on that success, then you as the retiring owner have the same exposure to failure as before the sale, without the management control to do anything about it.

One-third of this country's family-owned businesses will experience leadership changes in the next five years, according to a joint study by Arthur Andersen and the Massachusetts Mutual Life Insurance Company. Family-owned firms account for a majority of the businesses in this nation. According to Ross

Nager, director of Arthur Andersen's Center for Family Business in Houston, Texas, "Management and ownership succession can be disruptive for any company, but it is particularly difficult in the context of the family relationships that exist in these businesses."

The most important thing the owning families can do is protect the transaction against default—to the extent that they can. Doing so is absolutely critical if proceeds from the sale of a business are to be a significant portion of someone's retirement income. There have been numerous instances where owners have sold successful companies and retired to softer climes only to discover that the new owners had run the business into the ground. Owners in their mid-60s or older have been forced to come out of retirement in an attempt to revive their business and protect their buyout. However, by the time the installment payments stop, it is often too late to return the business to its sale value.

Often, an owner turns the business over to an associate with no more than a handshake or a hastily drawn agreement. A business sale under these terms is the same as an unsecured loan. Handshakes appeal to our frontier spirit, an ideal of the way business should be conducted. However, that is no longer realistic. You must treat the sale as more than an unsecured loan because you may well have liability for the acts of negligence or dishonesty of the purchaser.

Consider this. If a majority of businesses fail even though the owner toils 70 hour a week, what is the likely outcome if the purchaser dies or becomes disabled before the completion of the installment buyout? Business purchase and sale agreements, when they exist, rarely consider the death or disability of the purchaser and the impact either could have on the reliability of future installment payments.

CASE STUDY

Put yourself on the beach in the Virgin Islands, retired two years, when your banker calls on your infrequently used cell phone to say they have not received the check from your old company for the 25th installment. You sold out for a small down payment and 120 installment payments over the following 10 years. After numerous unreturned phone calls to the purchaser, you ask your lawyer to check out the problem. He calls a week later to tell you that the stress of the new business gave the new owner a heart attack. There is no news about the company itself.

When you arrive back in the States, you head directly to the business. The employees, few of whom are familiar to you, are wandering rather aimlessly around the building. You collar one of your old employees and ask what has happened. He recounts the heart attack story, but adds that no one knows what to do because the purchaser played his cards so close to the chest. He tells you about all your loyal customers who have taken their business elsewhere. What is your recourse?

If you hadn't addressed this problem in your purchase and sale agreement, there is little you can do except begin proceedings for default on the note. However, you don't want to precipitate the second heart attack, so you do nothing. Eventually, the business shrinks to below the point at which you have any hope of recouping your payments.

Does this sound farfetched? If it does, you will be shocked to learn how many good businesses are sold without any formally drafted agreement.

Would the financial situation be better if the purchaser was your son or daughter, or some other close relative? No, actually it could be much worse. Enforcing the terms of a handshake agreement with a family member is a lose-lose proposition. If you sue for the stopped payments, you face family alienation. If you don't sue, you will probably lose your capital. Some sales to family members are intended to be part sale and part gift. Others are intended to be *arms-length transactions,* meaning they are supposed to resemble transactions between strangers. Problems between family members arise when the transaction is not clearly defined.

The death of the purchaser can create even more difficulties. The seller is forced to deal with the executor or the attorneys for the purchaser's estate. The agreement between the buyer-decedent and the seller is now subject to corroboration only by the seller. The executor's responsibility is to the purchaser's heirs, not the seller. Any difference of opinion will result in a sharply drawn line between the needs and obligations of the two parties.

If you plan to sell anything on an installment basis, what can you do to protect the payments you expect to receive after the transaction? And what can a buyer do to protect his or her assets and heirs, while living up to the obligation to complete the purchase?

SOLUTIONS

◆ **Treat any purchase and sale of a business interest as a legal transaction.** Use an attorney. While this advice may sound self-evident, far too many good businesses are sold without adequate documentation or tax planning. At the risk of sounding defensive of the legal profession, more deals have gone sour from lack of lawyering than bad lawyering. This does not mean there are not incompetent attorneys—you know there are. Begin the search for a good general-purpose business lawyer well before you need one. For more difficult issues, rely on specialists. If the sale of your business involves potentially complex tax issues, hire a tax lawyer. Again, search through the state bar association. If your state has certified specialties, lawyers will usually list themselves by specialty in the telephone directory's Yellow Pages.

◆ **Insure installment sales if the purchaser is an individual and is to be an active part of the business.** Require life insurance and disability insurance as part of the agreement. Make sure that the beneficiary has an obligation to complete the purchase. This can be accomplished by using a trusteed agreement (depicted in *Table 3.5*). Or, the seller can own the policies and be the beneficiary.

◆ **Purchase an insurance policy face amount equal to the total value of the sale, less any down payment received at the closing.** Use decreasing-term insurance that tracks the annual decrease in the principal amount of the outstanding note. For example, if you sold your company for $1,200,000 with $200,000 at closing and the balance in equal installments over 10 years, a purchase a 10-year decreasing-term policy with an initial face amount of at least $1,000,000. Negotiate to have the purchaser pay the premiums even though you own the policies.

◆ **Aim for a cash sale if possible.** Be leery of agreeing to an installment sale solely for tax reasons. If an installment sale is the only way, then agree only if you can obtain adequate assurances that the purchase will be completed regardless of subsequent circumstances. Examples of such assurances would be adequate security for the loan you are making to the buyer, and adequate life and disability insurance to complete the sale if the purchaser dies prematurely or becomes disabled.

◆ **Protect yourself with provisions allowing early intervention in the event of default on payments.** Don't allow the purchaser to keep you on the sidelines while the business degenerates into a worthless shell. Reserve the right to repossess the business at the first sign of default. Have your attorney address this issue in the agreement.

◆ **If you sell to a relative, do so only after you consult a tax expert.** There are tax rules that can undo the tax advantages of the installment sale. The *second-disposi-*

tion rule is just such a rule. If you sold your business to your son, for example, on the installment basis, this is a *related-party sale*. Assume you have a zero dollar tax cost basis in the business and you sell for $500,000 over 10 years. The gain of $50,000 each year will be taxed as received. However, what if Junior changes his mind, resells the business a year later (the second disposition), and continues to pay you on the installment-sale basis? You must report the remaining gain of $450,000 ($500,000 − $50,000 = $450,000) in the year Junior sells, even though you may not receive any money ahead of schedule. The remaining tax of $90,000 ($450,000 gain x 20 percent capital gains tax rate) is due when you have only $50,000 of income. Use professionals to help you sell, even to relatives.

◆ **Consider a self-canceling installment note (SCIN).** A SCIN provides that the balance due under the purchase and sale agreement is forgiven upon the death of the seller. This will cause the forgiven amount to be included in the seller's estate for federal estate-tax purposes, but it removes from the estate any appreciation that the business has had since the sale. The courts lean toward no further tax problems for the purchaser. Consult a tax attorney.

◆ **Consider a private annuity.** If your primary motivation is to generate an income for your life and you have an estate in excess of the personal-estate-tax exemption of $625,000 (increasing to $1,000,000 by the year 2006), consider a private annuity with someone you trust. A *private annuity* is an unsecured promise to pay income for the life of the annuitant based on the fair market value of the asset and the "seller's" life expectancy.

Consider, for example, an annuity based on an asset with an appraised value of $1,000,000. The moment the transaction is agreed to, the asset is removed from the seller's estate for federal estate-tax purposes. The recipient of the property makes payments for the

seller's life, even if that is another 50 years. The risk
for the buyer is that he or she will end up paying far
more than the asset is worth. And the greatest risk for
the annuitant is that the purchaser will arbitrarily cease
making payments. The promise to pay the annuity payments cannot be secured by the asset. The private
annuity is a "trust-me" vehicle.

RECOMMENDED ADVISERS

Get a business valuation from your **accountant**
before you decide to sell the enterprise, in order to
assure yourself of a fair price.

Find an **attorney** well versed in business agreements by checking with state bar associations and
local Yellow Page directories for specialists. Use that
attorney to draft the purchase and sale documents.

SEE ALSO

◆ **Problem 18:** *Business Continuation and the Closely
Held Corporation* to review the types of agreements
used to insure business continuation contracts.

PROBLEM 25

DIVORCE AND THE
FAMILY BUSINESS

Divorce threatens to break up more than just the marital relationship. It can undermine the very existence of a closely held
business and it can create severe obstacles for family enterprises. Frequently, the best solutions are the ones adopted
well in advance of the separation, solutions that assume the
relationship will not last as long as the wedding vows
promise.

WITH OVER 40 PERCENT of today's marriages ending
in the courts and over 50 percent of closely held businesses family owned, it is reasonable to infer that many
of these ventures enter into the settlements of broken

marriages. In mom-and-pop businesses where both spouses work in the family enterprise, divorce rends their partnership at work as well as at home. How does the court make a fair and equitable distribution of the assets in these cases?

What about the "sole" proprietorship in which one spouse controls the business but the other is an active assistant without being listed as an employee? What is fair in this situation? The questions multiply if the non-operating spouse leaves both the business and the relationship, and the remaining spouse must now hire a replacement at the same time that the court requires the payment of alimony. In many businesses, especially proprietorships, a spouse may put in long hours and take no fixed compensation. Their business income (not salary) shows up on the joint return. How will the courts value their respective contributions to the business?

A different problem arises when the primary source of family income has been the breadwinner's business and now the courts are looking to that income for alimony and child support, as well as the continuation of a standard of living for the business owner. Judges are not necessarily astute business people, and some of them are capable of making horrendous estimates of a business's ability to generate future income.

Multigenerational family businesses introduce an extra layer of complexity. Many such businesses are large and successful. Some even employ the spouses and children of family members. What happens when the owner's daughter-in-law decides to divorce the son, yet wants to retain her position as vice president of marketing? To complicate the issue, what if 80 percent of the son's net worth is in corporate stock in Dad's business?

What is at stake in many multigenerational family businesses goes beyond the matter of an equitable distribution of a couple's assets. The divorce now involves employment and ownership of the company's stock. What does Dad have to say about the divorcing daughter-in-law's ownership of the company's stock? Does Dad as CEO of the company have the right to fire her just because of the divorce? What if the divorcing couple's children were also working in the business?

SOLUTIONS

◆ **Use prenuptial agreements to protect assets acquired before the marriage.** Prenuptial agreements strike many as somehow contradictory to the ideal virtues of marriage, such as trust and honesty. However, as anyone who has witnessed a large number of contested divorces will agree, too often when the relationship goes bad, so do notions of fairness, not to mention trust. A prenuptial contract makes good sense whenever one of the parties brings substantial assets to the relationship, especially if the assets include a successful business that one party has built and owns.

Attorney William F. Etherington III, of Beale, Balfour, Davidson & Etherington in Richmond, Virginia, recommends prenuptial agreements "especially in second marriages. With a first marriage, they can really dampen things." He sees great value in prenuptial contracts with older clients and those widowed or divorced and possessing sizable assets, which could easily include a closely held business interest.

◆ **Consider the use of an FLP with restrictions on the transferability of a business interest to nonfamily members, including spouses.** Restricting the transfer of the family-business interest does not mean the spouse is left without recourse to any assets. It just protects control of the family-business interest from falling into the hands of nonfamily members because of a divorce settlement or court award. The FLP operating agreement can provide for a buyout of the family member's interest in the event of death or disability of the related party. It is just divorce that hamstrings the parties, by prohibiting the partnership asset from passing outside the blood relations of the family.

◆ **Use restrictive marital trusts to prevent subsequent spouses from inheriting family businesses.** Some estate owners are concerned that upon their death, the surviving spouse will inherit a business interest outright, remarry, and enable a subsequent spouse to end up controlling or inheriting a stake in the enterprise. The way to avoid this result is to pass the business interest into a *marital-deduction trust,* so called because it qualifies for the estate-tax marital deduction despite the fact that the property's ultimate distribution may be limited. In such a trust, income can be payable to the surviving spouse for life, while the assets of the business are controlled by a trustee who is instructed how to protect the interest from subsequent spouses or in favor of children and other family members.

◆ **Negotiate before your arbitrate. Mediate before you litigate.** Try to agree on a reasonable settlement before calling in the expensive legal warriors, especially if your state has no-fault divorce laws. Attorneys have their place in our society, but they are used far more frequently in divorces than they need to be. At $150 to $300 an hour, attorneys' fees of tens of thousands of dollars for divorce are not unusual. Typically, the parties feel vulnerable and fearful that they will not be treated fairly. Sometimes it is the lawyers who take advantage.

Negotiation can involve just the two parties seeking a dissolution of the marriage. Try to agree on a fair property settlement without the rancor that ends up costing both of you legal fees and emotional energy. If negotiation fails, try to mediate the divorce and property settlement issues. Mediation involves bringing in a third-party professional to help settle the dispute.

If both parties to mediation agree to let the decision of the mediator be binding on them, the mediation process is called *arbitration*. It avoids the need for a trial, ensures privacy of the agreement, and is invariably less expensive to the parties who must shrink their assets to be divided by the amount of the fees. Long after a divorce trial is completed, the parties often bemoan the amount of money they wasted on attorneys' fees out of anger and revenge.

◆ **Check with your state bar association for the names of arbitrators in your vicinity.** Look for and interview for one that has experience in divorce and the division of business assets. Contact the American Arbitration Association for referrals (*see the "Resources" appendix*).

If you are marrying into or divorcing away from a family business, secure a commitment for nonfamily-owned assets. You will not want to own a minority interest in a family-owned business because without control, the interest is really of value only on paper. The controlling stockholder or partner decides whether any profits are to be paid to the other owners, and whether there is any value to owning a minority interest. You are better off with real estate, securities, bonds, or cash. Once the relationship is irretrievably broken, you should opt for assets that are liquid (saleable) and easily valued. This suggestion does not imply that you should settle for less than your fair share of the marital assets. It does mean that you want to be free to chart your own course, without being tied to the forces that control the family business.

RECOMMENDED ADVISER

 See your **lawyer** before the marriage if you bring significant assets to the relationship. Consider prenuptial agreements restricting access to the business interests and assets, especially if you are embarking on a second or subsequent marriage.

SEE ALSO

◆ **Problem 22:** *The Family Business* to understand the difficulties of owning part of a family business and the value of the FLP in protecting against transfers of the family business to nonfamily members.

◆ **Problem 30:** *Separation and Divorce* to explore in greater detail the problems inherent in financial planning during a divorce.

◆ **Problem 45:** *Family Problems* to learn about the problems experienced by the superwealthy in a separation or divorce.

PART

4

Investment
PROBLEMS

OST AFFLUENT
people, in addition to not considering themselves
wealthy, don't consider themselves to be
sophisticated investors. You might wonder, then,
how they got rich. Unlike their less-moneyed peers,
those who have earned financial security tend to
invest conservatively and rely on the advice of
experts. Anyone aspiring to their degree of wealth
can learn a lot from their humble attitudes toward
money and investing.

The threshold problem is finding a trustworthy
and talented financial adviser. With so many
institutions and individuals competing for your
business, how do you choose?

Problem 26 explains why you should consider a
financial planner and how to find one, including
questions to ask at the interview.

Next, it pays to revisit the fundamentals of

investing with the principles of asset protection in mind. In a world of almost limitless opportunities for allocating your money, it's easy to lose sight of the basics. *Problem 27* helps put these issues in perspective according to your individual needs.

Problem 28 addresses specific ways to save and invest. The landscape has changed dramatically in the past 20 years. This book presents a new map.

People with wealth are often paying someone for professional advice and money management. *Problem 29* walks you through your alternatives, separating the truth from the hype.

PROBLEM 26

FINDING THE BEST FINANCIAL ADVISER

What a wealthy person needs most is someone who can help create a complete financial plan and then

execute it. Unfortunately, that person or that firm is often difficult to find. There are confusing distinctions among the institutions and people offering advice about your finances. This
Problem clears the air about these various types of advisers and
explains how to choose the best ones for you.

CONSOLIDATION AND DEREGULATION in the financial-services industry over the past decade have increasingly blurred the lines between banks, insurance companies, stockbrokerages, broker-dealers, and their
investment representatives. Banks own stock-brokerage firms, mutual funds, and trust companies. Stock-
brokerage firms own life insurance companies, trust
companies, and money-market funds, as well as other
company-owned mutual funds, called *proprietary funds*.

Finding a top-notch planner among so many aggressive competitors should be easy. However, there just
aren't enough people who are qualified. The development of a financial plan is "people" driven and
"people" executed. While we are moving toward com-
puter-driven planning (certainly computer output is
the heart of the written plan today), you still need a
good planner asking the right questions, gathering the
pertinent data, prioritizing your objectives, providing
the planning recommendations, and perhaps execut-
ing them as well. Almost any financial institution has
the technology to create an impressively detailed, computerized financial plan. However, will they have anyone local with enough training and experience to
stand by it, stick with you, and provide alterations if
their tailor-made program no longer fits you perfectly?

Most financial institutions teach their people to
sell products before they teach them how to provide
the most basic planning services. Banks teach tellers
how to sell certificates of deposit (CDs) and even
annuities. However, only a handful of bank person-
nel can develop a financial plan. Stockbrokerage
firms teach brokers to recognize simple needs, such

as the need for retirement capital or cash savings, and then propose products to meet these needs, such as individual retirement accounts (IRAs) or CDs. Some brokers don't even do that much planning, preferring instead to hawk stocks over the phone to people they don't know.

And yet, there are experienced stockbrokers who can deliver very sophisticated plans. Some of the most sophisticated planners are insurance agents. How, though, do you find the planners among the product pushers?

A search by job title won't help you much. For example, there are no industry standards governing what a representative of a stock-brokerage firm is to be called. Common euphemisms today range from "investment representative" to "financial consultant." Is someone 22 years old with six months' experience really a "financial consultant" worthy of investing your hard-earned dollars?

The fact is, anyone can call themselves a financial adviser or a financial planner. How do you recognize the genuine article? Should your main adviser be a fee-only planner? A qualified stockbroker? A qualified life insurance underwriter? An independent investment representative for a national broker-dealer? A registered investment adviser? The right answer could be a yes to any of the above. With the computerized technical support available today, any one of these people might be a "financial adviser" worthy of your patronage.

SOLUTIONS

◆ **Ask your attorney and accountant who they recommend.** Ask for more than one name from each. These advisers are frequently in a good position to know who is doing a good job for their clients. Most estate-planning attorneys and CPAs have referral relationships with planners. Ask who they like and why. Don't hesitate to ask if the recommender stands to receive any referral fees or other considerations apart from reciprocal referrals.

Interview the candidates as though you are asking them to go to work for you. After all, you're doing just that! If you stop to think of the stakes involved, you'll realize that this person is a critical teammate of yours. If this were an employee of your company, he or she would be an important executive, your chief financial officer. Ask to see samples of his or her data-gathering documents, the written plan itself, and the systems available to monitor the plan. Ask for a resume and verify the claims it makes.

The following are some questions to ask the planner in the interview:

How long have you been in financial planning, and with whom were you affiliated during that time? You should be interested in the length of time and the breadth of experience the prospective planner has in the business. You can also ask former associates about the planner.

Describe your average client in terms of income, net worth, and occupation. If you are the owner of a closely held corporation, for example, with no plans to retire in the next 30 years, you shouldn't be overly anxious to work with someone whose practice caters to retirees.

Do you recommend a wide range of products, or do you stick to mutual funds and annuities? Some planners believe that all the investment needs in the world can be solved with mutual funds. They can't.

What experience do you have with life insurance, disability-income insurance, and annuities? Having a license is not enough. Most wealthy people rely heavily on life insurance to preserve estates and pay taxes.

Ask for a list of clients you can contact to enquire about the planner's recommendations, and follow through. Here are some questions to ask the references:

How long has the planner handled your affairs?

To what extent does the planner make and monitor your investments?

Do you have regular annual, or more frequent, reviews?

Does your planner ever call with good investment or planning ideas?

Does the planner keep you informed about relevant changes in the tax laws?

Has the planner ever expressed an investment philosophy to you, and can you state what you believe it to be?

◆ **Look for experience and education.** Financial planning is not about calling you to push the "stock of the week" or a new underwriting by the employer firm. It's about getting you committed to a program and accomplishing your financial objectives. You need to find someone with more than a decade of experience in providing financial-planning services—education funding, retirement and business succession planning, charitable gifts, wills and trusts, insurance analysis, and investment management.

There are several degrees and designation programs that let you know that someone has at least met a set of minimum educational standards for the job of planner:

— *Certified Financial Planner (CFP).* Awarded by the CFP Board of Standards in Denver, Colorado, this is the most common designation. CFPs pass a series of exams covering the spectrum of financial planning, including retirement, taxation, estate planning, education funding, and more, and they agree to abide by a code of ethics. A CFP designation does not guarantee that its holder is a competent planner. It tells you they have had exposure to the training necessary to do financial planning. Continuing education is a part of the program.

— *Chartered Financial Consultant (ChFC).* This designation is awarded by the American College in Bryn Mawr, Pennsylvania. It is less well recognized and regarded because it is issued by the same organization that awards the CLU (chartered life underwriter) designation to insurance professionals, and is often thought to be an insurance designation. It is not. The ChFC is comparable to the CFP in course content and difficulty. For example, holders of the ChFC designation may sit for the CFP exams without taking any additional courses. Continuing education is also required.

— *Certified Public Accountant (CPA).* This is the designation that requires the most arduous training. Unfortunately, financial planning is not a necessary component of the education. When CPAs decide to offer financial-planning services or sell mutual funds, they have to become qualified just as someone coming from any other discipline. CPAs have their own designation evidencing financial-planning training: *personal financial specialist (PFS).* Someone with this designation should have the necessary training to complete a financial plan.

There are also several official-sounding titles that have no value when applied to financial planning:

— *Registered Investment Adviser (RIA).* Anyone who manages money for individuals can register to become an RIA. If a firm or individual manages more than $25 million, they must register with the Securities and Exchange Commission (SEC). There are no tests, no courses, and no education requirements, initial or continuing. RIAs are not permitted to use the letters after their name. While you do want a money manager to have this certification, there is nothing inherent in the RIA that suggests that its holder has any experience or training in "financial planning." *(See Problem 29 for a discussion of money management, as contrasted with financial planning.)*

— *Registered Representative (RR).* Anyone who passes the examination required by the National Association of Securities Dealers (NASD) in order to sell securities is an RR. The exam satisfies the NASD that the person understands the *products,* such as stocks and mutual funds, not the *needs* that give rise to the product as a solution. A stockbroker by any other name is still a stockbroker, and you need to look beyond that level of sales qualification when you are selecting a planner.

◆ **Ask about compensation and fees for services.** Your choosing the right person is always more important than how they choose to be compensated. You should always know how the planner is to be paid—for the initial study, for the ongoing review, and for investment management, if that will be part of the arrangement. Top-quality advisers and planners all make healthy six-figure incomes regardless of whether they charge fees or receive commissions. If you have the right person, he or she will recommend what is best for you without regard to compensation. If you have the wrong person, he or she will find a way to overcharge you and take advantage of the compensation structure, whatever it is. Fees are not necessarily cheaper than commissions, especially for long-term buy-and-hold investors. And charging a fee does not make a planner or adviser more competent, or 100 percent objective.

The most common compensation arrangements are:

— *Fee-only planning.* The planner charges a fee for developing the plan. The fee should be based on some objective standard, such as the time it takes to gather the information and present it back to you, or a flat rate based on the size of your estate. You can spend up to $250 per hour, or about $5,000 for an entire plan.

— *Fee-based planning.* Some planners charge a flat fee for the planning and investment advice and execution. For example, fee planners may charge for the investments under management on a schedule tiered at 2 percent up to $500,000, 1½ percent on the next $500,000, and 1 percent for assets in excess of $1 million. Usually the fee-based planner works in conjunction with a discount broker, such as Charles Schwab, to provide trading at reduced fees or mutual funds without commissions, called *no-load funds*. This arrangement does not always mean there will be no further charges.

— *Commission-based planning*. Some planners choose to represent firms that prefer commission-based compensation, such as some brokerage firms. In this case, you pay nothing directly for the planning, but agree to do your product purchases through the planner on a commission basis.

No single arrangement is superior to another in all circumstances. Find the person with the most experience and training whose investment and planning philosophy most closely coincides with your own, and who has a reputation for honesty and fair dealing. You should unabashedly seek references and verification of their experience. Wealthy people understand the need for competent counsel and don't mind paying for the advice. Those with minor assets are more likely to quibble over compensation. Don't overpay, but expect to write some checks or pay some commissions for quality advice, whether investment, legal, or accounting.

◆ **Concentrate on building a relationship.** Financial and estate planning are ongoing processes, not one-time events such as selecting a college or paying off a loan. Seek out someone you trust. You deserve to feel comfortable that this person will place your needs above their own—the only lasting definition of a professional.

◆ **Never buy an investment over the telephone from someone you don't know.** "Never" is not too long a time for this rule. Do business with the people with whom you've decided to build a relationship. Where possible, especially in the early stages, do business face-to-face. You can tell a great deal when you are eye-to-eye. Most investors who complain of bad investments bought them over the phone from a broker whom they didn't know. If these salespeople had any experience, they wouldn't be cold calling you. To get yourself on the list that restricts telemarketers from soliciting you over the phone, contact the Direct Marketing Association *(see "Resources" appendix)*. Write to:

Telephone Reference Service
Direct Marketing Association
P.O. Box 9014
Farmingdale, NY 11735-9014

Request that your telephone numbers be added to the list of consumers who do not wish to be contacted by telephone for marketing purposes. Be sure to sign the letter.

◆ **Don't give your broker or anyone other than a professional investment manager with whom you have contracted in writing the authority to trade your account.** Even if you choose a passive role in your investments, keep the final decision-making authority to yourself. The only exception should be the hiring of a full-time investment manager, as outlined in *Problem 28*.

◆ **Focus on relationships, not the speed of transactions.** The quality of the time your planner proposes to spend in the data-gathering steps will dictate the future course and quality of your plan. It is not surprising that our leading financial institutions are striving to become more transaction oriented, focusing on ATM-like solutions to financial needs. This appeals to most people. However, if you were like most people, you wouldn't be reading this book.

RECOMMENDED ADVISERS

Interview the most experienced, best-trained, most reputable **planners** you can find, and hire the one with whom you feel you can build a relationship.

Ask your **accountant** to recommend a trustworthy and competent financial planner with whom he or she has personal experience.

Seek the same recommendations from your **attorney**, and from any wealthy and successful people you know.

SEE ALSO

◆ **Problem 28:** *Finding the Best Investment Vehicles.*

◆ **Problem 29:** *Professional Money Management.*

PROBLEM 27

CREATING THE BEST INVESTMENT PLAN

Being wealthy does not mean the same thing as being savvy about stocks, bonds, and real estate. Often, a high net worth or six-figure income results from building a business or developing a career specialty. Being savvy about investing really starts with recognizing that you need a professional planner. Being investment savvy is also about understanding your own risk tolerance.

THE FACT THAT most wealthy individuals do not consider themselves wealthy may help them stay that way. In the U.S. Trust Company study cited in the Introduction, only one-third of the affluent people surveyed considered themselves "very good" financial managers or investment managers. In fact, more respondents rated themselves "very good" in estate planning than financial planning.

Despite their self-effacing attitudes, wealthy (or on-track-to-be-wealthy) individuals spend more time on their financial affairs than their less-successful contemporaries. Thomas J. Stanley and William D. Danko, in their revealing best-seller, *The Millionaire Next Door,* found that prodigious accumulators of wealth (PAWs) "allocate nearly twice the number of

hours per month to planning their financial investments as [u]nder [a]ccumulators of [w]ealth
(UAWs) do." The UAWs had difficulty finding the
time to plan their investments. PAWs didn't.

Affluent people with annual incomes in excess of
$200,000 or net worth greater than $3,000,000 surveyed by the U.S. Trust Company presented an interesting picture of their risk tolerance. The survey asked
them to compare themselves to other people when
considering risk. Forty-three percent considered themselves less willing to take risk than others. Twenty-seven
percent considered themselves to be "average risk
takers." Only 11 percent said they were "much more
willing" to take risk than other people.

One of the explanations for this conservative bent
is that some wealthy individuals have assumed greater
risks in creating their wealth, especially if they started
a closely held business or professional practice.
Another likely explanation is that having accumulated
significant assets, most were unwilling to risk losing
them. Stanley and Danko would probably argue that
these people lived a frugal lifestyle that perpetuated
their affluence, and that they were attentive to their
finances and comfortable being conservative.

What is the best approach for you? How is an
investor with above-average intelligence supposed to
wade through this world of information overload?
Look to the fundamentals!

SOLUTIONS

◆ **Follow the six basic rules of investing:**

1 *Create your financial and estate plan.* You have to take
the time to develop a financial and estate plan—a
compilation of your objectives and a road map of the
best avenues to reach them. The plan could include a
budget, retirement plan, education plan, and an
investment plan or a business succession plan.

2 *Diversify your investments.* This is the art of putting

your eggs in more than one basket. Experts disagree on just how many different stocks, bonds, or mutual funds satisfy the requirement, but you will know when you are not adequately diversified.

There are several approaches to diversifying your investments. Some advisers tackle the subject from the perspective of *asset allocation,* a program of distributing your money among different categories of investments by some formula or advisory service. For example, a mutual-fund company may recommend that investors divide their investable dollars among a money-market fund for safety of principal, a growth-and-income fund for capital appreciation using blue-chip stocks, and two growth funds for appreciation utilizing both large- and medium-sized companies with long-term growth characteristics. Asset allocators frequently offer automatic services that readjust your portfolio as the adviser's allocation percentages change, or as strong growth of one asset class over another creates an imbalance.

Another diversification strategy might place more emphasis on purchasing stocks in different industries and bonds of varying maturities, and readjusting the portfolio as the recommending firm changes its opinions of the prospects for the near and intermediate-term future. Value Line, an investment advisory service, recommends investing in companies within over 100 industries that their experts believe will achieve better than average results.

What is the best approach to diversification? There isn't one that has clearly been proven to my satisfaction to be superior to all others. The important condition to avoid is being underdiversified.

3 *Buy high-quality investments.* For your key objectives, buy only quality stocks, bonds, mutual funds, or annuities *(see Problem 28)*. If you have excess funds to play with, use only those funds for unproven stocks, risky bonds, or speculative real estate ventures.

Regard highly speculative investments as an alternative to a spree in Las Vegas or Atlantic City.

How do you know if a stock or bond is a quality investment? Ask a reputable stock-brokerage firm how they classify that particular stock or bond. If it is classified as "aggressive," ask why.

4 *Exercise discipline in your investment habits.* If you need to invest new monies periodically to reach your objectives, develop a specific plan as to the types of investments you will buy and stick to it. Don't be concerned with the movement of the stock market day to day. Avoid getting caught up in media hype about the markets and interest rates. Scrambling through the paper each morning or surfing the Internet to check your portfolio is like driving from New York City to Los Angeles and checking the map every mile. By the time you get to Ohio, you're going to be a nervous wreck! What the market or the price of any one stock does on a daily basis is often irrational. Over time, however, a company's stock price reflects its underlying earnings. Most people end up selling their winners and holding onto their losers when they try to get back to even. Don't water your weeds and tear out your flowers.

5 *Invest for the long term.* Warren Buffett of Berkshire Hathaway, arguably the most successful investor today, quips that the most advantageous holding period for a stock is forever. While that may be a shade too long for most of us, it's closer to the truth than what most investors practice. A buy-and-hold philosophy works for several reasons. First, investors operating from instinct usually sell their winners too soon. Second, the tax laws reward holding periods of at least 18 months and one day. Third, expenses are usually lower because you are not paying new commissions. Fourth, it's easier to know a small number of stocks or mutual funds well, than to guess the next chapters of a constantly changing list of stories.

6 *Understand what you are buying and why—before you commit your money.* Many investors make bad decisions because they did not understand the investment when they bought it. They acted on the advice of a friend who knew as little as they did, or relied on a magazine article or television interview about a stock or fund without considering its appropriateness for their needs. When they find out how it behaves in different market scenarios, they sell, often at the wrong time.

If your financial plan is not in place, finish that task first *(refer to Problem 28)*.

◆ **Determine your risk profile and choose your investments accordingly.** There are four approaches to accumulating wealth by your own honest efforts: saving, investing, trading, and speculating.

1 *Savers* choose safety-oriented vehicles that pay interest regularly and predictably, such as CDs, investment-grade bonds, mortgages, and mortgage-based assets such as collateralized mortgage obligations (CMOs).

2 *Investors* choose vehicles that emphasize growth by capital appreciation and, possibly, reinvested income, such as dividends or rents. The most common vehicles are common stocks, real estate, and packages of these, such as mutual funds and unit investment trusts (UITs), all explained in *Problem 28*. Investors use time as a key ingredient in their accumulation goals. Their investment horizons are longer than a year, typically 5 or 10 years, or longer.

3 *Traders* take a shorter-term perspective. Jeffrey B. Little, author of the gem *Understanding Wall Street*, defines a *stock trader* as one who "attempts to take advantage of small price changes and is less interested in intrinsic value. Stock certificates are merely pieces of paper to be bought and sold for a profit within a short period of time—sometimes days or hours."

4 *Speculators* are big risk takers. If you're not a professional at it, avoid the risks of rapid and complete losses inherent in speculation.

You can be a passive saver and a passive investor, but you cannot be a passive trader or speculator. The most successful traders and speculators do it for a living. The losers in the trading and speculating arena are the people brokerage firms make millions of dollars catering to, because they are the source of the rapid generation of significant commissions, called *churning*, when buying and selling are excessive. Don't trade or speculate with your serious money—the funds you need for retirement or to finance an education.

RECOMMENDED ADVISER

Hire a **financial planner** to develop a complete financial plan based on your goals and objectives.

SEE ALSO

◆ **Problem 28:** *Finding the Best Investment Vehicles* to make sure you understand the differences among the investment products available today.

PROBLEM 28

FINDING THE BEST INVESTMENT VEHICLES

There are more than 5,000 stocks listed on the New York Stock Exchange, the American Stock Exchange (AMEX), and the NASDAQ, and there are more than 8,000 mutual funds. There are scores of vehicles to keep up with, including CMOs, STRIPs, and TIGRS, UITs, VAs, variable life, derivatives, and hedge funds. And don't forget the need to invest overseas. In order to hire good help, you need to understand some fundamental facts about the different investment types.

THERE ARE JUST a few basic investment types. Everything else is packaging. The basic savings and investment vehicles are:

◆ Savings accounts and CDs

- Bonds
- Stocks
- Annuities
- Real Estate
- Commodities and collectibles.

Everything else you buy is a "package" assembled from among these basic vehicles. A *mutual fund* or a UIT is just a packaging of savings vehicles, stocks, or bonds. Insurance companies amass huge sums in *variable annuities,* which are simply annuities and mutual funds bundled together. *Options, puts,* and *calls* are just an alternative way to invest in stocks, albeit very aggressively. You don't even have to buy and manage a rental property on your own any more. You can invest in real estate investment trusts (REITs) or partnerships. Finally, you can invest in gold, silver, orange juice, or pork bellies. If you are a farmer or miner, you might invest in the same commodity you produce as a strategy to hedge against a poor crop or falling prices. Collectibles, such as fine art, porcelains, and antiques— often pitched as assets that can be currently enjoyed while they appreciate—are usually owned as individual assets, but they too can be "packaged."

If you understand the underlying investment, you can see through the packaging to assess its value.

◆ **Savings vehicles.** A savings or checking account at your local bank, savings and loan, or credit union typically pays a very low rate of interest—or no interest— and is one of the worst investment alternatives. Nevertheless, you should maintain cash in a liquid (easy-to-reach) place for emergencies and monetary needs in the short run. For most people, the right amount of cash is six months' income. If you are wealthy, three months' net income is usually sufficient. Look for competitive yields for this liquid money, rather than simply accepting a low bank yield.

A *certificate of deposit* is a debt instrument issued by a bank. You are lending your money to the bank for a stated time period, in return for a stated interest rate. If you invested in a $10,000 CD for one year and the bank promised you 6 percent for the year, your principal is secure because the federal government insures CDs through the FDIC (Federal Deposit Insurance Corporation), up to $100,000 for your accounts in each institution. At the end of the year, you receive your $10,000 back plus $600 in interest.

◆ **Bonds.** *Bonds* are also debt instruments. In essence you are lending your money to the issuer for a stated time period in return for a stated interest rate. One of the common misconceptions about bonds is that they must be held until maturity. In fact, they may be sold before maturity, and frequently are.

The safest bonds are U.S. government bonds. They are backed by the full faith and credit of the government. Short-term debt instruments, one year or less, are called *Treasury bills*. If the term of the original bond is 1 to 10 years, it is called a *Treasury note*. Debt issued for longer than 10 years is called a *Treasury bond*. Agencies of the federal government also borrow money from the public. These bonds are not usually explicitly guaranteed by the full faith and credit of the United States, but they are implicitly guaranteed.

Corporations borrow money from investors, too. They issue notes and bonds backed by the creditworthiness of the issuing company, which can be ascertained by checking the company's credit ratings. Most corporate bonds are rated by several privately owned agencies or companies, the largest of which are Standard & Poor's and Moody's *(see Table 4.2 for the ratings offered by these two agencies)*. The higher the credit rating, the lower the interest rate yield.

Municipal and state projects are frequently debt financed by *municipal bonds*. In order to encourage local and state governments to finance their own growth and development, Congress allows municipal-bond interest to be received tax free for federal income tax purposes. You can also receive bond income state tax free if you reside in the state where the bonds are issued, and possibly even free of city taxes, as is the case for New York City obligations held by New York residents.

Zero-coupon bonds. A *zero-coupon security,* according to *Barron's Dictionary,* is a "security that makes no periodic interest payments but instead is sold at a deep discount from its face value. The buyer of the bond receives the rate of return by the gradual appreciation of the security, which is redeemed at face value on a specified maturity date." Zeroes are issued by governments and governmental agencies, and often carry abbreviations like TIGRS, STRIPs, etc. They are just repackagings of the two fundamental components of a bond: principal and income. Taxes are payable annually even though interest is not received until the bond matures or is sold.

◆ **Stocks.** A *stock* is a certificate of ownership in a corporation. The two types of stock are *common* and *preferred.* The latter performs more like a debt instrument, with a stated dividend return. A *dividend* is the company's way of sharing its earnings and profits with the stockholder, with a cash payment each quarter. Not all profitable companies pay dividends, however. Some outstanding corporations reinvest all their profits back into growing their company.

Common stocks can be classified as growth and income, growth, or aggressive growth. *Growth-and-income* stocks pay a meaningful dividend, say at least 2 percent. These include stocks considered *blue chips;* that is, stocks with long histories of growing profits and dividends. General Electric is an example. *Growth-stock* companies concentrate more on the growth of sales and earnings, without any particular concern for paying out dividends. *Aggressive-growth* stocks of newer, more speculative companies carry greater risk.

◆ **Annuities.** *Annuities* are long-term vehicles issued by insurance companies. They can be classified by time and by guarantee.

By time, an annuity is either immediate or deferred. An *immediate* annuity is an income-producing vehicle and comprises a relatively small portion of the annuity business. You pay a premium to the insurance company and they begin to pay you income within a month or so.

Most annuities are accumulation, rather than income, devices. Called *deferred* annuities, these grow tax deferred until money is withdrawn from the contract, either in a lump sum or as income. One of the biggest drawbacks to a deferred annuity is that, at the death of the annuitant, the beneficiary pays the tax on any gain in the contract.

Annuities can also be classified according to the guarantees made by the issuing insurer. Insurance companies issue fixed and variable annuities. A *fixed* annuity guarantees a stated return, invests your premium as part of the general assets of the insurer, and can be considered a safe investment only as long as your life insurance company is considered financially sound.

With *variable* annuities, you, not the insurance company, are responsible for the investment results. You choose from a menu of mutual funds with differing objectives and characteristics, as well as different managers. Variable-annuity assets are not commingled with the general assets of the insurer. They are kept in separate accounts and are not subject to the claims of creditors if the company should fail.

◆ **Real estate.** Real estate can be owned for investment purposes and includes apartments, commercial buildings, rental homes or condominiums, and raw land. You can also invest in real estate by lending to purchasers of real estate, taking back mortgages as evidence of your loan.

◆ **Commodities and collectibles.** Commodities can be purchased for investment, although most serious commodities buyers are professional traders or farmers trying to hedge against bad years in the marketplace or disappointing crops. Collectibles, such as antiques, art, or baseball cards, usually are a by-product of the enjoyment of the asset or hobby.

PACKAGES OF THESE basic investments comprise the vast majority of popular offerings. The most common are mutual funds, UITs, REITs, mortgage pass-throughs, zero-coupon bonds, and STRIPs. Their popularity is attributable to the ability of the average investor to join with other investors to pool resources for investment purposes. Also, most incorporate the expense of professional investment managers into the funds.

◆ **Mutual funds.** A *mutual fund* is an investment company. It invests in stocks, bonds, cash instruments, or some combination of these. According to the Investment Company Institute (ICI), which serves as a spokesperson for the industry, a mutual fund has eight distinguishing characteristics:

1 *Liquidity.* Owners of mutual-fund shares may sell their investment for cash any day that the markets trade.

2 *Diversification.* Investors can own more securities than they could purchase or keep track of on their own.

3 *Professional management.* Each fund is run by a manager or managers with experience in portfolio analysis.

4 *Choice.* There are a variety of funds for meeting different investment objectives.

5 *Flexibility.* Investment in a "family of funds" allows the investor to choose from and move money among a variety of funds all managed by the same company, such as Fidelity, Vanguard, Putnam, and Goldman Sachs. This can save fees and expenses, and it offers conveniences such as consolidated monthly statements.

6 *Accessibility.* Mutual funds can be purchased over the telephone directly from the fund family, through

discount or full-service brokers, at many local banks and savings and loans, and through financial planners and even accountants (in some states).

7 *Regulation.* Funds are regulated by the SEC and have to deliver a "prospectus" to every investor.

8 *Growth.* Since the 1920s, when the first mutual funds were created, the industry has grown to represent approximately 100 million shareholder accounts, with more than $2 trillion under management.

Mutual funds are sold with or without a sales commission—that is, load or no load. The *load* refers to the commission. No load generally means no advice; there is no one to pay a commission to, unless you are hiring a fee-based financial planner and paying a fee for recommendations. However, even fee-based planners who claim to have no stake in where you invest may be receiving ongoing commissions on assets with the fund company. Ask if this is the case before you assume a fee planner is more objective than a commissioned planner.

In the interest of keeping it simple and cutting through all the rhetoric, if you know enough to do your own investing, you may be better off if you buy no-load funds. However, if you are like most people and don't consider yourself a knowledgeable investor, find a good adviser and expect to pay for his or her advice, through either a commission or a fee.

In addition to the load, mutual funds spend a small percentage of their net assets to pay the fund managers and the expenses of reporting and operating the funds. This number can range from less than 0.5 percent to over 2 percent. Newer funds typically have higher annual expenses, until they raise sufficient assets to spread the expense among more investors. Beware of fund companies that do not cut expenses but actually increase the pay to compensate managers when they become more successful.

◆ **Unit investment trusts (UITs).** A *unit investment trust* is an investment alternative that falls somewhere between owning an individual portfolio and owning shares in a mutual fund. According to the ICI, "a UIT's portfolio is fixed, that is, it invests in a basket of securities and holds them during the life of the trust, which may run for many years. In contrast, the portfolios of mutual funds and closed-end funds change as fund managers buy and sell securities." A UIT is a packaged portfolio of stocks or bonds—such as corporate, government, or municipal bonds—or growth, growth-and-income, or international stocks. They are frequently organized by theme, such as the Baby Boomers Trust, offered by Van Kampen American Capital, which has a fixed portfolio of stocks that appeal to investors who are 35 to 50 years old and conscious of the companies that cater to their needs, such as Gucci and Delta Airlines.

UITs are liquid and the commissions are generally lower than those charged by a load mutual fund.

◆ **Real estate investment trusts** are packaged real estate investments. By investing in a REIT, you share in a large, diversified portfolio of properties you could not otherwise afford. REITs generally pass their rental income through to the investor. You can own apartments, office buildings, even medical complexes. These are good, rising-income funds, meaning that the better-performing REITs actually increase their dividends paid out to investors year after year. REITs trade like individual stocks, with the accompanying commissions lower than those charged for load mutual funds.

◆ **Mortgage pass-throughs.** When financial institutions lend money to home buyers, they take a mortgage in return as evidence of the loan obligation. That mortgage becomes an income-producing instrument. These individual mortgages are then packaged together and sold to investors. This may be done at the time of the original loans or later. The lending

institution gets new cash with which to make new
loans, and the purchaser of the loans has a stream of
principal and income repayments. Such bundles of
loans repackaged as CMOs or real estate mortgage
investment conduits (REMICs) generally offer a
higher rate of return on your investment than comparable alternatives. The return may be 1 percent
higher than 30-year Treasury bonds.

Given this honking traffic jam of investment vehicles,
how do you choose the best ones for your needs?

SOLUTIONS

◆ **Different assets have different characteristics. Identify
the ones that match your long-term investment
objectives.** There are five fundamental characteristics
of any savings and investment vehicle: safety, liquidity,
income potential, capital-appreciation potential, and
tax advantages. If you understand each characteristic
and the objectives in your plan, you can ask how a recommended investment meets your needs. Don't rely
on the sales representative or even the planner to do
that for you, even though they should. Ask specifically
how the investment works, and how it stacks up in each
of the five categories (see TABLE 4.1, on the following
two pages).

◆ **Know the different protection vehicles for savings and
investments.** Use them where necessary. There are a
number of layers of protection for investors, but their
characteristics are frequently miscommunicated and
widely misunderstood.

— *FDIC protection.* The FDIC is a U.S. government
agency that insures deposits in banks up to $100,000
per depositor, per institution. If you have more than
$100,000 in CDs, use more than one institution.

— *SIPC protection.* The Securities Investor Protection Corporation, also established by Congress, insures
securities and cash in brokerage-firm accounts against
the failure of the member firm. After a first effort to

4.1 INVESTMENT CHARACTERISTICS

INVESTMENT	SAFETY OF PRINCIPAL	LIQUIDITY
CD	Yes, FDIC limits	Yes, with penalty
Money Market	Yes	Yes
Government Bond	If held to maturity	Yes
Municipal Bond	If held to maturity & high enough quality	Yes, if high quality
Corporate Bond	If held to maturity & high enough quality	Yes, if high quality
CMO	If held to maturity	Yes
Utility Stock	No	Yes
REIT	No	Yes
Growth and Income Stock	No	Yes
Growth Stock	No	Yes
Aggressive Growth Stock	No	Yes
Penny Stock	No	Maybe
Commodity	No	Maybe
Fixed Annuity	Yes, if insurer is safe	Yes
Variable Annuity	No	Yes, with penalty
Collectible	No	No

merge the failed firm with another firm, the SIPC then steps in to liquidate the firm's assets and pay off the firm account owners. SIPC covers securities and cash up to a total of $500,000 per investor, with cash limits of $100,000. Most firms carry excess liability insurance that covers accounts up to $25 million or more. SIPC does not cover market losses, such as fluctuation in the value of a stock.

— *Bond insurance.* Many brokerage firms add insurance to the bonds they sell before they market the bonds to the public. This insurance covers both the interest and principal of the insured bonds. Municipal bonds are most frequently insured. The effect is to make the insured bond an automatic AAA-rated bond.

INCOME	CAPITAL APPRECIATION	TAX ADVANTAGES
Yes	No	No
Yes	No	Yes, if tax-free fund
Yes	Some, the longer the maturity	Yes, state tax free
Yes	Some, the longer the maturity	Yes, federal tax free and potentially state also
Yes	Limited	No
Yes	No	No
Yes	Yes	No
Yes	Yes	No
Yes	Yes	No
No	Yes	No
No	Yes	No
No	Yes	No
No	Yes	No
Yes	No	Yes
Yes	Depends on choice of funds	Yes
No	Yes	No

— *Bond ratings.* Bond ratings help you decide whether the offered bond meets your criteria for safety. The two largest rating services are Moody's and Standard & Poor's. Their ratings are shown in TABLE 4.2, *on the following page.* When you purchase a bond from a broker, ask the rating.

— *Insurance-company ratings.* Insurers are also rated for financial soundness. As many annuity buyers learned over the last two decades, not all annuity carriers are created equal. Some have failed. Remember that fixed annuities are only as safe as the insurance company that issues them, and even though they speak of guarantees, they are only referring to the promise of a declared rate of return. Look at TABLE 4.3, *shown on page 213.*

4.2	BOND RATINGS	
STANDARD & POOR'S		MOODY'S
AAA	**Highest Quality**	Aaa
AA+		Aa1
AA	**Strong Quality**	Aa2
AA-		Aa3
A+		A1
A	**Good Quality**	A2
A-		A3
BBB+		Baa1
BBB	**Adequate Quality**	Baa2
BBB-		Baa3
BB	**High Yield/Speculative**	Ba

NOTE: Parallel ratings by S&P's and Moody's are not necessarily equivalent.

Don't view the savings and investment features of life insurance as a reason to buy insurance you don't need. Variable life insurance should not be bought as an investment. In fact, no life insurance should be bought as an investment. Buy life insurance because you need financial protection against premature death, or as wealth replacement. Once you've made that determination and decided the amount of protection you need, ask which policy best suits your premium needs, considering the time the policy will likely be in force. *Universal life,* permanent insurance that is interest rate sensitive, and *variable life,* a permanent policy relying on the investment returns of underlying mutual funds, are just alternative ways of financing the purchase of life insurance. Both are viable approaches to paying premiums when you have a need for permanent insurance; that is, a need likely to exceed 15 years.

4.3 INSURANCE COMPANY RATINGS

A. M. BEST CO.	STANDARD & POOR'S	DUFF & PHELPS	MOODY'S	WEISS
ALL THE FOLLOWING ARE CONSIDERED SUPERIOR OR EXCELLENT RATINGS				
A++	AAA	AAA	Aaa	A
A+	AA	AA+	Aa	
A		AA		
A-		AA-		
ALL OF THE FOLLOWING ARE CONSIDERED GOOD RATINGS				
B++	A	A+	A	B
B+		A		
B		A-		
B-				
ALL OF THE FOLLOWING ARE CONSIDERED FAIR OR ADEQUATE RATINGS				
C++	BBB		Baa	C
C+	BB			

TIP: Only buy insurance from companies rated Superior or Excellent in the ratings above.

NOTE: Parallel ratings are not strictly equivalent. Any rating below those illustrated are below acceptable quality.

RECOMMENDED ADVISER

Use a **financial planner** to define your objectives, develop your plan, and recommend vehicles to you.

SEE ALSO

◆ **Problem 3:** *Insufficient Cash in the Estate* to review uses of life insurance to pay taxes.

◆ **Problem 26:** *Finding the Best Financial Adviser* to understand how the right adviser combines with the best vehicles to accomplish your financial-planning objectives.

PROFESSIONAL
MONEY MANAGEMENT

While the set of skills one needs to invest well can be learned, many affluent investors are accustomed to relying on professionals for advice on matters for which they lack either the knowledge, the time to acquire the knowledge, or the interest. Accounting, legal, and investment help are the most common examples.

PRIVATE INVESTMENT MANAGERS, those who provide fee-based investment services, are more readily available to those with wealth than those aspiring to wealth. Many managers have minimum limits for investment. Some will not accept accounts less than $10 million, others $1 million. This allows them to spend more time with each client. It also helps to attract investors who are more knowledgeable and sophisticated, and more likely to appreciate the services of an individual money manager.

At the other end of the spectrum of managed money is the mutual fund. Remember, one of the primary advantages of a mutual fund is professional management. However, with a mutual fund, there is no one-on-one relationship with the managers. They are investing according to a declared objective and you are welcome to join in for the ride, but they will be investing for everyone just the same. However, a well-selected group of mutual funds can often perform as well as privately managed money—for less in fees. A good broker or planner can help structure such a mix of funds.

Given the fine art of packaging, so well refined on Wall Street, it was just a matter of time before the stock-brokerage industry figured out how to present a middle-ground vehicle between private money management and mutual funds. It is called a *wrap account.*

Often it just adds an extra level of expense without the addition of significant services.

Another innovation from Wall Street is the *contractual fee for service* on an existing account. It is a way for brokers to charge a fee for assets under management that previously sat producing little income for the broker because the account had no trading activity. Hypothetically, the fee discourages churning. In many cases, it is a way of overpaying for a portfolio to remain inactive.

Busy, wealthy, and successful people are quick to recognize they can't do everything well themselves. They hire money managers. How should you go about doing that?

SOLUTIONS

◆ **Realistically assess your needs and resources.** If your objective is to fund a comfortable retirement and you have sufficient assets to accomplish that goal already, you can afford to be conservative in the selection of investment alternatives and you can probably avoid management assistance and fees. High-quality bonds or bond mutual funds can accomplish the job with very little risk. On the other hand, if your objective is to amass as much wealth as humanly possible, you will want to hire the best managers money can buy.

If you have decided to be a passive investor and to leave the asset selection to a professional, study your options in TABLE 4.4, *on the following two pages.*

If you are going to select an investment manager and give him or her the authority to make investment decisions, use a full-time RIA, not a broker or a financial planner. You will be hiring someone who *manages* investments for a living, not someone who *sells* investments or plans for a living. You should be hiring an expert with a verifiable track record. You will pay a fee for their professional services. Look for fee schedules that have declining percentages as you commit more

4.4   INVESTMENT-MANAGEMENT ALTERNATIVES

TYPE	EXPERIENCE	COMPENSATION
Stockbroker or Planner	Maybe—ask for references and résumé	Usually commissions; can be fee-based
Fee-based planner	Maybe—ask for references and résumé, designation	Fees based on assets under management
Wrap accounts	Maybe—depends on who is making investment decisions	Fees based on assets under management
Independent asset manager or trust company	Usually	Fees based on assets under management
Mutual funds	Usually, although some funds have inexperienced managers	Load funds have commissions. No-load = no commission. Annual expenses for assets under management

funds to the manager. A typical schedule might be 2 percent up to $500,000, 1.5 percent on the next $500,000, and 1 percent above $1 million. This means that if you invested $1.5 million under this schedule, you would pay:

```
0.02 x first $500,000   = $10,000
0.015 x next $500,000 = $7,500
0.01 x next $500,000   = $5,000
                $22,250 total annual fee
```

◆ **Hire your investment adviser diligently.** The first step is to ascertain your investment objective: taxable income, tax-free income, growth and income, growth, or aggressive growth.

The second step is to decide on the dollar amount

ACCOUNTABILITY	SERVICES	TIPS
Monthly statements	Planning possible; wide range of services if full-service firm	Do not grant broker or planner authority to trade account
Monthly statement should be furnished monthly or quarterly	Planning is the reason to use minimal statements	Compare fees and commissions based on likely pattern
Monthly or quarterly	Minimal statements	Check total costs as wrap accounts tend to be more expensive
Quarterly statements	Planning and banking services	Original asset management services, especially trust companies
Monthly or quarterly statements	Only if provided by a broker or planner	Best alternative for most investors

you will be investing. This makes it possible to determine if there are managers that are excluded because of the size of your initial investment.

The third step is to gather a list of potential managers that fit your criteria as to objective and size. Almost all the major brokerages can give you a list of the investment managers they recommend. If you have a broker you work with, ask for his or her firm's approved list. You don't need 100 names—just enough to give you a variety to choose from.

◆ **Interview the prospective managers.** If they balk because of the size of your investment, you have a feel for the personal care you will receive. If your money is going to be a drop in their bucket, you're probably better off with a carefully selected portfolio of mutual funds.

◆ **Study the investment manager's performance history (track record).** Industry standards require that a manager maintain a verifiable and accurate compilation of the firm's historical performance. Among other information, you should find out how long the manager has been at this business. You should concern yourself with the return in relation to the risk assumed. Ask for a graphical depiction of risk-adjusted return, called a *scattergram*. It shows where the investment manager stands relative to the appropriate standards for that fund, both as to return percentages and risk.

Growth funds measure themselves against the Standard & Poor's 500 Index. If growth is your objective, you ideally want a manager whose style gives you returns above the S&P 500, with risk below that of the index. Growth-and-income funds may compare themselves to the Dow Jones Industrial Average, made up of 30 of the largest blue-chip stocks in America today. An aggressive or small-cap fund usually measures its performance against an index of smaller and less-proven companies, such as the Russell 2000. Tax-free income can be measured against the Lehman Brothers' Muni Index, and taxable income against either the Lehman Brothers' Government Index or its Aggregate Index. The value of any measuring rod is in how usefully it compares the manager's performance to an "unmanaged" collection of stocks or bonds. These indexes, and others, can be found any weekday in the *Wall Street Journal* or the financial section of most newspapers. Another outstanding reference is the *Chase Investment Performance Digest*, published annually *(see the "Resources" appendix for details)*.

◆ **Ask the manager to describe his or her style of investing.** For equity (stock) portfolios, you want to know if the manager follows a growth or a value model. *Growth managers* concentrate on revenue and earnings growth among other indicators. *Value investors* focus more on companies that are undervalued by the market. At different times in the economic cycles, growth portfolios outperform value portfolios, and vice versa. You should probably have both value and growth in your portfolio.

Does the manager invest in large-cap stocks, mid-caps, or small caps? Each category has its own performance histories and expectations. The smaller the companies, the greater the risk and potentially greater return, on average. However, if low volatility—measured by swings in the overall value of the portfolio—is an objective, large-cap stocks are the answer.

Another question is whether the manager favors a top-down or bottom-up approach. The *top-down method* studies trends in the economy first, then searches for companies in those industries that should thrive on those trends. The *bottom-up methodology* prefers to search for good companies without particular regard to the overall economy or trends.

◆ **Ask about turnover ratios.** Unless you are investing in an IRA or other retirement plans, you will be taxed on any capital gains and income generated by the portfolio. The 1997 tax laws reward *low turnover,* meaning infrequent sales and repurchases of stocks and bonds. Assets held for 18 months and a day are taxed at 20 percent. Assets held for more than 12 but fewer than 18 months are taxed at the maximum rate of 28 percent. Assets sold within a year of their purchase are taxed at your ordinary income rate, which could be as high as 39.6 percent, before adding in your state tax, if any. A manager should be able to quote you turnover ratios for any portfolio he or she oversees. A ratio of 0.35 means that a little over one-third of the portfolio holdings are sold in a year, on average.

◆ **Make sure you understand the timing of the fees.** The fee structure should be explained fully. Ask for a "disclosure form" that details the agreement between you and the manager. Ask if you'll be charged any fees to exit the program. Make sure you understand whether the manager deducts his or her fees from your assets or if you pay separately. These fees are usually tax deductible as investment expenses. If possible, pay these fees by a separate check and let you funds grow.

If your broker provides other valuable services, such as planning, investment advice, and managing your IRA, consider using the brokerage firm's selected list of investment managers. The firm will keep your account, the investment manager makes the decisions, and your broker should be able to share the fee at no extra expense to you. The broker is compensated for his or her time, so don't be shy about asking detailed questions to find out how your broker's arrangement works.

If you want to stick with mutual funds, choose an asset allocation fund or program. Many wealthy investors are attracted by the prestige of a private money manager when a carefully selected portfolio of mutual funds will do as well, if not better. For example, building a portfolio of mutual funds may give you more control and better returns than a typical arrangement in which brokerage firms sell asset management plans for smaller sums of money, and merely commingle your funds with the investment manager's existing fund. Here you are buying a mutual fund anyway, just under a different name. Look before you leap.

Load mutual funds may offer reduced commissions, called *break points,* for larger purchases. If you invest more than $50,000 with the fund family, typically the total load drops from 5.5 to 4.5 percent. At $100,000 it falls to 3.5 percent, and at $250,000 to 2.5 percent.

Be wary of converting your existing portfolio from a commission-based account to a fee-based account. Many investors own excellent portfolios that they rarely change, especially if they inherited the account. Some investors, such as Warren Buffett, rarely buy or sell stocks. He believes in buying good-quality stocks and holding them until they are no longer good-quality stocks. If this is your philosophy, you are not paying much in the way of commissions, so don't jump at the stockbroker's offer to switch your portfolio to a fee basis. It pays the broker whether you sell, buy, or sit.

If you are a frequent buyer and seller, a fee-based commission schedule might make sense. Run the numbers based on your transactions for the prior year or two. Compare those broker commissions to how much you would have paid in fees.

If the fee encourages you to become an even more frequent trader, remember that the income tax on short-term gains is up to 39.6 percent and that you are frequently better off if you buy quality vehicles and hold.

RECOMMENDED ADVISER

Make sure you have a financial plan with objectives before you select an **investment manager**.

SEE ALSO

- **Problem 26:** *Finding the Best Financial Adviser.*
- **Problem 28:** *Finding the Best Investment Vehicles* to understand the benefits of buying mutual funds for long-term wealth-accumulation objectives.

PART 5

Family
PROBLEMS

F AMILY PROBLEMS generate more than just emotional costs. They can pose lifelong threats to the preservation of your wealth. Some of these difficulties are preventable. Others can be managed by risk-assumption techniques, such as insurance. Still others can be planned for and minimized.

Approximately 40 percent of marriages end in divorce, and problems of separation, custody, and child support have become commonly experienced—if not commonly anticipated—events. Even if you start a relationship with lofty intentions and sensible aspirations, you can realistically lay some groundwork for a dissolution, if one occurs. *Problems 30 through 33* give you ideas for wealth management in these situations.

One of the most overlooked areas of wealth protection is safeguarding your assets against erosion in the event of a long-term disability. *Problem 34* offers solutions to this threat.

With the mixed blessings of living too long hanging over your own wallet, it is easy to forget your obligation to your parents. *Problems 33 and 34* consider the financial troubles that can beset three or more generations living under one roof and the issues of long-term care.

Problem 35 shows you the most effective ways to fund education expenses. Looking through the fog of likely costs, this Problem has some solid recommendations for paying college or secondary-school bills.

Problem 36 addresses the special problems of loans and gifts to family members, especially minors.

SEPARATION AND DIVORCE

Planning for separation and divorce doesn't make either event more likely to happen. Agreements such as prenuptials can address such issues as the division of assets before disruptive emotions enter into the fray. In addition, there are devices for dealing with financial issues without the often crippling legal and accounting expenses that arise in heavily contested divorce proceedings. Smart solutions exist, even if you think it's too early—or too late—to look into them.

WHEN TWO PEOPLE enter into a partnership that is supposed to last their lifetimes, no wonder its unraveling is so gut wrenching and financially contentious. Only rarely do the partners make equal financial contributions, and yet money often becomes the focal point of most divorces, as though dollars were the only way to measure a contribution to the relationship.

The collapse of a business, like the collapse of a marriage, tends to be emotional, expensive, and elongated. Yet, as we saw in *Problem 25, Divorce and the Family Business,* neither commercial nor conjugal partners are quick to face these questions going in.

With more and more two-wage-earner families, the problems of an equitable division of current assets and future income have become more complex. Back when only the husband worked and the wife assumed primary responsibility for the children, courts had an easier time dividing the estate. Often, they simply tried to lop it into two halves. Nowadays, both parties are likely to have careers, or at least training for a career. This can lead to disputes about what training, earning potential, and work experiences make each party worth in the job marketplace.

Courts and lawyers in most jurisdictions do not regard making the divorce process easier and less expensive as their chief responsibility. It is not unusual for legal fees to exceed $100,000 for a process determining how the parties will divide only $1 million or so—frequently driven by the lawyers' assertions that adversarial proceedings will yield more than good-faith bargaining. Even in states that have enacted no-fault divorce laws, legal fees continue to seriously erode the monies that could otherwise be used for the welfare of the children or the litigants.

The high incidence of divorce has also paved the way for a high incidence of remarriage. The parties are frequently older, if not wiser. They often have more assets than they had the first time around. And yet, there is a natural reluctance to discuss and resolve financial responsibilities before the marriage ceremony, perhaps out of fear that it will create a rift that dooms the relationship.

Usually, problems begin as soon as a couple separates. How are two households going to carry on where one existed only weeks before? Money immediately becomes the focus, especially if one of the spouses is not employed outside the home. Moreover, many wealthy couples don't *feel* wealthy—even though they may have valuable assets, they don't have much extra income after expenses. And we're not just talking about those who live beyond their means. Many farmers, professionals, and owners of businesses pour most of their profits back into the enterprise.

The division of retirement-plan assets can be an especially charged issue when one partner has been working in the home, raising children, and entertaining the spouse's business customers, while the other has built up assets that were to fund their joint retirement. Equally problematic is the situation in which both parties have careers with separate retirement plans, but one plan is much better funded than the other.

The right to an ongoing income is a big source of discord. When is a partner entitled to *alimony*, defined as income for a divorced spouse?

Child support and custody are discussed in *Problem 31*. It can cost a lot to fight over something that is beyond price.

The ultimate irony is that divorce—the very process designed to make sure the parties walk away with an equitable division of the assets—often is a major source of financial difficulties, whether by forcing untimely liquidation of a house or securities, setting up a hardship for one partner, or eroding hard-earned assets with legal and accounting fees.

SOLUTIONS

◆ **Negotiate first; if unsuccessful, arbitrate.** Avoid litigation if possible. Explore the nonlitigation process in your home state, usually called *alternative dispute resolution*. The emphasis is on resolving differences without the acrimony and expense of litigation.

Negotiation is defined as two people sitting down face-to-face and trying to reach a settlement on their own. *Mediation* is also a process with the two disputants sitting down, but adding a third party—ideally a professional—to help with the discussions and negotiations. *Arbitration* is a formal legal process with a professional arbitrator, where the decisions reached are binding and used to avoid a trial. Alternative dispute resolution is private and the conclusions are confidential. Attorney Hanan Isaacs of Princeton, New Jersey, is chairman of the Dispute Resolution Section of the New Jersey Bar Association and a professional mediator, arbitrator, and trial lawyer. Isaacs believes that the old adversarial system of resolution is too often characterized by parties trying to find the "meanest, baddest litigator," when the emphasis should be on sitting down to find a compromise.

◆ **Enter into a prenuptial agreement covering both assets and earnings.** Despite the negative connotation of prenuptial agreements, they have an often overlooked positive attribute: the parties discuss money *before* the marriage. Since money can be one of the sore spots in any marriage, the parties are better off seeing how their future partner addresses the difficult questions before the ceremony. If there are minimal assets or if both parties are young and embarking on their first marriage, no agreements are necessary. However, the conversation is a great idea anyway, whether you're sorting through this yourself or advising someone else, including your children and heirs.

Start by raising the issue of finances. Try to reach an understanding of how the family bills are to be paid, savings to be generated, and investments to be managed. Discuss your respective feelings about risk and volatility. If these are issues too difficult or incomprehensible, hire a financial planner to walk through the options with you.

Prenuptial agreements can be revocable or irrevocable, but most should be changeable by the parties. They should address not only separation and subsequent divorce, but also prolonged illness and disability.

Often there is a sizable disparity between the assets of the two parties, especially where second or subsequent marriages are involved. The prenuptial agreement protects the assets if the marriage is not successful. If time dispels the fears of dissolution, the parties can dispense with the agreement. A simple prenuptial agreement should cost no more than a will and trust.

◆ **Even if you don't adopt a prenuptial agreement, decide on the rights to retirement-plan assets earned before the marriage.** Couples should agree how pension, profit-sharing, 401(k), and individual retirement account (IRA) monies would be divided after a divorce. It would not be unreasonable for two middle-aged workers to agree that each should keep their own plan accumulations. Young married spouses might contemplate retaining their own retirement assets, at least as long as each works.

If there is no prenuptial agreement for retirement

plan assets, use a QDRO. A *qualified domestic-relations order* (QDRO) is a court-approved order for distribution of retirement-plan assets. Use of a QDRO can avoid the current taxation that would result if one spouse handed a lump sum from the plan to the other. Whether the assets are left in the existing plan or rolled over into a new IRA, the tax can be deferred until the funds are needed at retirement. This is advantageous because often the *nonparticipant spouse,* that is, the spouse who was not contributing to the plan, needs a retirement fund, not the cash. If you are the nonparticipant spouse, avoid the temptation to take the cash—unless you absolutely need it to live on currently.

◆ **Review your estate plan after a marriage or a divorce.** Often divorced couples, already reeling from legal fees, don't want to spend time or money reviewing wills and other estate-planning documents. This can be a serious mistake. Consider the situation where the divorced husband remarries and dies without changing the beneficiary on his group life insurance, his deferred-compensation plan, or his 401(k) plan. His new wife would receive none of these assets. His ex-wife would receive $1 million as a windfall.

◆ **Check the ownership and beneficiary designations on all life insurance policies.** Believe it or not, life insurance is often overlooked by the divorcing parties and the courts. For many, this can be a significant portion of the decedent's estate, especially with the heavy use of life insurance in estate planning today. You should review the coverage and ownership to make sure the appropriate parties are protected. You can use the insurance to protect ex-spouses and children after a dissolution. And do not forget that some insurance— permanent plans such as whole life, universal life, or variable life—can have cash surrender values. These cash equivalents should be addressed in any agreements. Finally, be mindful of your insurability. If you have become uninsurable due to health conditions, be very hesitant to give up the ownership of any life insurance or disability-income insurance.

◆ **Consider the creation of an irrevocable life insurance trust (ILIT) to ensure the payment of proceeds according to the property settlement agreement.** The ILIT *(see pages 77–78)* can satisfy obligations to a prior marriage and family without distorting your current estate plan. This is especially advantageous where there is a subsequent marriage and new family responsibilities.

◆ **Take advantage of COBRA-mandated health insurance protection.** The Consolidated Omnibus Budget Reconciliation Act (COBRA) provides that employers with 20 or more employees with group health insurance must make coverage available for dependents of terminated employees where there is either a divorce or a legal separation. This does not always afford you the best coverage at a reasonable premium. However, if there are any ongoing medical problems that are considered preexisting conditions, it may be the only affordable choice. Apply for COBRA coverage and use it while you shop around for your own policy. Learn about the cost advantages and coverage disadvantages of managed-care plans before you commit. Read Ellyn Spragins's book, *Choosing and Using an HMO*.

◆ **Where advantageous, arrange for tax-deductible alimony or separate maintenance payments.** Lump-sum settlements are not tax deductible. Alimony paid in installment payments can be deductible if it is paid in cash rather than in real property or other assets; and if it won't continue after the death of the recipient; if the parties don't live together; and if the divorce agreement states that the payments are to be deductible as alimony. Child support is not deductible.

Alimony is taxable upon receipt by the spouse. Whether it is advantageous to have the payments considered alimony or not depends on the facts and which party is being considered. The key to coming out on top is to ask your tax adviser.

◆ **Reinvest alimony into an IRA.** The Tax Reform Act of 1984 permits alimony to count as earned income for purposes of funding an IRA. Divorced spouses who have not been the primary breadwinner in the family often have received little information and even less advice as to their own retirement planning. Consult a financial planner to determine whether you are better off with the traditional tax-deductible IRA or the new Roth IRA, where deposits are not tax deductible but withdrawals at retirement are tax free.

RECOMMENDED ADVISERS

Consult an **attorney** about a prenuptial agreement. When divorce seems imminent, seek out arbitration channels through the state bar association before you automatically hire lawyers with reputations for being the best fighters. The most contentious are often the most expensive.

Get a realistic assessment of your tax situation from your **accountant** before and after the dissolution. This is important for both spouses.

At the very least, consult with your **planner** about the new division of property and begin to consider your new objectives.

With your **life insurance agent**, reconsider your beneficiaries in light of your new marital status.

SEE ALSO

◆ **Problem 25:** *Divorce and the Family Business* to anticipate the impact of divorce on family-owned businesses.

◆ **Problem 31:** *Child-Support Responsibilities* if children are in the picture.

CHILD-SUPPORT RESPONSIBILITIES

For many divorcing Americans, child support is less an obligation to be shouldered than a responsibility to be cherished. For the wealthy or aspiring-to-be-wealthy, a parent's financial objective should be to provide the best childhood and education. The most monetarily effective plans are those that make the interests of the children the focal point.

THE FIRST CHALLENGE for divorcing parents is to separate their current emotions from the child's present and long-term needs. This is not a text on the psychology of children of divorce; our aim is to assist you with the financial considerations. However, parents can have a priceless impact on the well-being of a child by keeping their offspring out of the conflagration. All the money and planning in the world will not fill the void left by an acrimonious divorce that used the child as a pawn in the game.

The child's current needs should dictate the required level of child-support payments. These payments are sometimes so high that the paying parent detests the ex-spouse and the agreement, and even resents the child. Courts that support this kind of financial retribution are often guaranteeing the child more harm than protection. If there is to be a "punitive" element to the settlement, it should go toward the education or long-term needs of the child, rather than child-support payments that just disguise a higher living standard for the custodial spouse.

Wealthy parents often send their children to private secondary schools. Yet, property settlement agreements frequently overlook the expense of funding tuitions at any level other than college. Many prep schools charge in excess of $20,000 per year for boarding students, and not much less for day students. Primary-school tuition can easily top $15,000. Three years at a good prep school, combined with four years at a private university, can cost $150,000 or more. Add graduate school and the number could exceed $200,000. With five children, a divorced parent could be out $1 million just for education expenses.

Don't fall into the trap of favoring decisions that make more tax sense than common sense. The results can be disastrous. Uniform Gifts to Minors Act (UGMA) accounts, discussed in detail in *Problem 36*, are an example. In an effort to place assets beyond the grasp of either parent, divorcing parents often establish UGMA accounts with stocks, bonds, or mutual funds. The parent named on the account as custodian can withdraw monies to pay for the child's basic living needs. Income and capital gains are taxed to the custodial parent until the child is 14, at which time the income is taxed to the child. This tax shifting at age 14 is usually a small advantage compared to the potential problems created, because the remaining assets pass automatically to the child upon reaching the age of majority.

There are many cases where stocks placed in a UGMA grew far greater than anyone would have guessed, often amounting to more than $250,000. If the child decides not to go to college, the money is still his or hers, at majority, which could be 18 or 21, depending on the state. The prospect of an irresponsible child driving off with $250,000 in a checking account holds little appeal for most parents, yet it happens all the time.

Another problem is that of the death or disability of the parent responsible for support and education. It is one thing to require continuing support during your ex-spouses's lifetime, but another to ensure the successful completion of that obligation if that other parent stops earning a living due to death or disability. If the decedent remarries and has a second family, the problem gets larger and the likelihood of resolution after the death smaller. Read on for solutions to these problems.

SOLUTIONS

◆ **Aim for a reasonable agreement.** Don't go after everything your partner has as a tactic to end up with what you actually hope to get. Negotiators in every sphere have discovered the benefit of win-win negotiations, where both sides get what they want. Start by trying alternative dispute resolution, especially mediation, involving a professional experienced in resolving domestic disputes.

◆ **Use trusts to fund the education needs of children, especially if funding in advance of when needed is required.** Trusts can create the same income-shifting possibilities as UGMA accounts, without the loss of control of the assets at the child's majority. The parents can select an independent trustee, such as an attorney or a trust company, if they cannot work together civilly for the child's benefit. If the child does not need the funds for college or schooling at whatever level, the trustees can withhold the monies well beyond the age of majority—say until the child learns to be more responsible—or the trustees could even redeploy the funds for siblings who need and will appreciate the money for their education needs.

◆ **Take advantage of the new education IRA.** While the $500 limit each year is not a huge amount to set aside, every dollar counts. Remember that the new IRA is limited to $500 per child, not per parent. The deposit can be tax deducted and the funds accumulated tax deferred. When withdrawn, the amounts are not taxable. If not expended for education, they may be rerouted to other siblings.

◆ **Do not be too conservative with education funds.** There is a tendency to be too safety conscious with monies invested for education. Use equities for accounts that will be in existence for 10 years or longer. True, bonds deliver their returns at a guaranteed time, but you may be able to set aside less money in the long run if you assume a little more risk. Use a financial planner to project the differences.

◆ **Use a financial planner to build a model education fund.** Most planners have computer programs that can estimate the current contributions necessary to fund an education well in the future. Some even have built-in projected tuition increases for major colleges. Try to agree on the extent of education funding that is to be provided, primary and secondary, college and graduate school. Consider the possibility of loans and grants, although the wealthier the parents, the less likely their children are to qualify for need-based financial aid. Also, the farther away the need is, the less reliance you should place on assumptions of aid. Don't

5.1   EDUCATION PLAN

REQUIRED INFORMATION	EXAMPLE
Age of student	Age 5
Years until enrollment	13 years
Today's college cost	$29,435 Princeton
Assumed rate of inflation	5.05%
Assumed return on investments	Option 1: Zero coupon Treasuries
	Option 2: 8% compounded annually
Amount accumulated to date	$0

PROJECTED EXPENSES AT TIME OF COLLEGE ($29,435 TODAY INCREASED AT 5.05%)

Year 2010	$55,847
Year 2011	$58,667
Year 2012	$61,631
Year 2013	$64,742
Total	$240,887

INVESTMENT REQUIRED	ZERO-COUPON TREASURIES	8%
Lump sum today	$107,081	$78,835
Annual deposits		$9,974
Monthly deposits		$831

SOURCE: EDWARD JONES INVESTMENTS

be unrealistic in your choices of colleges. Not everyone is a candidate for Princeton, Harvard, or Yale. There are hundreds of quality institutions that cost a fraction of these more visible–name schools. Consider the impact of inflation on tuition. Actually, inflation has lagged the rise in the cost of tuition for most colleges and universities over the last several decades. Use a cost of tuition increase assumption of 5 to 7 percent. TABLE 5.1, *at left,* gives a sample education plan. *(See Problem 35 for a more detailed discussion of education funding.)*

◆ **Enlist the aid of grandparents.** Your parents and sometimes even those of your ex-spouse can be invaluable in divorces. They frequently are capable of being more objective than you and consequently can serve as excellent trustees. They are also a source of potential help in funding a college education. Again, take care to avoid UGMA accounts where the funds to be accumulated could reach significant proportions—say the amount you would feel comfortable with in your offspring's pocket if he or she drops out of school and heads for the border. The tax benefits rarely outweigh the risk of a child walking away with a large chunk of the assets.

RECOMMENDED ADVISERS

When negotiating your way through divorce and child-support issues, use an **attorney** who under stands the importance of minimizing legal and accounting fees to draft trusts to benefit the child or children.

Use your **planner** to estimate the expense of currently funding a future education. Coordinate trusts or accounts to meet the projections with a provision that addresses potential shortages.

SEE ALSO

◆ **Problem 30:** *Separation and Divorce.*

◆ **Problem 35:** *Funding Education Expenses* to learn more about the alternatives and considerations when planning educational costs.

MULTIPLE FAMILIES

A frequent by-product of divorce is multiple families. When a divorced parent remarries, he or she often assumes responsibility for another family. Whether by joining the new spouse's family, starting another one with their own children, or both, the legal and financial responsibilities can be significant.

THE PSYCHOLOGICAL IMPACT of multiple families is a potential source of stress in current relationships and in financial and estate planning. Alimony and child-support responsibilities can make subsequent marriages more difficult because of the continuing outflows of cash to support existing obligations. Often, second spouses take issue with these expenditures, especially if they have not had families of their own or are contributing a sizable share of the new family's income.

Dividing assets and income into three categories—mine, yours, and ours—is not unhealthy so long as the divisions are made through positive discussion and not by default. This is especially important when the apportionment of money and time is required because of the children from prior marriages or relationships. For many couples, the segregation of income and assets occurs after the joining together, even though the prior responsibilities predated the relationships.

Adoption of a new spouse's children is another big financial issue in multiple families. There is possibly no act that can signify one's commitment to a relationship more than adoption. However, as with any child-rearing issue, this is a step that should not be taken lightly. Once someone adopts a new spouse's child, the entire financial responsibility of paying for education and raising the child to maturity or majority—whichever comes first—becomes theirs to share. With a family of four children, this could be financially equivalent to cosigning a $5,000,000 loan for the other spouse.

Multiple families also put pressure on the estate-planning needs of second spouses. Will and trust arrangements need to provide for both families—the first according to the terms of your property settlement agreement, at a minimum, and the second according to your conscience and your remaining means. If you have not reviewed your plan from the first relationship, you are probably ensuring that someone will be left in a painful situation. The same goes for your life insurance planning. Sometimes courts obligate the divorcing parents to retain life insurance for the benefit of an ex-spouse or the children. When the parent remarries, the new spouse and children also need protection. The result can be a doubling of the need for insurance. And, possibly a doubling of the premium.

SOLUTIONS

◆ **Review your financial and estate plans at the time of divorce and again before remarriage.** Know the extent of your obligations and responsibilities before taking on new ones. Involve your potential spouse before tying the knot so that there are no illusions about the family finances. Honesty up front can help minimize confrontations later. Include in your discussions not just the legal obligations but also what you feel are the moral obligations to prior spouses and children. It is better to know the limits of your new spouse's sympathies and generosities before the remarriage.

◆ **Review your insurance policies upon divorce and again before remarriage.** A court order often helps determine the appropriate level of insurance for divorced parents. Rerun the capital-needs analysis (CNA) *(found in Problem 6)*, with the new marital status assumptions and all its responsibilities. If you are to be the custodial

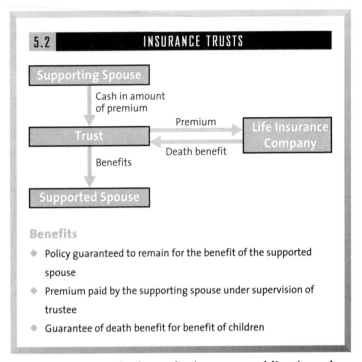

5.2   INSURANCE TRUSTS

Supporting Spouse

Cash in amount of premium

Trust   Premium   Life Insurance Company

Death benefit

Benefits

Supported Spouse

Benefits

◆ Policy guaranteed to remain for the benefit of the supported spouse

◆ Premium paid by the supporting spouse under supervision of trustee

◆ Guarantee of death benefit for benefit of children

parent, try to tie down the insurance obligations during the divorce process by having the agreed-upon life insurance owned by a trust that the ex-spouse cannot control *(see* TABLE 5.2, *above)*.

◆ **Utilize corporate trustees for multiple-family needs at your death.** It is usually unfair and almost always unwise to leave your current spouse with the responsibility of doling out funds to children from a prior marriage, not to mention ex-husbands or ex-wives. Just as an executor's, this is a lousy job, with lousy pay. Avoid the conflicts and time drain on your current family by establishing trusts to handle the investment of funds, receipt and reinvestment of insurance proceeds, and the decisions as to what are legitimate education expenses. These can be education trusts, as explained in *Problem 31* or marital trusts, discussed in *Problem 5*.

Consult your **attorney** about the best way to meld past and current responsibilities, including the adoption of children and the use of trusts. Ask how to change your estate plan to remove the burden from current spouses of dealing with financial obligations to past spouses.

Have your **insurance agent** review your policies upon remarriage to ensure there is sufficient protection to provide the required or desired dollars for your ex-spouse and children from that marriage, as well as your new familial needs.

Have your **financial planner** review your financial plan at any change in your marital status or when adding children.

SEE ALSO

- ◆ **Problem 30:** *Separation and Divorce* to understand the general considerations accompanying a dissolution of a marital relationship.
- ◆ **Problem 31:** *Child-Support Responsibilities* to understand the funding of your children's needs after dissolution of a marriage.
- ◆ **Problem 33:** *Sandwich-Generation Planning* to consider the obligations to your parents that are often overlooked until they are approaching your doorstep.

PROBLEM 33

SANDWICH-GENERATION PLANNING

The term *sandwich generation* is used to describe the cohorts of adults responsible not only for their own children living at home, but also for their aging parents. Hit hardest are single parents who find themselves short of both time and money in trying to care for children as well as parents.

ACCORDING TO ONE government study, the average woman in this country will spend 17 years raising children and 18 years caring for her parents. If these phases overlap, she is in the "sandwich." Women bearing children at an older age, the increased longevity of our parents, children living with their parents while in their 20s and 30s, and inflation eroding our parents' income all contribute to this squeeze.

The problem can become even more acute if the parent needs nursing-home care or some other form of health care not covered by Medicare. As was discussed in *Problem 15*, most nursing-home services are not covered by Medicare, and your parent may not qualify for Medicaid.

The estate-planning considerations of people in the sandwich generation have something in common with the multiple-family models in the preceding Problem. Here the financial responsibilities of both children and parents may survive you, the primary breadwinner. To what extent do you want to provide for your children after your death? And what about parents who may need to live with you?

SOLUTIONS

◆ **Address the problem of parental support before your parents need to move in.** This seems elementary, but a large number of families are unable to discuss the possibility of parents as dependents because the parents refuse to share their financial affairs with their children. To impress upon your parents the importance of planning while there is time, have a heart-to-heart talk with them about the need for you to plan for their dependency, even if it is just a remote possibility. Include your brothers and sisters if there is a chance you will be sharing the responsibility with your siblings.

◆ **Explore the availability of long-term-care insurance for your parents as well as yourself.** Long-term-care insurance provides a daily sum to be used in the event of

confinement in a nursing home or, under some policies, for home-health care. If the responsibility is likely
to fall on your shoulders, consider protecting your own
assets in the event your parent(s) need this care. If you
will be sharing the cost with siblings, share the cost of
the premiums—typically $1,200 to $1,800 a year for a
65-year-old receiving a $100-a-day benefit. And if you
are a candidate for living with your children, try to buy
the coverage for yourself. The chances of using the policy are better than one in three, and the average stay in
a nursing home exceeds 2½ years. Remember, the
insurance company only insures those who qualify
medically, so don't wait to buy the coverage until there
is a major health threat *(see Problem 15 for details)*.

◆ **Make sure you and your parents have current estate
plans including durable powers of attorney and health
care directives.** Make sure you understand their wishes
as to artificial life support and that they have commu-
nicated their preferences in a legal document that is
enforceable *(see Problem 17)*.

◆ **Boost your own life insurance death benefit to cover
your parents' needs.** If you are the primary source of
support for your parents, make sure you have sufficient insurance on your life to see them through to the
conclusion of theirs. Have your life insurance underwriter add your parents' income needs to your Capital
Needs Analysis (CNA) as laid out in *Problem 6.*

◆ **Make sure you have adequate disability-income insurance.** If your children and your parents rely on you
financially, you absolutely must make certain your
income is protected in the event of disability. This coverage may be available through your employer. If not,
purchase it on your own.

If you have enough assets to replace your income,
you may choose to pass on the disability insurance. For
example, if you have $75,000 of salaried income and a
stock and bond portfolio of $1,500,000, you could con-
vert your portfolio to income-producing bonds and

easily replace the salary. On the other hand, if your $1,500,000 is in raw land or illiquid non-income-producing assets, purchase the disability income insurance. Tips on how to best purchase this insurance are found in *Problem 34.*

◆ **Discuss the situation with your children.** Make sure your children understand the financial, logistical, and physical responsibilities of caring for aging parents. If they are made part of a team effort rather than part of the problem, they will benefit from the experience without feeling that the grandparents are taking time and resources away from them.

RECOMMENDED ADVISERS

Make sure your **attorney** advises you on what can and cannot be done with your parents' assets. Be slow to enter into schemes to deplete your parents' assets so that they qualify for Medicaid.

Have your **planner** update your CNA when it becomes apparent you will be supporting your parents. Use the results of the analysis to upgrade your life insurance coverage *(see Problem 6).*

SEE ALSO

◆ **Problem 6:** *Insufficient Income for the Heirs* on the uses of a CNA in estimating the amount of life insurance you should carry.
◆ **Problem 15:** *Living Too Long and Long-Term Care.*
◆ **Problem 34:** *Extended Illness and Long-Term Disability* to ward off threats to your wealth caused by a long illness or disabling injury.

EXTENDED ILLNESS AND LONG-TERM DISABILITY

Extended illness and long-term disability deplete our emotional and physical assets. No matter whether you are the person disabled or the caregiver for a stricken family member, you are faced by falling income, increasing expenses, and dramatic changes in lifestyle. Disability is not age specific; it can occur at any time. There is no way to prepare for the emotional expense, but there are steps to lighten the financial burden.

AN EXTENDED ILLNESS during childhood is always a tragedy, especially if the outcome is the child's death. No training course exists to prepare a parent for the shock of learning of a child's illness for the first time. Nor is there any way to appreciate the astronomical cost of health care in these situations. If you are wealthy, you undoubtedly have health insurance. However, your coverage may not be adequate.

Disability during your working life can confront you with increasing medical and care expenses coupled with a drop in income, especially if a disabled breadwinner is in a personal-service business such as law, medicine, or accounting.

The chances of suffering a long-term disability during your working career are much greater than death at the same age *(see* TABLE 5.3, *below)*.

The impact of these statistics can be brought home if one considers the "big four" diseases: hypertension (high blood pressure), heart disease, cerebrovascular disease (stroke), and diabetes. These four are the leading causes of death among working adults age 45 to 65. With the advances in modern medicine, the death rate from the four has actually declined. Unfortunately,

5.3	RISK OF DISABILITY

RISK COMPARISON OF LONG-TERM DISABILITY AND DEATH

Age 30	Disability 4.1 times more likely
Age 40	Disability 2.9 times more likely
Age 50	Disability 2.2 times more likely

there has been an accompanying 55 percent increase in chronic, long-term disability during the same period of time. Jeff Sadler, author of the insurance industry text, *Disability Income*, explains, "While life spans are getting longer, it's due in large part to sustaining a lengthy disability instead of death." Sadler stresses that for most people, their "greatest asset is their ability to work and earn an income."

The various studies on wealth and affluence tend to include both those with high net worth and those with high income. U.S. Trust Company, in its study of "affluents," included those with adjusted gross incomes (AGIs) of $300,000 and above. Many of these people would not have enough set aside to maintain their current standard of living if they were disabled.

Extended illness at retirement age is discussed in *Problem 15*. However, the health conditions that lead to a need for nursing-home care can start before retirement.

SOLUTIONS

◆ **Review your health insurance annually.** If your coverage is provided through an employer group, make sure it has high enough limits. For the wealthy, the greatest threat is the "extraordinary" claim, in excess of $250,000, that could begin to threaten the upper limits of your health insurance plan. If your coverage has a maximum of $250,000 per illness or $250,000 for your lifetime, add to your coverage on an individual basis. Million-dollar claims are not as unusual as you might think, and this should be the minimum acceptable upper limit to your coverage. If you are the owner of a small business or professional practice, increase the limits for all employees under the plan. The cost to upgrade your protection will vary significantly depending on where you live. If you are wealthy, it is going to be worth the cost.

◆ **Review your need for disability-insurance income**

insurance. Enlist the aid of a professional life insurance underwriter. Realistically assess the ability to convert some of your assets to income-producing assets. This is critical. Professionals and executives, for example, are especially vulnerable to a loss of income because they often create wealth more from their high current earnings than from the increasing value of their business assets.

If you own a closely held business, realistically assess the business's ability to continue your income. If most of your net worth is tied up in your business, how likely is it that you will be able to convert that business into a lifetime stream of income in the event of your disability? (If it were easy to do so, you probably would have done it already.)

◆ **Adopt a salary-continuation plan.** The Internal Revenue Service (IRS) can disallow deductions for wages paid to sick and injured employees, including the owner, if there is no plan specifying the terms of such payments. This can be especially severe if the person receiving payments is an owner; in such a case the payments are considered dividend distributions if the business is profitable.

In order to establish a plan, put it in writing, such as a corporate resolution. Second, communicate the plan to your employees. Self-insure to the extent you as the employer feel comfortable with the exposure. Provide commercial insurance policies beyond the self-insured amount. For example, an employer could promise to pay employees an income for up to two weeks while disabled, then a short-term, disability-income insurance plan could pay benefits for up to 26 weeks. Thereafter, only executives and highly compensated employees could receive benefits under long-term insurance policies for the term of the absence, up to age 65. A certain amount of discrimination by income is permissible, but let the insurance agent make that determination.

◆ **Consider the tax treatment of disability-income plans.** If the premiums are deducted currently by the employer, the benefits will be taxable income as received. However, if the premiums are not deducted, the income is not taxed upon receipt.

◆ **Do not rely on Social Security or Medicare for disability income.** Buy your own insurance policy. Some people assume that Social Security replaces lost income. To qualify as "disabled" under Social Security, an individual must be: 1) covered because of sufficient years under the system, *and* either 2) disabled, or expected to be disabled, for at least 12 months, *or* 3) disabled for at least five months by a condition likely to result in death. The disabled employee cannot be employed in any substantially gainful activity. This definition is just too confining and restrictive to rely on. And Medicare pays no disability benefits whatever.

Long-term disability is a greater threat than short term. From a perspective of protecting your wealth, you should devote more money to covering the catastrophic claim than the small claim. Self-insure to the extent you have adequate wealth to absorb the small claims and the loss of income for the first few months.

◆ **Take advantage of deductibles and elimination periods to reduce premiums.** Health insurance premiums can be lowered by agreeing to a high deductible. You assume the responsibility of expenses, up to an agreed-upon level. This lowers the insurance company's exposure as well as its expenses, because for them, the smaller claims are more expensive to administer. In disability insurance, the elimination period is the equivalent of a deductible. You assume responsibility for income replacement up to a specified number of days of disability, such as 90 or 180. Thereafter, the insurance begins to pay. Increasing your elimination period from 30 to 90 days can reduce your annual premium up to 25 percent.

Financial planners usually recommend you have three to six months' net income on hand as a cash reserve. The threat of a disabling illness or injury is one of the reasons for this fund. If you have significant stocks and bonds, less of a cash reserve may be necessary since the securities could be converted to cash.

◆ **If you are a business owner, consider business overhead–expense insurance.** What happens to the business expenses when the owner is disabled? Usually nothing. Bills continue to come due each month regardless. If disability will expose you to continuing bills at the office, plant, or practice, as well as bills at home, buy business overhead insurance. It should cover the bills for a year or two, or long enough for you to decide what to do with the business and to execute your plan. If you intend to cash out, it's easier to sell an ongoing concern.

◆ **Consider purchasing long-term-care insurance before you need it to lock in your insurability.** If you are in poor health now, you may not qualify for insurance at all, or be limited to buying special policies at much higher premiums, called *rated insurance*. If you need long-term-care insurance to protect your assets, consider buying the coverage now while the premiums are lower and your health is good. If you build your assets to the point at which you no longer need the coverage, you can always let it lapse. When do you reach that point? When your income producing (or those that can easily be converted into income producing) assets are sufficient to provide an income to live on indefinitely without working. If you need $60,000 annually to live, then $1,000,000 at 6 percent would be sufficient for the near term. However, remember that inflation means you will need even more than your original $1,000,000. Let your planner show you how much is necessary to fund a lifetime of income, including inflation.

RECOMMENDED ADVISER

Review your policies with your **insurance agent** for protection against catastrophic health claims and disability. Compare the relatively small premium increase to the potential depletion of your assets.

SEE ALSO

◆ **Problem 15:** *Living Too Long and Long-Term Care.*
◆ **Problem 20:** *Death or Disability of the Sole Proprietor.*

PROBLEM 35

FUNDING EDUCATION EXPENSES

A quality education does not have to break the bank, especially if you start to accumulate soon after a child is born. You can find investment vehicles that will keep ahead of escalating college bills. And you can be savvy about how to title your funds to maximize growth and minimize taxes.

A PARENT'S WILLINGNESS to fund education expenses reveals a lot about their values and priorities. Parents can find themselves facing room and board and tuition expenses not only for college, but also for private elementary, high school, and graduate school. Today, they are asked to pay for tutors, extracurricular activities, and prep-school expenses.

In the U.S. Trust Company's survey of wealthy people, approximately 70 percent were willing to pay for the expenses of a private college, 85 percent for a public college education. Only 58 percent of the parents said they would pay for graduate school. Funding education is a high priority among the wealthy, but not without some reservations about the ultimate well-being of the child.

If you are wealthy, the grant-in-aid solution—need-based scholarships and grants—is unlikely. Your child's education is likely to be on your nickel. Saving money for college costs is still the best solution.

The challenge, of course, is finding a vehicle that offers a good return without undue risk. It would be disheartening to have the value of your assets fall 30 percent just as your child needs the funds for tuition.

You may also have at least some concern about how to allocate education dollars for a child who may or may not use them intelligently. The most extreme case is the child with a significant UGMA account who decides to take the money and head for the beach.

SOLUTIONS

◆ **Start building an education fund as soon after your child is born as you can.** Compare the annual outlay required to accumulate $100,000 *(see* TABLE 5.4, *below).*

◆ **Use equities or equity mutual funds during the early years.** If you have more than seven years to accumulate funds, invest at least a portion of the monies in growth or growth-and-income stocks or mutual funds. Compare the historical returns of various asset classes when deciding how to invest your money.

Kristin Davis, author of *Financing College*, recommends an allocation of up to 100 percent in equities

5.4	EDUCATION ACCUMULATION				
SAVINGS $100/MONTH	TOTAL	4%	7%	9%	12%
20 years	$24,000	36,800	52,397	67,290	99,915
15 years	18,000	24,691	31,881	38,124	50,458
10 years	12,000	14,774	17,409	19,497	23,234
5 years	6,000	6,652	7,201	7,599	8,249
SAVINGS $250/MONTH	TOTAL	4%	7%	9%	12%
20 years	$60,000	91,999	130,991	168,224	249,787
15 years	45,000	61,728	79,703	95,311	126,144
10 years	30,000	36,935	43,524	48,741	58,085
5 years	15,000	16,630	18,000	18,997	20,622

for accounts of elementary-school children or younger. She lightens the stock allocation as the child nears college. While the students are in junior high, she advises 75 percent in equities and 25 percent in fixed income; in the freshman/sophomore years in high school, 50 percent in equities and 50 percent in fixed income; and in the junior and senior years, 25 percent in equities and 75 percent in fixed income. When the students start college, she suggests having everything in fixed-income assets. Match this guideline with your own risk tolerance, but realize that buying short-term certificates of deposit (CDs) for a two-year-old is too conservative, primarily because of the impact from the rising costs of an education.

◆ **Consider the tax ramifications of your investment choices.** The use of stocks and mutual funds can make it easier to take advantage of capital gains rates at 20 percent. Remember, if the funds are in your name, they will be taxed as your assets. However, the expected tax savings of putting them in your child's name in order to have them taxed in the lower bracket of the child may not be worth the risk of the child walking away with the assets—without the education.

◆ **Use UGMA accounts sparingly.** The assets in UGMA accounts belong to the child. During minority, the custodian may use the funds for the child's support, including education. However, the money belongs to the child at majority *(see Problem 36).*

Make sure the UGMA assets are reasonable in relationship to the needs of the child. For example, if you have a child who is a poor student and highly unlikely to attend a prestigious private college, don't warehouse money in a UGMA account.

◆ **Use the new education IRA.** Starting in 1998, each child can have an education IRA funded to the extent of $500 per year, from whatever source, such as parents, grandparents, or other friends. While the annual limit of $500 per child doesn't go very far in today's college, you should take advantage of this special IRA.

The IRA is to be used for qualified higher-education expenses, which include tuition, room and board, books, supplies, and fees. *Higher education* means college or graduate school.

As with all IRAs after the Taxpayer Relief Act of 1997, there are limits based on the tax status of the contributor. Single taxpayers with an AGI of $95,000 begin to lose their eligibility to contribute. At $110,000, the eligibility disappears completely. For married taxpayers, eligibility phaseout starts at $150,000 and is total at $160,000. If you are a high-wage earner, look for others to make the contributions on behalf of your children, including the child with summer-job money.

If all the funds are not used for qualified educational expenses before the account holder reaches age 30, the money must be distributed. Since the account holder will be under 59½, there will be a 10 percent penalty tax added to the taxable income of the entire fund balance. However, if the account is rolled over into another education IRA for the benefit of someone in the account holder's family, the tax is deferred and, in most cases, eliminated because withdrawals for qualified expenses are tax free.

◆ **Look into state education plans.** Some states now have education plans for residents that make it easier to accumulate funds for their children. By paying a premium of sorts, the parent is guaranteed a level of funding that pays part or all the tuition expenses for public schools in that state. Each state has an office that serves as a state grant agency. Contact this office to find out about available resources in your state.

Find out if there is a prepaid plan that allows parents to set aside monies at today's tuition rates for their child's future education. There are differences from state to state, so learn all you can before you set aside any money. In some plans, if your child goes to school out of state, there is a low interest rate on your accumulated funds. Over half the states have such plans in effect, or legislation pending to create a plan.

◆ **Consider trusts.** When there are several children to educate and the expenses are likely to include prep schools and graduate schools, consider the use of a trust fund to shift the taxable investment income from your tax return, and to overcome the problem with UGMA accounts at majority. The monies may be used only for education, but if a child decides to skip school, the monies accumulated for his or her benefit could be used by the next in line. Unused funds could be distributed years later or be used for grandchildren, thus avoiding the mandatory-distribution problem of an education IRA.

◆ **If loans are necessary or just preferred, consider a home equity loan in order to deduct the interest.** You can deduct the interest on a home equity loan, but the loan is then your responsibility. If the loans are to be the student's responsibility, be sure to shop around. The loan alternatives today are numerous and their terms varied. When you select repayment terms, remember how difficult it was to save money in your first job. If the loans are too large, the graduate develops a sense of futility about the prospects for getting out of debt.

RECOMMENDED ADVISER

Consult your **financial planner** for a schedule of periodic investments to fund education expenses over time. Read *Financing College* by Kristin Davis *(see the "Resources" appendix section at the end of this book).*

SEE ALSO

◆ **Problem 26:** *Finding the Best Financial Adviser.*
◆ **Problem 28:** *Finding the Best Investment Vehicles.*
◆ **Problem 36:** *Gifts to Minors* to understand the tax ramifications of gifts to your children.

GIFTS TO MINORS

Parents, grandparents, and other family members have always sought means of making more meaningful gifts to children. State laws seek to protect the rights of children. The confluence of the two objectives resulted in the Uniform Gifts to Minors Act (UGMA), a law adopted by the states and now in the process of revision as the Uniform Transfers to Minors Act (UTMA). It is important to understand the law before gifting financial assets.

GIFTS OF CASH or other financial assets take on special significance because of tax laws. As discussed in Part 1, "Estate-Planning Problems," any individual may gift $10,000 in cash or assets to any other individual in any calendar year without incurring a gift tax or the recipient's owing any income tax. This estate-planning vehicle encourages parents and grandparents to make gifts to their minor children and grandchildren for specific purposes, such as a college education.

Grandfather Ed Yucated has been advised by his accountant that he should begin to pare back his estate in order to avoid the imposition of estate taxes at his death. Ed understands the logic and is interested in seeing that his four grandchildren are well educated. His certified public account (CPA) told him to gift $10,000 to each of them under UGMA and that he needed to have four accounts set up to create the UGMA gifts. Ed called his broker to establish the accounts and said that he wanted to make the gifts with the understanding that the monies only be used for education. Any problems?

For starters, unlike the education IRA, the monies cannot be restricted for educational use only. And if the child drops out of school prior to receiving any of the monies, the custodian, the person designated as watchdog of the funds in the account, is obligated by law to transfer the assets to the child at majority age, which is 18 or 21 depending on the child's home state. If Ed wants to control the disposition of the assets, he needs to name himself as the custodian. However, at Ed's death a successor custodian will have to be named. That successor will be able to make the decision how to expend the funds, but only until each child comes of age and takes control of them.

CASE STUDY

Grandmother Strings wants to gift $10,000 a year to her only granddaughter but is not happy with her son-in-law and the way the child is being raised. She has asked her banker to establish a UGMA account and wants to be able to decide whether to give any of the money to the child when she sees how the child turns out on her 21st birthday. Can she do that?

Sorry, Grandma, no strings attached. One of the drawbacks of these UGMA and UTMA gifts is that they are irrevocable. The funds must be used for the child's support and education, and any balance must be transferred to the child's name at majority.

CASE STUDY

Grandfather Pitcher would like to make a lasting gift to his grandsons, all of whom seem to like baseball, Pitcher's passion. Grandpa has a very valuable collection of original baseball trading cards. He wants to gift them under UGMA. Can he?

One of the reasons why states are converting from the UGMA to UTMA is to permit transfers of any kind of asset. The older UGMA only allowed gifts of cash, securities, and sometimes life insurance policies. The new, expanded version allows real estate interests, tangible assets, and intangible assets, as well as gifts from trusts and estates. Each state has its own version of either UGMA or UTMA.

The acts present an easy, affordable means of making a meaningful gift to children, but there are restrictions. How do you decide whether to use UGMA/ UTMA, a trust, or an outright gift of $10,000 per donee each year?

SOLUTIONS

◆ **Use UGMA or UTMA accounts for gifts of moderate size and when you are willing to part with the funds completely.** The accounts allow family and friends to make gifts that can make a difference, such as for education or support. The primary advantage of uniform-account gifts is the convenience and lack of expense of establishing the account. Every bank, insurance company, stockbrokerage, and any other financial institution has the capability to start and maintain the account. There is no need for a trust document to be drafted and administered.

The big drawback is the loss of control over the funds once the minor comes of age. Therefore, avoid these accounts for large gifts or larger accumulations of money if they are not likely to be spent by the time the child reaches 18 or 21, depending on your state of residence.

◆ **Consider a trust for larger gifts or gifts with enough time ahead to grow into large sums.** There is no limit to the number of custodial accounts or the amount of money that can be established for a minor. If you and your parents or grandparents are in a position to set aside $10,000 each year for a newborn child, or $50,000 annually, sit down with your parents and grandparents and discuss a trust. A UGMA account with $50,000 a year deposited and growing at 7 percent will end up with over $500,000 by the time the child reaches college age. That could be a significant windfall for the child at 18 or 21. The trust funds on the other hand, could be used for education and the principal for some future date or event, such as a wedding, birth and education of the next generation, or for the child's siblings, if any. The trust is more expensive to administer, but the control it offers may be worth the expense.

◆ **Match the investment vehicle with the timing of the funds' withdrawal.** If the child is two years away from college, you won't want to buy an aggressive-stock mutual fund with a contingent-deferred sales charge that penalizes you for withdrawing money for any purpose. Some investors with children close to their matriculation date prefer to use government securities because of their safety *(refer to Problem 35)*.

◆ **Understand the tax ramifications of the income on the assets.** Because the child is the beneficial owner of the assets, he or she is the taxpayer—all the unearned income in the UGMA and UTMA accounts is taxed on the minor's tax return. However, there are different rules for children under age 14 than children 14 and above. For children under age 14, the first $650 of income incurs no tax. The second $650 is taxed at the child's bracket. All unearned income above $1,300 is taxed to the child at the parent's highest marginal tax bracket. At age 14, the unearned income is taxed at the child's bracket.

From a planning standpoint, aim for investments that generate less unearned income in the early years if the income is going to exceed $1,300. To put the income in perspective, $20,000 in corporate bonds at 6.5 percent will generate $1,300 of unearned income per year.

There is no required income tax filing by the custodian.

◆ **Be aware of federal and state gift-tax laws.** Gifts to UGMA and UTMA accounts qualify as present-interest gifts and therefore, can fall within the $10,000 per year per donee exclusion. However, some states permit extending the age of majority for these accounts. If the extension is taken, gifts after the extension may not qualify for the annual exclusion under the gift-tax law. In addition, some states do not have gift-tax laws that are complementary to the federal $10,000 exclusion. Check with your tax accountant.

◆ **Be aware of the federal estate-tax laws.** If one of the purposes of making gifts is to remove the assets from your estate, do not name yourself as custodian of a UGMA or UTMA account. If the donor of uniform-gift assets dies while serving as custodian, the assets are included in the donor's estate.

◆ **If you live in a community-property state, ask your tax adviser how best to make the gifts.** Community-property states have different estate-tax results.

Check the laws in your state before using UGMA or UTMA assets to purchase life insurance or annuities. While most states allow the transfer of insurance policies into these accounts, not all states allow uniform-gift accounts to purchase a policy on the child's life. Ask your attorney or tax adviser.

RECOMMENDED ADVISERS

 Consult your **attorney** about sizable gifts, and the advisability of trusts rather than uniform gifts to minors.

 Consult your **tax accountant** for advice on the application of federal and state income, estate, and gift-tax laws for establishing UGMA/UTMA accounts in your family.

 Ask your **financial planner** how to best invest the child's gifts *(review Problem 28)*.

SEE ALSO

◆ **Problem 35:** *Funding Education Expenses* for more advantages and disadvantages to using UGMA accounts.

PART 6

Liability
PROBLEMS

NE OF THE greatest threats to your financial well-being today is liability for your actions (or failure to act) in situations where the courts can hold you accountable. Usually, these are situations where there has been some bodily or psychological injury to someone or damage to property they own. Losses can wipe out fortunes literally overnight. If you are working to maintain the wealth you have amassed, shielding yourself from such judgments is a cost of doing business.

The first line of defense against liability claims is your own proper behavior. Unfortunately, however, people of significant means cannot afford to rely on that alone. Litigation over matters of liability are at an all-time high. Without judging the causes of the increase, the lesson is to have adequate insurance to protect yourself and your assets against warranted and frivolous claims alike.

Insurance should serve two needs: covering legal costs so you can be adequately defended against claims of liability, and indemnifying you for any financial losses as a result of liability. Insurance is also your best line of defense against Mother Nature and the actions of others.

This Part examines the areas of liability that the wealthy are most likely to encounter. Read about your potential exposure and then use this book to find and consult a top-quality insurance agent.

PROBLEM 37

LIABILITY AND LOSS AT HOME

There are two types of financial threats involving your home. One is actual damage to your house and the contents inside. The other is bodily harm to you, your family, and guests (even if uninvited). Your first line of defense is to eliminate or at least minimize the risk. Your second—insurance—is complex and confusing, and sometimes adversarial.

YOU (OR SOMEONE you delegate the responsibility to) are the risk manager for your property. Your first step should be to do a survey to anticipate Murphy's Law—what can go wrong, will—before it invokes itself.

Start with physical assets. What can go wrong? Your house and its contents are susceptible to damage from fire, lightning, wind, rain, hail, snow, ice, flooding, mud slides, sinkholes, tornadoes, hurricanes, explosions, collisions, physical attack, and any number of other perils. Are any particularly likely (do you live in a flood plain?) and how dire would their consequences be (would your hillside house in Oakland, California, be a total loss in a brushfire?)?

Is there any way of minimizing the risks? Often a great deal can be done. You can reduce the threat of damage from fire by storing combustible materials away from sources of heat. You can clean chimneys annually. Remove old paint rags from the bag next to the furnace.

Is there any way to reduce the potential for loss? Smoke detectors do not reduce the chance of a fire, but their early warning can reduce the extent of the damage. This could be the critical difference between rebuilding a garage and walking away from a complete loss of your home.

Next, what about bodily damage to you and your family? What about your guests? If a visitor suffers a loss of property or physical injury in a fire in your home, what can you do to protect yourself (and them) against the loss? And what about an uninvited guest, someone who decides to swim in your pool while you are vacationing out of the country? Or a thief who breaks his neck falling down a flight of stairs while burglarizing your home? Or the guest who drinks too much at a dinner party at your home and then causes (or has) a fatal accident after leaving?

The final area of concern should be your possessions, especially valuables that cannot be replaced. Art and antiques frequently come to mind first, but those who have experienced the loss of a home due to fire often feel more strongly about photographs and mementoes of special occasions. What can you do to minimize the loss of these items or to replace their value?

SOLUTIONS

◆ **Find a good property and casualty agent or agency.** If you are more interested in low cost, defer the selection of an agent until you have shopped around for the lowest premium. If you are more interested in the best advice, search out and interview candidates for the job of being your agent. Start with the Yellow Pages in your phone book, under "Insurance: Property and Casualty." Look both at *captive agents* (those who represent a single company) and *independents* (those who will seek proposals from several companies for you). Remember, you will almost never find the absolute lowest premium, and even if you did, it wouldn't be for long because insurers change rates frequently.

◆ **Buy "special-form" homeowners insurance.** Homeowners insurance protects you against three threats: 1) the loss in value of your real and personal property, 2) the loss of use of your home, and 3) personal liability.

There are now six different forms of standard homeowners insurance, designated by number, from HO 00 01 to HO 00 08, skipping 05 and 07. Among wealthy homeowners, the 03 form is the most common. It is referred to as the "special form" and provides the broadest coverage for your real property, and can provide extensive coverage for your personal property as well. The 03 form pays for all losses from all perils, unless they are specifically excluded.

Condominium owners need to purchase HO 00 06

coverage. This coverage is designed specifically for owners of condominiums. The owners' association will have its own policy to cover the common areas and liability for its property, but you, as a unit owner, must have your own coverage as well. Be sure to check with the association to see what limits you are required to carry.

Request 100 percent replacement-cost coverage. The standard 03 policy insures your home against damage for 80 percent of the cost to rebuild at today's cost. Increase your coverage to 100 percent. The typical premium increase to cover replacement cost rather than actual cash value is 10 to 15 percent. Premiums can vary dramatically from state to state.

◆ **Purchase "comprehensive" personal-property coverage.** The standard homeowner's policy pays the actual cash value loss of the contents of your home. You want to change that coverage to the replacement value, which is what the comprehensive policy covers. The difference can be illustrated by considering the replacement of a diamond engagement ring that may have cost $10,000 when purchased but would cost $30,000 to replace today. The standard policy pays $10,000, while the comprehensive pays $30,000.

◆ **Add an "inflation guard" endorsement to the policy.** This automatically increases your coverage (and, of course, your premium) each year to help offset inflation. You select the increase percentage. The historical rate of inflation suggests a 3 or 4 percent annual increase in coverage.

◆ **Know what property is excluded from the basic coverage and decide whether to insure it separately.** Typically the 03 form excludes damage to land, structures on the property used for business, rental structures, and vehicles not used to maintain the property, such as large boats, golf carts, snowmobiles, and jet skis. To insure these items, you need to add coverage to the basic form. Ask your agent before you take the all-terrain vehicle home or before you start any construction.

◆ **Insure your property against floods and earthquakes if a threat.** Flood damage and earthquake damage are usually explicitly excluded from coverage under the standard 03 policy. If you live in an area threatened by these perils, buy the coverage separately. (Those living in flood plains have to have flood insurance.)

◆ **Purchase special coverage for valuable items.** If you own expensive jewelry, art, antiques, or other collectibles, ask your agent if you need to separately list these items in your policy application, or if you are required to purchase a separate personal-property floater policy in order to cover them. Take photographs or videotapes of these items and store the pictures in a safe-deposit box, even if your current insurer claims it is not necessary. Save receipts from each purchase. This will help with income taxes as well. Have special assets appraised every three years.

◆ **Maximize your policy limits and purchase "umbrella coverage" to layer on top of the basic policy.** The basic 03 form covers the contents up to 50 percent of your home's insured value. The typical policy has a limit of $100,000 for liability losses, $1,000 limits on medical expenses, and $500 for physical damage to the property of others. Increase the contents coverage, if necessary to the actual fair market value of the contents. Increase the liability dollar amounts to the maximum allowed under the contract, then buy an "umbrella" policy. The umbrella functions to increase the total limits by layering another policy on top of the basic 03 policy. It should also dovetail with your automobile insurance policy. The umbrella coverage also provides protection against liability often excluded under your basic homeowner's policy, such as claims against you for slander, libel, and invasion of privacy. You should increase your liability to at least $1 million and probably much higher. Most insurers can issue policies up to $10 million. Ask your agent how much each additional $1 million of coverage raises the premium.

Don't confuse an excess liability policy with an umbrella policy. The former is more restrictive. Buy the umbrella coverage.

◆ **If you use your home for business, make sure your business assets are covered.** The typical policy regards business assets as excluded. The same is true of parts of the property being rented to someone.

◆ **Use deductibles to lower the cost of insurance.** The higher the deductible, the lower the premium. Ask your agent what other ways exist for lowering the premium, such as installing smoke detectors and security systems. When it is affordable, make these additions.

◆ **Check into the availability of rate reductions at age 55 or when retiring.** Many insurers reduce rates when homeowners begin to spend more time in their homes. According to Jean Salvatore of the Insurance Information Institute in New York City, "Some insurance companies will give you discounts of around 10 percent." The rationale is that retirees spend more time on the premises, and that occupied homes are less vulnerable to burglaries, fires, damage caused by failing pipes, and similar physical events.

RECOMMENDED ADVISER

Find a highly qualified property and casualty **insurance agent**. Look for agents or agencies with significant years of experience and a good company behind them.

PROBLEM 38

LIABILITY AND LOSS IN YOUR AUTOMOBILE

The insurance industry estimates that there were 33.9 million motor vehicle accidents in 1994 in this country. In them, 43,000 people died and approximately 5,885,000 people were injured. The economic loss from these accidents has been placed at $110,500,000,000 by the Insurance Information Institute. With these odds, it's almost impossible to contemplate a lifetime behind the wheel without an accident. As if these were not grim enough statistics, there are approximately five auto thefts for every 1,000 cars on our streets each year—one every 20 seconds. It stands to reason we should be adequately insured. But what is adequate?

MOST STATES HAVE financial-responsibility laws, making automobile insurance compulsory. There is plenty of variation, however, in the types of insurance you are required to carry. And the "minimum insurance required" should not interest the aware driver anyway, because that level of protection is not adequate.

A *personal automobile policy* (PAP), a contract between the policyholder/driver and the insurance company, traditionally has four parts: Part A covers bodily injury and property damage; Part B covers medical payments; Part C provides coverage against damage caused by uninsured motorists; and Part D covers the insured automobile itself.

Part A, liability coverage, is designed to pay damages—including interest—assessed against you, the insured, for the benefit of the injured party, either for bodily injury or property damage, as a result of an automobile accident found to be your fault. Most insurers express the limits of their Part A coverage as three numbers. The first is the maximum they will pay for bodily injury to any one person. The second is the limit for bodily injury to all persons involved in the accident. The third is the actual dollar limit for damage to property. So, $100/$300/$50 describes a policy that restricts bodily injury payments to one person to $100,000, everyone in the accident to an overall limit of $300,000, and a maximum liability for property damage to $50,000.

The liability part of your policy typically insures you, (the named insured), your spouse and family members, an individual driving with your authorization, any person or organization that can be held accountable for your driving, and you and your family members driving someone else's vehicle. The insured person usually lists the automobiles to be covered in the policy, but newly acquired autos are automatically covered for a period of time (as are rental cars) without specifically listing them.

This liability area is where the greatest threat to your wealth lies. Despite attempts to put reasonable tort reform before the public, litigation over liability is a huge business. In 1991, according to the Insurance Information Institute, the American civil-liability system cost $132 billion, or 2.3 percent of our gross domestic product (GDP). Yet, only 22 cents of every dollar spent on lawsuits actually compensated the parties for their actual or economic losses. The most controversial part of a tort lawsuit is the money claimed for "pain and suffering"—awards above and beyond actual expenses that supposedly compensate for psychic or psychological damages. In 1991, they consumed 21 cents out of each dollar. Of the remaining 57 cents, 15 cents went to the claimants' lawyers, 18 cents to defense costs, and 24 cents to administrative expenses. While the civil-liability system covers much more than just automobile-related liability, cars trigger a disproportionate share of litigation.

Part B coverage for medical payments is designed to pay for medical expenses incurred within three years of an accident for the insured, the insured's family, and any other person in an insured automobile. Fault is never an issue or cause for exclusion. The coverage usually is payable even if the insured is covered elsewhere, such as by another driver's insurance or your own health insurance at work. The typical policy limits the medical payments to $5,000 or $10,000 per person.

Part C provides uninsured-motorists' coverage—essentially insurance to protect the insured—in case the other driver in an accident is uninsured or under-insured. The offer of coverage is mandatory in most states, although the insured can opt not to take it. This uninsured and underinsured protection is relatively inexpensive.

Part D is usually referred to as physical damage coverage and is designed to pay for damage to the automobile. Collision coverage pays for damage caused by an automobile accident. Other-than-collision coverage insures against damage to your automobile by causes other than an accident, such as hailstorm or hurricane damage. This is sometimes referred to as *comprehensive coverage*. With just collision coverage, only collisions are covered.

SOLUTIONS

◆ **Find a good property and casualty agent or agency.** Finding a good, experienced agent representing quality companies is frequently more important than saving a hundred or so dollars on your premiums. *(See the "Solutions" section of Problem 37 for tips on how to find an agent or agency.)*

◆ **Buy the maximum automobile liability protection you can buy.** Go for the highest coverage-A limits. The chances of suffering a loss in an auto are just too great to ignore or downplay. Dovetail the automobile coverage with your liability umbrella coverage, introduced in *Problem 37*. Make sure there are no gaps in coverage. There is often a real advantage to using a single insurance company for your home, auto, and umbrella coverage. You'll increase the likelihood of finding an excellent matching of coverage under the three policies.

◆ **Push your underwriter to tell you all the factors that you can control to lower your premiums.** The type of car you drive is a major factor, and not just because of its cost. Some cars are far less attractive to thieves. Some cars have a higher safety rating. Write to the Institute for Highway Safety at 1005 North Glebe Road, Arlington, Virginia 22201, and request the *Highway Loss Data Chart*. A less-popular car may save you money because it is less in demand on the theft market. Cars with antilock brakes, automatic seat belts, and airbags also reduce your premiums because they make your car safer.

◆ **Increase your deductible.** Raising your deductible from $200 to $500 usually results in a 15 to 20 percent decrease in collision and comprehensive premiums.

◆ **Drop collision and comprehensive coverage on much older cars.** When you car's value starts to approach the premium, it's time to drop the collision and comprehensive coverage. If you're paying $500 a year for collision and comprehensive coverage on a car worth $2,000 and have $10,000 in money-market savings, forget the coverage. Assume the risk yourself. Janet Bamford in *Smarter Insurance Solutions* recommends dropping collision coverage when the value of the car falls below 10 times the annual premium. Let your cash reserves be your guide.

◆ **Avoid drinking-and driving-offenses and moving violations on your driving record.** These dramatically increase your premium, especially drunk driving. The liability coverage under your automobile insurance will not defend you against criminal charges, such as drunk driving.

RECOMMENDED ADVISER

Find a good **insurance agent**, experienced in property and casualty liability, as outlined in *Problem 37.*

SEE ALSO

◆ **Problem 37:** *Liability and Loss at Home.*

◆ **Problem 39:** *Liability Problems in Your Business* if your automobile is used in your work.

LIABILITY PROBLEMS
IN YOUR BUSINESS

Most business owners fortunate enough to be considered wealthy have insured their businesses against the traditional perils, including theft, wind, and fire. However, there is a great deal more to threaten a business today than the traditional villains of Mother Nature and dishonest mankind. Today's threats reflect the technologies of the times and the popularity of using the legal system as a way of seeking entitlement and revenge.

AS A BUSINESS OWNER, one of the first questions to ask is, what are my exposures to liability and loss? Ideally, the question is posed before the doors open for the first day of business, because the liability and losses can easily precede the opening. A manufacturing company has property, plant, and equipment in place before the first widget comes off the production line. Two lawyers forming a new firm sign leases, purchase furniture, and drive from place to place before they send out their first bills. Their liability started when they formed their new venture, whether or not they entered into a formal written agreement.

You have liability for the products you manufacture or sell, or for the services that you provide. Every transaction has the potential for disappointment and possibly even a loss on the part of the purchaser, and is therefore one of the areas where liability can be attached to your business, if not to you, the owner, personally as well. However, it is not the only area.

Most businesses have a location—offices, a plant, or some other site where business is conducted. Owners have a responsibility to maintain a safe workplace, not just for employees, but also for visitors.

Does the business do anything that could pose a threat to the environment? Most business owners would say no, even though they have a heating-oil tank on the premises. Anyone who has experienced a leak from either an underground or aboveground tank can testify to the time and expense of meeting the environmental standards. Your business can be held accountable to federal and state environmental agencies in all sorts of ways, from providing an unsafe workplace to damaging the underground water supply with pollutants. A savvy insurance agent will alert you to these potential violations.

Almost all companies authorize some business use of automobiles. Each trip to a client's office or pizza delivery is a potential lawsuit. When an employee makes a trip to the local bank to make a business deposit, guess who's liable for their negligence behind the wheel.

One area of liability law attracting special notice these days is *employment-related practices.* This encompasses job discrimination, sexual harassment in the workplace, violations under the Americans with Disabilities Act (ADA), and wrongful termination. If you are an employer or even a manager interviewing for employees, you are vulnerable to claims in this area. According to Maryellen Alvarez of the Insurance Resource Center in Charlotte, North Carolina, "One of the primary reasons for the increase in employment-related suits is that in 1992 these suits were changed to decision by jury. Prior to 1992, these cases were decided by a judge. Interpretation—'trial by employees!'" And here's a trap: most general-liability policies specifically exclude these types of claims from your coverage.

We tend to associate the phrase "professional liability insurance" with medical and legal malpractice, perhaps by surgeons, accountants, architects, and engineers. However, the list of businesses needing to protect themselves actually includes computer consultants, financial planners, management consultants, family and marriage counselors and psychotherapists of all kinds, nurses and other health therapists, home inspectors, and dozens more. Professional liability policies protect the professional against malpractice suits and breach-of-contract actions.

According to the Insurance Information Institute, over 12 million Americans operate businesses out of their homes. Many assume that homeowners' insurance protects the business and its assets. This may not be a safe assumption. Typically, there are low limits on business assets, such as $2,500 for equipment in the home. And homeowners' insurance usually does not provide liability protection if a customer or client is injured in your home.

Once you hire employees, state law may make you responsible for providing workers' compensation insurance. This coverage provides some monies toward medical costs for injuries on the job and for income replacement until the worker recovers and returns to work.

Where do you start in plugging all these potential leaks to your wealth?

SOLUTIONS

◆ **Find a qualified agent or agency.** You need a professional with experience insuring businesses—not all property and casualty agents have it. An independent agent often has greater choices to represent you, although many independents only represent a handful of companies.

◆ **Insist on quality, safe companies.** Learn how to check out the safety rating of your insurance company using the rating services and the state insurance commissioner's office *(refer to Table 4.3, in Problem 28)*. Ask for the company's A. M. Best rating, or their credit rating from Moody's or Standard & Poor's. Only use the top-rated companies.

◆ **Separately insure your home business.** The typical homeowner's policy excludes business liability. You should be able to purchase a business owner's package or a few separately issued policies that will cover all of the traditional business risks discussed in this *Problem*.

An excellent resource for the small-business owner is a book written by Dr. Sean Mooney, CPCU (chartered property casualty underwriter), a senior economist at the Insurance Information Institute, entitled *Insuring Your Business*. The book is available by calling the institute at 212-669-9250.

◆ **Purchase employment-related practices insurance for your business as soon as you hire employees.** This policy protects you against lawsuits for sexual harassment, wrongful termination, discrimination, and similar types of claims. Your general-liability policy usually excludes this coverage. This is affordable coverage for most employers; you should not assume it is only for major corporations. Legal fees alone could exceed $100,000 just to defend yourself and your business from a claim.

◆ **If you can be insured under a professional liability insurance policy, buy the coverage.** You may be able to purchase the protection under a business owner's policy (BOP), or you may have to take out a separate policy. Whichever form is available to you, get the protection. The policies will shield you and your associates acting within the scope of their duties. And it covers the expenses to defend lawsuits, whether they are justified or not.

◆ **For professional practices, implement a loss-protection program.** According to the Lewis-Chester Group in Summit, New Jersey, some of the techniques that can be employed include:

— Establish billing practices at the beginning of the client relationship. This will tend to minimize disputes over your fees or billings to your customers.

— Use engagement letters, contracts, and whatever other means are available to define the services to be provided.

— Avoid conflicts of interest.

— Obtain the appropriate credentials and certifications and participate in continuing-education courses if required in your specialty. These will help support your claims of professionalism in the performance of your duties.

— Avoid giving specific warranties and performance guarantees.

◆ **Check with your agent or your state insurance commissioner's office to determine your responsibilities under workers' compensation laws.** This coverage is frequently mandated, so you need to know the requirements. If your business is incorporated, you personally will be covered, along with your employees. However, remember that workers' compensation applies to on-the-job injuries and usually runs out long before recovery, if any. It is not long-term-disability insurance that protects you whether you are injured at work or not. If you are a high-earning business owner or executive, don't rely on workers' compensation for your protection against sickness or accident.

RECOMMENDED ADVISER

Find an **insurance agent** or agency with expertise in working with comparable businesses. Ask for references and check them until you've talked to enough owners that you're convinced the agent understands your business needs.

SEE ALSO

◆ **Problem 28:** *Finding the Best Investment Vehicles* for a discussion of the safety ratings of insurance companies *(refer to Table 4.3).*

LIABILITY PROBLEMS OF OFFICERS, DIRECTORS, AND TRUSTEES

In another era, leaders were looked upon with respect and reverence for their commitment to their corporations and their philanthropic interests. Today, they are regarded by many as just part of the pool of litigation targets. The sophisticated executive or volunteer knows enough to protect against that one disgruntled employee, shareholder, or patron who can find a lawyer to press their claims, justified or not.

THE MOST DIRECT exposure from liability is as an officer or a director of a business, especially a publicly traded corporation. However, even the closely held–corporation officer or director has liability exposure. And it can come from any number of angles, including employees, shareholders, competitors, regulatory agencies, and consumers.

Lawsuit allegations typically fall under three categories: mismanagement, misrepresentation, or material errors or omissions in the disclosure of financial information. Insurers offer directors and officers (D & O) liability insurance. Some insurers go beyond D & O coverage to protect executives who are not directors.

Executives today are likely to serve on outside boards, both profit and not for profit, often at the encouragement of their own corporations. Any board position carries with it liability exposure for the actions of the board, and indirectly the corporation. In general, a nonprofit director owes a duty of loyalty, obedience, and diligence in the execution of his or her role. Very few board members ever ask if there is D & O coverage that protects them from unwanted litigation. This is especially true of volunteer directors of charitable boards. These nonprofit organizations can be just as guilty of improper employment-related practices, such as sexual harassment or wrongful termination, as a business corporation. They can be held liable for slander, libel, and financial mismanagement.

State legislatures in many jurisdictions have tried to limit the exposure of directors of nonprofit organizations. However, a state can only limit the application of its own laws, not those of the federal government.

Fiduciary liability attaches to the employer's role in the administration of the business's retirement plans. Many executives that fall under the definition of a fiduciary under the Employee Retirement Income Security Act of 1974 (ERISA) have personal liability for the assets in these plans. This means that their personal assets are at risk. A fiduciary includes any individual who has discretionary authority or control with respect to the management or administration of the retirement plans and its assets. Fiduciaries can be sued by plan participants, beneficiaries, or the U. S. Secretary of Labor. In addition, the Treasury Department and the Pension Benefit Guarantee Corporation also have jurisdiction over fiduciaries. Many executives take this responsibility too lightly.

Finally, there is the unseemly, yet real, threat of kidnapping and extortion. The insurance industry has responded to the problem with kidnap/ransom insurance.

SOLUTIONS

◆ **Provide D & O liability insurance for your business's management team.** It is unfair and sometimes impossible to recruit the finest talent to your team without adequately protecting them in the execution of their duties. Remember that litigation is not just about right and wrong any more, if it ever was. Buy D & O insurance with generous limits, and highlight its place in your package of employee benefits.

◆ **Ask your insurer if he or she has coverage that supplements the basic D & O liability.** Chubb, for example, issues an executive liability and indemnification policy that "protects directors and officers against losses resulting from lawsuits alleging misrepresentation, mismanagement, and material errors or omissions in the disclosure of financial information." It offers up to $50 million of coverage, worldwide protection, advancement of defense costs as incurred, and severability of coverage with respect to each director and officer.

◆ **If there are pension or profit-sharing plans including 401(k) plans, purchase fiduciary liability insurance.** Many employers adopted the 401(k) alternative when Congress placed caps on the income that could be taken from the defined-benefit plans so popular in the 1970s and 1980s. However, shifting the investment burden to the individual, as under 401(k), does not absolve the employer of all liability for investments. Some employers provide too few fund choices for employees to have meaningful alternatives—an issue that may pull some companies into court.

Make certain your insurance covers both employee-benefits liability and breach of fiduciary duty by trustees and others handling the investments and administration. Typical limits are $25 million.

◆ **Use experienced firms to manage qualified plan assets and administer the plans in accordance with ERISA standards.** It is critical to hire competent fiduciaries, investment managers, and plan administrators. The larger, prototype plans are frequently the ones most likely to satisfy ERISA requirements, and are sometimes the least expensive alternative. They can be found through mutual-fund companies, insurance companies, and larger national banks. Some critics of 401(k) offerings claim that the expenses attached to the plans are too high. Sometimes they are, but don't focus on cost alone. The quality of administration, investment performance, and personal service are just as important.

◆ **If you serve on nonprofit boards, make sure the organization carries D & O liability insurance for its board.** The term "nonprofit" tends to disguise the true nature of many organizations that fall under the penumbra of the 501(c)(3) tax shelter. Many hospitals, universities, nursing homes, and foundations have significant earnings and profits. They encounter all the potential causes of action that for-profit businesses face, and enjoy no ethical halo in the eyes of their employees. The Lewis-Chester Group reports that "over 50 percent of all D & O claims against nonprofits involve improper employment-related practices, such as wrongful termination, discrimination, breach of contract, and sexual harassment."

Insurance coverage for outside directorships can be applied for by the corporation that employs the executives that are encouraged to serve on these outside boards. Chubb Insurance uses an outside-directorship liability (ODL) system to issue a separate policy for this protection. "It is a separate coverage with separate limits," says Ted Merritt of Princeton, New Jersey's Merritt Insurance Agency, a representative of Chubb. "Your company's D & O policy won't run up against the problem of depleting its policy limits and exposing it to adverse claims experience."

◆ **If you are a visible executive with a heavy international travel schedule, purchase kidnap/ransom insurance.** The first concern of any kidnap and extortion policy is the safe return of the kidnap victim. However, these acts are frequently about money, as well as making a political statement. There are not many companies providing the coverage, but with the increasingly international exposure of executives and employees, it pays to protect them and the business from these threats.

RECOMMENDED ADVISER

Find an **insurance agent** with experience in these areas.

PART 7

Charitable-
Giving
PROBLEMS

HE PRESSURE IS on the federal government to drastically cut funding for all manner of causes, from food stamps to National Public Radio. As long as there are tax dollars supporting public programs there will be disagreements over which are most worthy. In the public arena, you act with your vote and your political contributions. In the private sphere, you act with your time and your charitable contributions.

Problems 41 through 43 address the challenges of reconciling the desire to be charitable with our instincts for self-preservation. For most wealthy Americans, there is a limit on how generous they can be and still maintain their current standard of living, retain an adequate portfolio, and sustain their families. The right balance varies with each individual's sense of obligation to family and to the public weal.

Tax laws recognize and encourage philanthropy because Congress realizes that to the extent the people satisfy the nation's charitable needs, the government is free to spend elsewhere. Tax planners have responded by creating vehicles designed to facilitate public generosity.

Problem 41 explains the rules for charitable giving. *Problem 42* describes gifts of partial interests—charitable gift annuities, charitable remainder trusts, and charitable lead trusts. The final problem, *Problem 43,* explores the world of foundations, public and private, and the limited window of opportunity to create a lasting impression with your own foundation.

CURRENT CHARITABLE GIFTS

True philanthropy is motivated more by altruistic motivations than by tax benefits. Still, the Internal Revenue Code (IRC) allows individuals and businesses to support "charitable organizations" on a tax-advantaged basis. The psychic and financial rewards make the consideration of current gifts and planned charitable giving compelling.

IN ORDER TO qualify for tax benefits, a donor must clear certain hurdles imposed by the IRC. The benefits could come in the form of deductions or credits that reduce your income, estate, or gift tax.

The first requirement is that the donee organization must be a "qualified" organization. The list of qualifying charities is found in Internal Revenue Service (IRS) "Publication 78," which should be available in your tax preparer's office, the public library, or by calling the IRS. In order to make that list, an organization must be one devoted exclusively to charitable, religious, scientific, educational, or literary purposes, or must foster amateur sports or prevent cruelty to children or animals. None of the organization's earnings can benefit a stockholder of the organization. The organization cannot be used to lobby or influence legislation.

An organization must file for the "qualified" status with the IRS. Approval is not automatic. You cannot rely on the philanthropic-sounding name of the organization, or even that the volunteers say they are a qualifying charity.

The donor cannot take a deduction for property or assets, except to the extent that it exceeds any value or benefit to the donor. Assume you are invited to a $100-a-plate dinner for the American Heart Association, a qualifying charity. Following a low-cholesterol diet plan, they serve a salmon dinner and good wines at a value of $35 per person. That means that in reporting your contribution, you may deduct only the amount in excess of the value of the benefit received—$65. With gifts in excess of $75, the charity should acknowledge the gift in writing and detail the amount that is deductible.

In addition, for all gifts in excess of $250 per year received by any charitable organization, the donee must submit a written acknowledgment of the gift to the donor. The donor should attach this acknowledgment, or at least a copy, to his or her tax return. A canceled check is not enough. This is true whether the gift is to your alma mater, the local hospital, or the Metropolitan Museum of Art.

The gift must be made in the tax year in which the deduction is claimed. And, if the gift is in excess of $5,000 in value and is not readily marketable, the donor must submit a qualified appraisal.

There are limits on the tax deduction allowed to qualifying organizations. There are two levels of deductibility: 50 percent and 30 percent. Which level applies depends on the type of gift and the type of charitable organization.

The general rule is that an individual is allowed a deduction each year of up to 50 percent of adjusted gross income (AGI) to churches, schools, hospitals, medical research, or to any organization that normally receives government or public support, as well as to federal, state, and local governments. Gifts for the use of these same organizations, or for the use of other charities falling outside the classes enumerated above, are considered 30 percent organizations.

CASE STUDY

Gifts of cash to a qualified charity are deductible up to 50 percent of AGI. Suppose Dr. Ty Ming sold a vacant lot for $300,000 cash and would like to make a gift to the Red Cross. Can he deduct the entire $300,000?

It depends on his AGI reported on his income tax form 1040. For example, if Dr. Ming has an AGI of

$150,000, he can deduct $75,000 in the current tax year. Does that mean he loses the deduction for the remainder of the gift? No. He can carry over the unused deduction of $225,000 ($300,000 – $75,000) for five years, or until used up completely, if sooner. If Ming's AGI remains level, he will exhaust the deduction in four years.

What about gifts of property other than cash? With the stock market appreciating dramatically in the early and mid-1990s, common stock has become a popular asset to gift.

CASE STUDY

Suppose Hyrum Tekk bought $10,000 worth of Super-Software stock that has now appreciated to $500,000. His alma mater is conducting an important capital campaign focused on upgrading computer sciences. Hy would like to make a meaningful contribution to recognize the part Old U. played in his success in technology. What should he consider before making the gift?

A good tax counselor will advise Hy Tekk that "the tax tail should not wag the generous dog." He or she should tell Tekk that he can deduct the full $500,000 value of the stock only if his AGI supports a gift that large. Hy Tekk has been successful, but not that successful. His average annual AGI over the past five years has consistently been $200,000. In other words, Hy will be able to deduct approximately $300,000 (five years of 30 percent x $200,000 AGI). Does that mean he shouldn't make the whole gift? That's Hy Tekk's call. After all, it is his money.

The rules for stock and real estate follow the nature of the capital asset, long term or short term. If the stock or the real estate is a short-term capital asset, held under 12 months, the allowable deduction is 50 percent. Long-term capital gain–asset limits are 30 percent. If an asset is gifted, which when sold generates ordinary income, the deduction ceiling is 50 percent of AGI. And if the gift is an asset that is related to the charity's primary function, such as a painting to an art museum, the limit is 30 percent. (If the painting is gifted to a hospital, it is 50 percent.)

Up to this point the discussion has focused on income tax benefits. However, gifts to qualifying organizations can also generate an estate-tax deduction. The most obvious requirement is that the bequest be made at the decedent's death. There is no limitation on the size of the deduction as there is with the income tax deduction. Again, the charity must qualify for the IRS's list. Much of the potential for creative tax planning around charities involves the gift of partial interests, discussed in *Problem 42.*

SOLUTIONS

◆ **Consult your tax adviser before making significant gifts.** Now more than ever, this nation needs philanthropic generosity. And the tax incentives are attractive enough to consider combining your propensity toward giving with the IRS's economic benefits in order to magnify the effect of your generosity. For some, your tax adviser is your accountant, for others, your tax attorney. Read *Problem 42* especially for ideas on giving of partial interests in your assets.

◆ **Know your tax options, but act on your charitable instincts.** Don't let tax laws govern your actions. Giving away money to a charity you don't care about, just for the tax advantage, makes less sense than taking the time to find a worthy object of your generosity.

◆ **Consider the gift of appreciated securities.** The tax deductibility of the full fair market value of the security is an example of tax laws helping you to magnify the gift. The gain in the appreciated stock, bond, or mutual fund escapes income taxation. The only limitations are the 30 percent/50 percent AGI rules. Make sure your tax adviser opines on the application of the limits *before* you make the gift.

◆ **Consider the gift of life insurance.** Life insurance death benefits always exceed the premium cost and hence are an excellent opportunity to leverage your charitable contributions.

CASE STUDY

Ms. Welloff is 55 years old, a happily remarried widow and mother of six children from her first marriage. She and her new husband are both financially secure and have decided that each should provide for their own family's welfare and not each other's. Ms. Welloff's deceased husband often stated that he wanted to do something special for his alma mater, Ivy U., but he died before creating any plan. Ms. Welloff has been giving away her excess income for many years, both to her grandchildren and to Ivy U. Her annual gift to the university averages $20,000 a year. She is torn between a desire to leave a major bequest to Ivy U. and her obligations to her family. Is there anything she could do to satisfy both?

Life insurance payable to Ivy U. may be the answer. She could use the annual $20,000 to pay a premium on her life naming Ivy U. as the beneficiary. At her death, the entire death benefit could pass to Ivy U. At age 55, Ms. Welloff could buy approximately $1,500,000 of life insurance. If she wanted a current income tax deduction for the premium, she would name Ivy U. the owner of the policy. If she is more interested in retaining control of the policy and its cash surrender value during her lifetime, the policy death benefit would be included in her estate at her death, but deductible as a charitable contribution for estate-tax purposes.

Save receipts for charitable gifts, especially over $250. The rules are tougher for substantiating gifts to charities. Know the rules before you make the gift and certainly before you file your tax return.

RECOMMENDED ADVISERS

Consult your **tax accountant** before making substantial gifts. Ask what substantiation you need for various gift levels.

Explore testamentary-giving possibilities with your estate-planning **attorney**.

SEE ALSO

◆ **Problem 42:** *Charitable Gifts of Partial Interests* to learn about the tremendous opportunity to make gifts that benefit both your family and the charity, and that can be tailored to your needs.

PROBLEM 42

CHARITABLE GIFTS OF PARTIAL INTERESTS

Many charitable people worry that they may be giving away assets that they or their heirs will need later. Consequently, they might want to consider gifts where they retain income until their death or give the current income to charity but retain the assets for their heirs. The IRC recognizes these gifts of partial interests, and planners have created interesting strategies for their implementation.

THE MOST INNOVATIVE area of charitable giving for most wealthy individuals is that of *planned giving*. This term is used to differentiate itself from the normal annual contributions requested from most charitable organizations. It encompasses testamentary and lifetime gifts of trusts, often of partial interests rather than of an entire asset or portfolio.

Gifts of partial interests were conceived in reaction to the desire of donors to help charities while retaining an income stream, or, the reverse, to provide an income for the charity while reserving the ultimate asset for the donor or the donor's family. Often, donors are able to improve their current standard of living while promising substantial benefits to the charity.

Mr. Dewrite is a 70-year-old widower with an estate valued at $1 million. His children are grown and financially secure. His church has been a mainstay of his life and he would like to do something out of the ordinary for the congregation. At the same time, he has watched his pension dissipate because of the fraudulent handling of his retirement funds by his prior employer. A friend suggested a charitable remainder trust (CRT).

Dewrite consulted a tax-attorney member of the church's planned-giving committee, who said he would run some numbers for Dewrite. The attorney asked Mr. Dewrite how a monthly income of just over $6,000 would work. Dewrite was excited because his common-stock portfolio of $1 million was only paying 2 percent, or about $1,667 a month. He had thought of selling the stocks, but his cost basis was so low he would have paid several hundred thousand dollars in taxes, even at 20 percent capital gains rates. The idea of a raise of more than $4,333 a month sounded very good. The fact that the CRT generated a charitable tax deduction was gravy.

How does the CRT function? (*See* TABLE 7.1, *at right.*)

In Mr. Dewrite's case, he gifts his portfolio into the CRT. The trustee then sells the appreciated stock for $1 million, without incurring a tax because it is sold inside the charitable trust. The trust pays an income to Mr. Dewrite for his lifetime at the agreed-upon 7.5 percent (that is, $6,250 a month). According to the church's trustee, the value of the *retained interest* (the income for life that Mr. Dewrite retains) based on his age is $434,680. The rest of the $1 million— $565,320—generates a charitable tax deduction in that same amount—the equivalent of 56.53 percent of a $1 million gift.

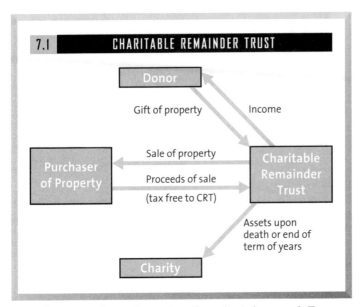

7.1 — CHARITABLE REMAINDER TRUST

Donor

Gift of property   Income

Sale of property

Purchaser of Property   Charitable Remainder Trust

Proceeds of sale
(tax free to CRT)

Assets upon death or end of term of years

Charity

Is there any benefit to the church right away? For one thing, the CRT might be able to invest that $1 million at better than 7.5 percent. It then gets a fund that is actually growing in addition to paying a lifetime income to Dewrite. The assumption is that there will be $565,320 remaining after the payment of the 7.5 percent. There could, in fact, be a great deal more— or a little less.

What if Mr. Dewrite had asked for a 25 percent payout each year? The IRS rules make the balance between the income needs of the income beneficiary and the tax deduction, based on reasonableness. He would have to check with his tax adviser to see what the upper limits might be on the income interest.

One of the requirements for the tax deduction is that the gift in trust must provide for either a "fixed annuity," a "unitrust," or a "pooled-income fund."

With a *fixed annuity*, the trust is obligated to pay the income beneficiary either a fixed dollar amount or a fixed percentage of the initial value of the trust, which must be at least 5 percent of the initial value. In addition, the income must be paid at least annually and the trust must be irrevocable. The grantor cannot name an income beneficiary yet to be born. The retained interest cannot be greater than a *life income* (that is, an actuarial prediction of income for the grantor's life), nor greater than 20 years if the grantor chooses a *term trust* (one that defines its length in years rather than for life).

The *unitrust* alternative is similar to the fixed annuity except that the interest income is defined as a fixed percentage of the trust assets, as recalculated each year.

The *pooled-income-fund* approach is actually controlled by the charity rather than the donor. The gifts of all other pooled-income donors are commingled and the grantors all receive a life income.

What about the situation where husband and wife are both still alive and in need of an increasing income, but only for as long as both or just one of them is alive? The answer: use the same kind of CRT vehicles as a single donor. Suppose Mr. and Mrs. Grant Orr, ages 67 and 64, loyal devotees of the art museum, have $1 million in real estate that is not income producing and has a $0 cost basis. The Orrs don't want to sacrifice $200,000 to taxes ($1,000,000 value − $0 cost basis = $1,000,000 gain x 0.20 capital gains rate), but are comfortable giving the property away after their deaths. They could establish a CRT with the $1 million and take a $75,000 annual income for their lives. They could generate a tax deduction of $226,140, or 22.614 percent. The trust could then sell the land for cash and invest the proceeds without the capital gains tax.

What if the facts were reversed and the potential grantor doesn't need the income for several years, but wants eventually to give the assets to heirs rather than to charity?

CASE STUDY

Ms. Goodheart, a 75-year-old widow with four grown and successful children, has inherited a small apartment complex from her father, valued at $1,000,000 with no mortgage. The annual income from the complex is $100,000. She had all the income she needed before the inheritance, living comfortably on her $100,000 per year pension. She is now concerned that the asset will result in an estate tax that did not exist before. She had kept her estate at the $600,000 level by making gifts to Stanford University. She would like her children to ultimately have the property, say in 15 years, but she doesn't want the income. She asks what can be done. A charitable lead trust (CLT) is a possible solution.

A CLT derives its name from the gift of the "lead" or income portion of the trust that passes to the charity. The donor transfers the property into a trust, specifying a fixed amount to be paid annually to the named charity for a specified period of time. When the period expires, the property passes to the donor's beneficiaries as outlined in the trust document. If the trust is funded during the donor's lifetime, income tax benefits accrue. If the trust is created under the decedent's will, it can generate significant estate-tax deductions.

Ms. Goodheart could create a testamentary charitable lead trust to receive the property at her death, have the income paid to Stanford for a term of years, then pass the remaining principal, or trust *corpus,* to her children *(see* TABLE 7.2, *on the following page).*

Ms. Goodheart decides to gift the property to the CRT. Income of 10 percent, or $100,000, is payable to Stanford for 15 years. At the end of that time, the property passes to the children. Ms. Goodheart gets a tax deduction for the present value of the annuity, which is the income stream payable to Stanford, equal to $326,820. (These calculations are based on complicated formulas derived from the IRC and IRS regulations.) The remainder interest, equal to $673,180, passes to the children. In 15 years, this would pass estate-tax free under the expanded unified credit of $1,000,000. Remember from *Problem 2, The Estate-Tax Bite,* the unified credit for estates and

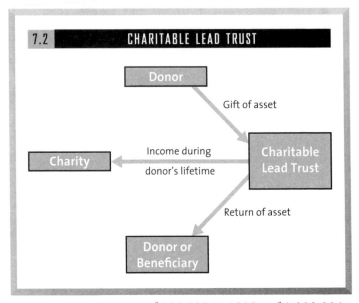

7.2   CHARITABLE LEAD TRUST

Donor

Gift of asset

Income during donor's lifetime

Charity ← Charitable Lead Trust

Return of asset

Donor or Beneficiary

gifts increases from $625,000 in 1998 to $1,000,00 in the year 2006.

What, then, are the problems associated with CRTs and CLTs? The most obvious is that the donor is giving away part of the asset. A gift of even a partial interest is a gift, after all. If the objective is to preserve wealth, giving it away seems to run counter to that philosophy. However, there is an answer found in a rather unlikely place.

SOLUTIONS

◆ **Ask your favorite charity about a charitable gift annuity (CGA).** This income vehicle is similar to a CRT. The donor transfers cash or assets to the charity, in return for an income. The income must be for at least one lifetime. However, it could be for two lifetimes, such as yours and your spouse's. It cannot, however, accommodate an income for say, five years, with the assets then reverting to the charity *(see* TABLE 7.3, *at right).*

Jennifer J. Alby, JD, director of Planned Giving at the American College in Bryn Mawr, Pennsylvania, says

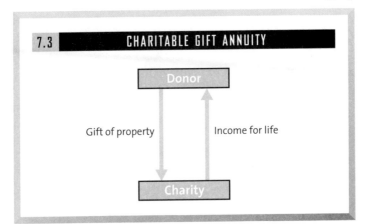

7.3   CHARITABLE GIFT ANNUITY

Donor

Gift of property   Income for life

Charity

that "CGAs are often promoted by charities as a useful way for a donor to make a charitable gift while retaining an income stream that will give the donor additional retirement protection." Basically, "the donor and the charity form an agreement, whereby the donor makes a donation to the charity in exchange for a life annuity backed by the assets of the charitable organization."

You do not want to use a CGA unless the charity is authorized to grant gift annuities, is financially strong enough to make you feel secure that its promise of an annuity for life will be fulfilled, and your state's laws encourage CGAs. Alby recommends that your tax adviser be someone acquainted with state laws.

◆ **Use a wealth replacement-trust to replace gifted assets for your heirs.** The wealth-replacement trust (WRT) is a tremendous addition to the CRT and CGA schemes to ensure that both the charity and your heirs get the most mileage from your assets (*see* TABLE 7.4, *on the following page*).

This is as close as you can get to donating your cake and eating it too. One of the common objections to the CRT (or any other gift plan) is loss of the use of the assets by the donor's heirs. Gene Kweeder, of Creative Financial Group in Pennsylvania, recommends two trusts. One should be the CRT that receives the

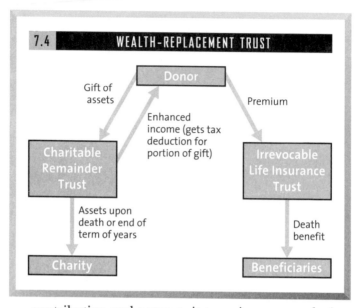

7.4 WEALTH-REPLACEMENT TRUST

Donor

Gift of assets

Premium

Enhanced income (gets tax deduction for portion of gift)

Charitable Remainder Trust

Irrevocable Life Insurance Trust

Assets upon death or end of term of years

Death benefit

Charity

Beneficiaries

contribution and converts it to an income-producing source. The second should be an irrevocable life insurance trust (ILIT) that buys a life insurance policy on the donor's life in an amount equal to the gifted asset. Reread *Problem 10* for a detailed explanation of ILITs. The premium is financed in part by the increased cash flow to the donor and in part by the income tax savings generated by the charitable gift. The donor gifts the premiums to the ILIT.

◆ **Consider a NIMCRUT.** A charitable remainder unitrust's income can fluctuate because the payout is based on a percentage of the trust assets' value. If the value drops, so does the income. A NIMCRUT is a *net income with makeup charitable remainder trust.* It provides that if the trust's income is insufficient to cover the payout in any given year, the trust can hold off on your payment until a future year. This can also be helpful if you donate an illiquid asset, such as real estate in a difficult market. The trust could take time to sell the property at a good price and not have to rush to provide your income.

If you wanted an ILIT wealth-replacement trust to supplement the NIMCRUT, you might have to use inexpensive term insurance until the real estate is sold, or defer buying the life insurance until the income starts. Or, the donor could designate sufficient current income to fund the ILIT until the sale of the property.

◆ **Use CRTs to diversify your portfolio.** Founders and early-team builders of successful companies often accumulate significant assets, but all in the one company's stock. These founders find themselves on the horns of a dilemma, faced with either paying a large capital gains tax, or remaining poorly diversified. A transfer of some of this stock into a CRT can lessen the lack of diversification because the trustee can sell the stock without incurring the tax, then reinvest to spread the risk. While the donor loses the actual asset, he or she can reap the benefit of the diversified portfolio by taking the income, and quite possibly use his or her tax deduction to buy wealth-replacement life insurance to offset the assets given away to the charity. This can be especially advantageous when the stock is not paying back dividends in the first place.

RECOMMENDED ADVISERS

Use an **attorney** to create the charitable trust.

Have your **tax accountant** show you the advantages of the charitable gift in dollars and cents.

SEE ALSO

◆ **Problem 43:** *Creating Your Own Private Foundation* to understand the tax and psychic rewards of taking an active role in giving away your assets.

CREATING YOUR OWN PRIVATE FOUNDATION

Charitable deductions have been recognized in the IRC since the Revenue Act of 1917, just four years after the enactment of the federal income tax. That earliest deduction was limited to 15 percent of the taxpayer's net taxable income. However, foundations actually predated the code in this country. George Peabody created an educational foundation in 1867. The Carnegie Foundation was established in 1905 and the Rockefeller Foundation in 1913. The overriding motivation for creating a foundation should remain philanthropic. Tax benefits should just make the process more affordable or generous.

ACCORDING TO THE foundation's Directory, published by the Foundation Center in New York City, there are more than 37,000 foundations in this country. Approximately 10,000 hold assets in excess of $1 million and control more than 96 percent of all the assets held by foundations. The other 27,000 or so are only responsible for 7 percent of the gifts from foundations, which is approaching $10 billion in grants.

Greg Barnard, chairman of the 1,500-member Council on Foundations in Washington, D.C., reported that his membership contributed in excess of $6.5 billion to charities in 1997. He believes the tax laws, especially those adopted as part of the Tax Reform Act of 1984, have provided "compelling incentives" for charitable giving. Barnard was concerned about the congressional proposal to discontinue the tax deduction for contributions of appreciated securities to family foundations. His worries have only been delayed by the Taxpayer Relief Act of 1997. It extended the more favorable tax treatment for one year, until May 31, 1998.

The Council on Foundations carefully watched the response when the favorable provisions of the Tax Reform Act of 1984 expired during 1995 and 1996, and then during the subsequent period when the act was temporarily revived. Council surveys revealed that the tax deduction for appreciated securities was a factor in the creation of at least 140 foundations, and that fully three-fourths of these will receive new contributions of stock because of the law's extension allowing tax deductibility of the full appreciated stock value.

Prior to a tax law change in 1969, a taxpayer could take a charitable deduction for the fully appreciated value of any asset transferred to charity. However, the 1969 changes sought to eliminate many abuses and nixed this deduction along with the rest. It created strict rules against self-dealing to eliminate excessive compensation and fringe benefits. It restricted the holdings of other business interests and risky investments. And it sought to strongly curtail the use of foundations to lobby and influence governmental actions. Running afoul of these provisions can, in the more severe cases, result in a confiscation of assets. This law helped to shape the foundation for the Tax Reform Act of 1984 that reinstated the deduction for appreciated assets.

There are two broad classifications of foundations: public and private. *Public foundations* encompass four categories of charities:

1 Churches, schools, medical facilities, and other charities with predominantly public or governmental support;

2 Charities that receive at least one-third of their funding from the public—including from ticket sales—and less than one-third from endowments;

3 Organizations supported by or closely affiliated with those in category 1; and

4 Organizations conducting tests for public safety. Public foundations do not have the same threatened restrictions on gifts of appreciated assets, nor are their rules for administration as restrictive as for the private foundations.

There are several different classifications of *private foundations:*

♦ **Independent foundations.** These are private and usually created by an individual by bequest. The Ford Foundation is an example of an independent foundation. Independents make grants to other tax-exempt organizations. In other words, they themselves are not conducting charitable projects—rather they are supporting the efforts of others. The tax laws require them to distribute approximately 5 percent of their endowment each year.

♦ **Company-sponsored foundations.** Corporations often start foundations for charitable purposes and fund them with gifts from earnings or stock. They are governed by the same regulations and tax provisions as independents. (These are not the same thing as company-sponsored, charitable-giving programs that make direct gifts to charities.)

♦ **Family foundations.** These entities are created by individuals and are usually family run. The Council on Foundations estimates that two-thirds of the foundations in this country fall into this category, holding some $86 billion in assets and making grants of $5 billion annually. They can have as little as $100,000 in assets.

♦ **Operating foundations.** These private foundations actually provide charitable services themselves, rather than just funding other programs. The Carnegie Endowment for International Peace is an example.

One interesting type of foundation that falls into the "public" category is the *community foundation.* This type of organization focuses on the local community and is usually funded by local donors, which is why the IRS considers this type to be public rather than private. They tend to focus on grants to charities in the community, employing staff and local directors to decide who should receive what funds. The oldest such foundation is the Cleveland Foundation.

Community foundations have a great selling angle. They offer more generous tax-deductibility provisions as well as lower expenses for start up and administration than private foundations. The Crossroads Community Foundation in western Boston provides prospective donors with a comparison sheet of private and community foundations. It itemizes the disadvantages of the private approach, including lower deductions for cash gifts (30 percent of AGI rather than 50 percent), a 2 percent excise tax on investment income, the 5 percent payout requirement, legal fees for start up, regulations against self-dealing, required public disclosure of activities and participants, and prior approvals required to grant scholarships.

There are some obvious advantages and disadvantages to creating your own foundation or to endowing a fund within a community foundation. How do you decide what's right for you, and how do you put your charitable intentions to work?

SOLUTIONS

◆ **Examine your charitable intentions.** If you are just looking for a way to escape taxes on the run-up in your stock's value over the past decade, look elsewhere than the private foundation. In fact, this is a great opportunity for a community foundation. And if your community lacks one, you could be instrumental in creating one and still not have the long-term commitment of the private approach. Community foundations often feature donor-advised funds because they cater to the preferences of the donors in their grants. Nancy Kieling, executive director of the Princeton Area Community Foundation in Skillman, New Jersey, prefers unrestricted donations because they leave the foundation free to decide among the hundreds of worthy applicant organizations that need financial assistance. She admits, however, the donor-advised funds do appeal to many of the potential donors.

◆ **Use private foundations to make a unique contribution.** The violinist Midori created her own foundation, Midori and Friends, to take classical music into New York public schools. She and other top-quality musicians under the foundation's program have played for more than 60,000 public school students in the New York area. While Midori's program is not the only one in New York to put good music at the reach of students, Melanie Smith, executive director, says, "What we have that's unique is Midori. It's her energy and vision that drive this program's success."

Russell B. Wright, president of the Wright Foundation in Newark, New Jersey, focuses on disadvantaged children in his hometown. He seeks out and supports deserving students by offering them grants to private boarding schools. The foundation supports over 100 students in preparatory schools and colleges.

The private foundation is an exceptional forum for putting your money behind your beliefs for the betterment of humankind.

◆ **Gear the structure to your family.** The way you conduct your foundation's business can be tailored to your family's talents, interests, and resources. By marshaling the talents of family members with different drives and skills, everyone contributes according to their own abilities. And, unlike the family business where the bottom line is the only way to keep score, the foundation can carry its own scoreboard, one tailored to the talent.

◆ **Use consultants.** The Council on Foundations maintains a database of consultants who provide references. These experts can help in the process from creation to operation. Dorothy S. Ridings, president and CEO of the council, has been an active advocate for favorable tax laws and truly effective foundations. The council should be viewed as a resource for families on the brink of moving toward a private foundation.

Use an **attorney** who specializes in foundations to create the entity and file for the proper tax status.

Ask your **financial planner** whether a local community foundation could help you reach your charitable-giving objectives and save you the expense and effort of administering your own foundation.

SEE ALSO

◆ **Problem 41:** *Current Charitable Gifts* to learn the general rules for the tax treatment of charitable gifts.

◆ **Problem 42:** *Charitable Gifts of Partial Interests* to understand the alternatives for giving away part of your assets while retaining either the income or the principal for yourself and/or your family.

PART 8

Superwealth
PROBLEMS

HE PROBLEMS OF the superwealthy—
people with a net worth of $20 million or more—
are like the problems of the merely wealthy, often
with just more zeroes attached. What differs,
however, is the range of solutions. Wealth does,
in fact, have its privileges. *Problems 44 through 47*
tell you about some that you can enjoy.

The estate-tax laws apply equally to everyone
with a taxable estate valued at $3 million or above,
extracting, in principle, 55 percent of that value
for the federal government. However, most of the
superwealthy pass on their assets for considerably
less shrinkage than 55 cents on the dollar. *Problem
44* explores some of their more innovative and
even aggressive techniques.

The superwealthy are not immune to family
difficulties, whether from divorce or children with
special needs. The snafus just get bigger and

usually more expensive. *Problem 45* looks at family problems on a big budget.

Superwealthy owners of family businesses sometimes assume greater risks in their planning. *Problem 46* addresses some of the techniques not covered earlier in this book.

In 1997, Ted Turner raised the standard for charitable giving with his $1 billion pledge for United Nations causes. This is a standard easily within the reach of most of the superwealthy, and in fact utilizes a vehicle that most of these individuals and families already control. *Problem 47* tells you how you can, too.

ESTATE-TAX PROBLEMS

The estate tax, adopted to reduce the concentration of wealth in the hands of a small number of individuals or families, has not accomplished its purpose. The vast majority of wealth in this country escapes the federal estate and gift tax. It happens by design and through a dedication to the belief that it is permissible to pay as few dollars in taxation as the law allows. The superwealthy in this country pay less tax proportionately than the merely wealthy. How do they manage it?

ACCORDING TO STATISTICS garnered from the Internal Revenue Service (IRS) and New York University economist Edward N. Wolff, three-fifths of the assets of the wealthiest individuals escape estate taxes at death. In 1993, for example, it is estimated that for individuals with estates between $600,000 and $1 million, 61.5 percent of their estate assets were subject to tax. For individuals with estates over $20 million, 31 percent of the assets were taxed—about half. What do the superwealthy know that the merely wealthy don't?

If there is one signal characteristic of the superwealthy, it is their willingness to seek help with their planning. In story after story, one finds an enlightened team of professionals dedicated to helping their clients minimize taxes. It sounds easier to afford this planning on $20 million than on $1 million. However, in many cases, there is some risk and significant expense involved.

When William Olsten, the founder of the third-largest temporary-help agency died, he left his family an estate of $115 million, primarily in Olsten Corporation stock. He left half of the stock outright to his wife, Miriam, and half in trust for their children, which would pass to them at her death. The distribution scheme would have resulted in the entire estate being taxed at Mrs. Olsten's death at 55 percent, or over $60 million, assuming no appreciation in the stock. What that meant to son and now-president of Olsten Corporation, Stuart Olsten, was loss of control of the company. The heirs would have to sell so much stock to pay taxes that they would lose effective control of the business their father had built from scratch.

What did Stuart Olsten do? "I started interviewing lawyers," he says, "and most of them said it was too late and we would just have to sell half the stock and write a check." That is, until he met Richard B. Covey, an attorney with the New York law firm of Carter, Ledyard & Milburn. Covey suggested that Miriam Olsten purchase her children's right to inherit the trust assets that they couldn't access until her death. The attorney actually placed a value on the use of the trust assets today, as opposed to some indeterminate time in the future. She used her Olsten stock to make the purchase. The technique, accepted by the IRS after negotiating the value of the trust interest, generated a capital gains tax but eliminated the estate tax.

Mr. Covey advised Mrs. Olsten that the transaction was "risky," but she decided to take the risk. The family won. Now the children are exploring ways of paying the significant tax at Mrs. Olsten's death, including the use of life insurance. A policy with a face amount of $50 million could be purchased with only $1.2 million in annual premiums.

In another case involving a potentially crippling estate tax, an aggressive family position paid off in the hundreds of millions. In 1979, S. I. Newhouse, the founder of the publishing powerhouse that owns *The New Yorker* magazine, died with an estate in excess of $1 billion. The family business was the largest asset, and the IRS, arguing that the control vested in the heirs made the stock even more valuable, levied a tax bill of $609 million. The heirs argued that the stock was worth much less because the voting shareholders who were family members would have been reluctant to vote against the decedent, but now were more inclined to be independent. This made all of the minority interests worthless. They litigated the issue in tax court, a special venue in the federal system, and, in 1990, the court agreed with the taxpayers and said the tax due was only $48 million.

The Newhouse case is not the only instance where the courts have not sided with the IRS when the stakes were high. Joseph H. Lauder, founder of the cosmetics firm named for his wife, Estée, died with an estate in excess of $100 million. The IRS claimed the estate owed $89.5 million in taxes. The family argued the tax should be $29 million. The discrepancy was based on differing valuations of the family stock. The court effectively split the difference after listening to the appraisers for both sides, valuing the shares at $50.5 million.

According to Donald C. Alexander, IRS commissioner during the 1970s, the service "has flubbed cases because it is outgunned." William D. Zabel, a New York estate lawyer and author of *The Rich Die Richer and You Can Too,* agrees. "The IRS, including its trial lawyers, is seriously undermanned and overextended. And this leads them in some cases to compromise where they might obtain substantially more by litigating."

This seems to be the contention in the case of the Pritzkers, the family owners of Hyatt Hotels. When founder A. N. Pritzker died in 1986, the IRS claimed the estate tax due was $53.2 million. The heirs claimed the amount due was zero. They argued that the family wealth had been successfully shifted to Bahamian trusts for the benefit of Pritzker's children and grandchildren. The case never went to trial. Just before the tax court was to hear the case, the IRS settled for $9.5 million. At the crux of the decision to settle was the inability of the IRS to uncover all the records of the family business and trusts. The Bahamian government has strict rules about financial privacy and the United States could not compel the Bahamians to disclose the details. Commentators saw the result as a win for the Pritzker family. Jay Pritzker, a son of the decedent, said that he thought "the government's people did an excellent job of collecting more than they were entitled to."

Tax planning is not the only rationale for using off-shore trusts. Duncan E. Osborne, of Osborne, Lowe, Helman & Smith, LLP, a law firm in Austin, Texas, says that the two most common reasons U.S. citizens opt for offshore trusts are asset protection and meaningful economic diversification. However, he calls tax planning, especially "establishing a vehicle for exemption equivalent trusts and generation-skipping transfer tax [GSST] exemption trusts" a valid and widespread motivation. *(Refer to Problem 5 for a detailed explanation of these trust vehicles.)* So is marital-deduction property planning, such as "establishing a vehicle for partitioning community property, spousal gifts, and QTIP [qualified terminable-interest property] trusts." In fact, Osborne says that "while it is not improper to take advantage of legal opportunities to protect assets, if the trust is later challenged, the existence of non-asset-protection motivations will help counter charges of fraudulent intent."

These stories have a common thread—talented and creative legal advice and support. You should spend considerable time and energy lining up your tax team now while the estate is growing.

SOLUTIONS

◆ **Assemble a great team of estate and financial planners early in your wealth-accumulation career.** At the heart of such a team is an excellent attorney. Financial planners and accountants usually play key supporting roles, especially in valuing businesses and providing insurance to prefund the estate tax.

◆ **Use life insurance to prepay estate taxes with discounted dollars.** Too often, wealthy estate owners recognize life insurance as the least-expensive way to pay taxes only after age and stress have combined to make them uninsurable. You must qualify medically for high-ticket life insurance. The longer you wait to buy insurance, the greater the risk that your health will no longer be good enough to qualify at standard rates.

Insurance companies sometimes issue rated policies—that is, contracts with higher premiums or lower benefits—in cases where your health is not good enough for you to qualify on a standard basis. This does not mean you have one foot in the grave. Insurance companies make a profit by having favorable claims' experience. Don't take rated policies personally; it's about their willingness to prefund your tax bill and your willingness to pay their premium.

◆ **Don't be afraid to take a little risk in your estate planning.** Just know what the risk is compared to the potential gain. Your advisers should be able to give you several alternatives for planning the disposition of your assets at your death, or even sooner. The risk is usually whether the IRS will accept your approach or valuation. Make sure your advisers explain the risks carefully. Realize that what makes them risks is uncertainty; therefore, even the explanation of the risks involves guesstimates. Put yourself in your heirs' shoes for a moment and then make your decisions based on your comfort level with the possible outcomes.

◆ **Consider offshore trusts if you have both asset protection and non-asset-protection motivations.** This is not an area for the weak of heart, but it represents a tremendously fertile ground for estate planning in the decades to come, largely because of the globalization of our economy and investments. As Duncan Osborne, author of *Asset Protection: Domestic and International Law and Tactics*, says, "The explosion in the U. S. litigation industry, capricious legislative bodies, and the volatility of markets and economies have sparked a powerful response. The buzzword in the 1990s among lawyers representing lawyers at risk is 'asset protection.'" It's also the key to lawyers protecting anyone. Offshore trusts can be tax- as well as asset-protection vehicles. However, Osborne believes the client must be willing to invest at least $1 million with foreign investment managers. Only use an attorney with considerable experience in offshore-trust planning if this approach appeals to you.

◆ **Consider an Alaskan trust for perpetual existence and creditor protection.** In 1997, the Alaskan legislature amended the Alaska Trust Act to permit trusts domiciled in Alaska to have a perpetual life, and to allow a client to be a beneficiary of his or her own trust and still provide protection from the claims of creditors. The first feature, perpetual life, makes it possible to avoid the *rule against perpetuities,* which limits a trust's existence to a term not to exceed the lifetime of one of the living beneficiaries, plus 21 years. The second aspect, creditor protection, is especially noteworthy because Alaska has no state income tax, sales tax, or trust-income tax. Bill Hunter of KeyCorp's Wealth-Management Division, with offices in Alaska, believes the Alaskan trust will appeal to many who are leery of offshore trusts. "Since many of our trust clients tell us they are more comfortable having their assets under American jurisdiction rather than having to deal with a foreign jurisdiction and court system, we think the legislation offers an attractive estate-planning option." Ask your attorney about the viability of these trusts in your situation. You do not have to move to Juneau to create such a trust.

RECOMMENDED ADVISERS

 Retain the best **attorney** you can afford for planning superwealth estates.

 Use **accountants** and firms with experience in dealing with the IRS on complex issues.

Use **financial planners** to run hypothetical probate alternatives and propose investment strategies to dovetail with estate planning.

 Find a professional **life insurance underwriter** who can help you find the right coverage for your estate-tax needs. Look for a CLU/ChFC (chartered life underwriter/chartered financial consultant) designation and someone with decades of experience in the advanced underwriting markets. Check for references and ask the prospective agent if he or she has ever written a case with a significant premium.

SEE ALSO

◆ **Problem 2:** *The Estate-Tax Bite.*
◆ **Problem 5:** *Excessive Joint Ownership with Spouses.*

P R O B L E M   4 5

FAMILY PROBLEMS

The family difficulties of the superwealthy are usually exacerbated by their wealth. Aside from the obvious conclusion that money can't buy happiness, are there any recommendations that can be made?

CERTAIN PROBLEMS SIMPLY don't exist for someone with superwealth. For example, the expenses of long-term care should not concern someone with a $20 million estate, unless it is all illiquid. Superwealthy individuals do not spend time fretting over the financial-aid forms for their college-bound children. And few dread facing the financial drain of having three generations under their roof.

On the other hand, wealth is no antidote to the pain of divorce and child custody, multiple families, or extended illnesses and long-term disability. A superwealthy 45-year-old who is paralyzed with a stroke may not need disability-income insurance and may be able to afford better treatment, but the disability remains.

The financial impact of divorce depends upon the lifestyles of the divorcing couple. The more lavish the predivorce standard of living in relation to earnings, the more difficult the adjustment. The courts tend to award alimony and child support based on prior lifestyle, rather than prospective income.

Divorce is problematic for superwealthy owners of closely held family businesses. Selling part of the business to raise the cash to fund the property settlement agreement could prove to be impossible. Yet, if a nonworking spouse is entitled to a portion of the assets, the court may be unsympathetic to claims that the business is not saleable.

Owners of successful, public, family corporations could have problems with voting control after a divorce if the shareholdings must be divided in order to satisfy the court.

Child-support obligations are usually not a financial burden as they are with the nonwealthy, but the superwealthy may be more likely to invoke the full measure of their law firm's arsenal to frustrate the spirit of the alimony and child-support agreements.

Multiple families can pull emotional strings as easily with superwealthy individuals as with less-landed contemporaries. The size of the prior divorce settlement might even be a bone of contention among the new couple. There are no easy answers to these abrasions to the emotions. However, with the superwealthy, the price tag for each failed relationship can seriously erode wealth and power within family businesses.

SOLUTIONS

◆ **Begin financial and estate planning early in your relationship with your spouse.** Your current plan is not binding in a court, but it might help you and your spouse come to grips with your real wealth and its limitations. Many divorce cases generate significant fees in the process of trying to uncover the hidden assets of the partner with the greater earning capacity. If both of you are part of the plan from the very beginning, you will know what exists and how it can be divided.

If you are not able to trust your spouse with the truth about your wealth, plan for your death and divorce right now. There is no plan called a "divorce plan," comparable to an estate or financial plan. However, you *can* seek legal advice and position your assets to protect your family and your holdings. Gifts into trusts and generous use of annual gift-tax exemptions can position assets beyond the reach of the courts.

If you know your predisposition toward lack of trust before the marriage, opt for a prenuptial agreement, explained in *Problem 30*.

◆ **Use trusts freely as part of a divorce settlement process.** Divorcing parents can agree to use trusts to fund child support and education objectives decided upon as part of the divorce process. This will remove any problems about timeliness or gamesmanship with the children's financial security. Trusts are advantageous over uniform gifts to minors act accounts because they do not automatically convert to the child's name at the age of majority.

◆ **Use allowances, trusts, and investment classes to teach your children financial responsibility.** One of the responsibilities of superwealth is training your children to be responsible in turn. This is not easy, especially if you have had to learn yourself as an adult. Too few parents deal with this problem before it becomes a fiscal disaster. Your children need to understand how difficult it is to earn money in order to appreciate the need to preserve it, especially if you are doing something philanthropic with the funds. Here are several things you can do:

— Get the children involved with the disposition of funds to charities.

— Make the children handle an allowance.

— Enroll your children in investment classes and investment clubs.

— Take your children to the workplace and let them start to understand what enterprise is all about.

◆ **Use trusts to protect children from themselves.** If your children are not financially responsible, use trusts to provide for their financial needs now and after your death. A corporate trustee can eliminate some of the animosity likely to fall on a family-member trustee, but corporate trustees are not without faults. They can be rigid in their approach to dealing with beneficiaries' financial needs and limited in their choice of investments. You can go a long way to eliminate the problems with corporate trustees by giving them clear guidance and wide latitude. In the trust document, spell out your hopes for your heirs. State how much discretion should exist in paying expenses for traditional and nontraditional education. This is the great advantage of setting up the trust before your death or incapacity: the ability to lay out your intentions to the trustees face-to-face as well as in writing. Meet with the trustees and your children. Let them get to know each other before they have to interact over the funds.

RECOMMENDED ADVISER

Rely on a good **attorney** to guide you through the alternatives to resolving family issues, short of litigation, if possible. Try alternative dispute resolution, as outlined in *Problem 30.*

SEE ALSO

◆ **Problem 30:** *Separation and Divorce.*
◆ **Problem 31:** *Child-Support Responsibilities.*

BUSINESS DISPOSITION PROBLEMS

When closely held businesses reach valuations measured in tens or hundreds of millions, planning for the disposition of the business interest becomes more difficult. The dollar amounts of the estate tax and income tax become alarming. It is difficult to find a buyer at these price levels. And, often owners want to keep the business in the hands of a small group, such as the family. Without planning, retention of the family business is less likely.

LLAMAR HUNT RECENTLY transferred 80 percent of the ownership of the Kansas City Chiefs National Football League franchise to his children. His objectives were to keep the business in the family and to reduce estate taxes. "It is the smart thing to do," said Hunt, age 64, and still actively running the business. "If you wait until you die, there are some huge estate taxes that would come due. I didn't want to have a situation where this large an asset would be hanging over my estate." Sports franchises command healthy values. *Financial World* magazine estimated the Chiefs franchise to be worth $188 million. At a 55 percent estate-tax rate, that would be $103.4 million in taxes due.

The gift of the 80 percent interest undoubtedly generated significant gift taxes, also at 55 percent. However, most of the future appreciation of the business value will be dispersed among the children, and perhaps the estate-tax bite will be many years in the future. In fact, the increase in the franchise's value from the time of the gift may have saved as much as $30 million already. It is likely the children were able to discount the value of the interests because they were minority interests, as discussed in *Problem 8*.

News media fortunes also carry significant values, as with the Newhouse publishing fortune discussed in *Problem 44*, which generated an estate in excess of $1 billion.

In fact, the IRS claimed a tax due of $609 million. But for the tenacity of the family's estate lawyers, much of the business could have been liquidated to pay the tax bill. Malcolm Forbes chose the life insurance route with his planners. It is reported that Forbes was insured for as much as $67 million. He was smart enough to know that the key to preserving the business for his family was to plan for the disposition of the business while he was still healthy, and long before he planned to step from the helm. His son, Steve, now safely at the head of the family business, is presumably taking similar planning steps for his own estate. He has certainly continued his father's tradition of legally avoiding taxes.

At the heart of all these great estates is the issue of business valuation. There is obviously more at stake with businesses of this magnitude. However, the solutions to the valuation problems are sometimes made easier by the size of the business and its comparability to other enterprises in the same industry, yet publicly owned, hence with readily available stock values. When you have to rely on an appraisal of a closely held business worth $1 million, there often can be less room to maneuver.

With time to plan your strategy for the disposition of the business, you also gain the advantage of planning for a favorable valuation. A business succession agreement can fix the value for estate-tax purposes in your estate. Waiting until the death of the majority owner to fix a value is tantamount to leaving the business valuation in the hands of the IRS.

SOLUTIONS

◆ **Address the issues of the competency of your successors before they become the owners in fact.** Betsy W. Townsend, CLU, ChFC, of the Townsend Company in Cincinnati, Ohio, a specialist in estate planning for owners of family businesses, believes that "identifying a successor is one of the most problematic tasks for any business owner." She worries that stereotypes, such as firstborn or male versus female, don't take into account the actual abilities of the children. She is likewise concerned about the problems created if only some, or none, of the children have the ability to continue the business. How will the passed-over children react? An equally difficult question is what to do if the children may in the future be capable, but aren't now. Townsend recommends *interim planning*, which includes a plan for management until the children are experienced enough, or demonstrate that they are not qualified. It may require a "golden-handcuffs" plan, encouraging key employees to "stay on to run the company until it can be transitioned to the children."

◆ **Recognize the inherent conflict of interest between those active in the business and those who are not.** The active owners will have different objectives than siblings without a voice. The managing shareholders usually are concerned with the long-term growth of the business. Silent, sibling partners are alternatively looking for income and a higher valuation for the stock. Townsend recommends "partnership or shareholder agreements to protect minority owners." Townsend also emphasizes the distinction between treating children "equally" and "fairly": "Most parents want to make certain that their children are treated 'equally.' This is very difficult to do in the family-business setting. First of all, the family business is often by far the largest asset in the estate, so 'equal' treatment would seem to indicate that even inactive children will receive a portion of the value of the business. But, the true value of the business interest to an inactive owner is seldom 'equal' to that of an active owner. On the other hand, the active children may argue that they are the ones who are treated unfairly if the inactive children are given cash (or similar assets) with a value equal to their share or ownership in the business. After all, cash comes without the element of risk or the 'sweat equity' required in running a family business."

◆ **Insure your estate-tax bill.** As explained in *Problem 3*, paying your estate-tax bill with discounted dollars for life insurance premiums is most often the least-expensive method. Take a page out of Malcolm Forbes's book, even if the insurance required is in the tens of millions. If you wonder how the business can afford to pay the premium, ask yourself how the heirs can afford to pay the tax.

RECOMMENDED ADVISERS

Create a disposition plan with an experienced **attorney**. Look for tax-saving opportunities in minority stock interests.

Contact your **insurance agent** to insure the estate-tax and cash-flow obligations under business continuation agreements (BCAs). Use irrevocable life insurance trusts (ILITs) as enumerated in *Problem 10*.

SEE ALSO

◆ **Problem 3:** *Insufficient Cash in the Estate.*
◆ **Problem 8:** *What's It Worth: Valuation Problems with the IRS* regarding minority stock positions.
◆ **Problem 10:** *Improper Beneficiaries and Owners* about using ILIT to fund the tax bite without increasing the size of your estate.

PROBLEM 47

CHARITABLE-GIVING PROBLEMS

Ted Turner's 1997 pledge of $1 billion for the benefit of the United Nations, a commitment of $100 million each year for 10 years, seems to be the largest gift ever for charitable purposes. This level of giving prompts us all to rethink our charitable intentions.

TURNER CREATED THE Turner Family Foundation in the early 1990s. The former head of Greenpeace USA manages the foundation and each of Turner's children sits on the board of directors. Turner's interests run largely to the state of our environment. In 1997, for example, the Turner Foundation approved $5.5 million in grants for habitat causes, $2.5 million for population causes, $1.8 million for water and toxic-waste issues, and $1.7 million for energy-related projects. One advantage of a foundation is that its grants can mirror the concerns of the grantor, rather than being a reflexive reaction to someone else's plea for money. The foundation route is proactive.

There is some correlation between current giving and the stock market. The Dow Jones Industrial Average, while not a perfect barometer for the rise of all stocks, increased from a 1,000-point level in the 1960s and 1970s to more than 9,000 by 1998. In 1970, the total charitable giving in this country was $25 billion. Today, the figure approaches $175 billion. The majority of that sum, 79.6 percent, comes from individuals. Only 7.8 percent comes from foundations, 6.9 percent from bequests, and 5.6 percent from corporations.

The link between the stock market and individual philanthropy is epitomized by Ted Turner's largess. His $3 billion net worth is largely in Time-Warner stock. The $1 billion pledged represents the appreciation on his stock in the nine months of 1997 leading up to the gift. If the markets continue to favor Time-Warner, he may be able to make the gifts annually without jeopardizing his voting-control position. This may become a useful lesson for proponents of philanthropy. Unfortunately in Turner's case, he announced the billion-dollar gift *before* consulting with his tax advisers. It is unclear just how he will fund his promises to the United Nations. However, with proper planning you can have your cake and eat it, too—Turner's impulsiveness notwithstanding.

When you reach the superwealth stage, your concern shifts from income needs to tax avoidance and creating something meaningful with your life's work.

The foundation is the perfect vehicle for rounding out one's purpose.

However, the ability to tax deduct the appreciation in one's stock may have a limited life. Unless Congress renews the tax deductibility of the appreciation in value, a very limited window in 1998 will have been the last chance to make a gift of appreciated securities to your private foundation while still reaping full deductibility of the stocks' share.

For superwealthy executives, much of their compensation comes in the form of stock options. If the tax deductibility of stock appreciation is to be repealed, executives will have to reconsider their gifts to private foundations and their timing.

SOLUTIONS

◆ **Create your own foundation.** Superwealth rewards may be greater for the good that you can do with your wealth than the show you can put on with your assets. Take advantage of tax breaks to create a charitable organization that grants money the way you choose to see it spent and invested. This requires an active role in the grant making.

◆ **Involve the entire family.** This is as much a part of the family heritage as the business that spawned the wealth. In fact, it should be more so, because the family foundation is a vehicle for family members who don't make business contributions to make a real difference nonetheless.

RECOMMENDED ADVISER

 See your **attorney** now to cope with the tax law changes.

SEE ALSO

◆ **Part 7:** *Charitable-Giving Problems* on charitable giving and its tax consequences.

RESOURCES

ACH OF THE *Problems* in this book has commanded considerable attention from writers and scholars. Many stand out if you want to go further into a particular topic. This appendix gives you additional writings and other resources, such as Internet Websites and periodicals, organized by Parts.

PART 1

ESTATE-PLANNING PROBLEMS

WILLIAM D. ZABEL'S *The Rich Die Richer and You Can Too* [John Wiley & Sons, New York, New York, 1996] is as enjoyable as the title suggests. While written in advance of the Taxpayer Relief Act of 1997, the conceptual presentation of estate-planning techniques is excellent.

For professionals such as attorneys, accountants,

financial planners, and insurance agents, two authors stand out. Donald F. Cady, JD, LLM, CLU, has written *The Field Guide to Estate Planning, Business Planning, and Employee Benefits* [the National Underwriter Company, Cincinnati, Ohio, 1997]. This book is updated by Cady annually by the National Underwriter Company. His e-mail address is: dfcady@ix.net.com.

The second prolific author for professionals is Stephan R. Leimberg, JD, CLU. He coauthored the best estate-planning book for planners, *The Tools and Techniques of Estate Planning* [the National Underwriter Company, Cincinnati, Ohio, 1995]. The latest version reflecting the 1997 tax law changes should be out soon. Also, look for the other books in that series, *The Tools and Techniques of Financial Planning*, *The Tools and Techniques of Employee-Benefit and Retirement Planning*; and *The*

Tools and Techniques of Life Insurance Planning, all published in 1993 by the National Underwriter Company.

Another source for the wealthy is called *The American Bar Association Guide to Wills and Estates; Everything You Need to Know About Wills, Trusts, Estates, and Taxes* [Times Books, New York, New York, 1995]. The Website address for the American Bar Association store is: http://www.abanet.org/store/home.html or try your local bookstore.

Internet users can access lists of estate-planning, probate, trust, and elder-law lawyers nationwide. Try the Website: http://www.ca-probate.com/links.htm.

Read *The Millionaire Next Door* by Thomas J. Stanley, Ph.D., and William D. Danko, Ph.D. [Longstreet Press, Atlanta, Georgia, 1996] for insights into the financial habits of millionaires.

The new demographics of the American landscape are described well by Gail Sheehy in *New Passages: Mapping Your Life across Time* [Random House, New York, New York, 1995].

There are a number of helpful IRS Websites. The Treasury Department publishes a daily newsletter entitled the *Digital Daily*. You can find it at: http://www.irs.ustreas.gov/prod/cover.html. Forms and IRS publications can be accessed at: http://www.irs.ustreas.gov/prod/forms_pubs/index.html.

There are several good resources for retirement planning. Read Mary Rowland's *A Commonsense Guide to Your 401(k)* [Bloomberg Press, Princeton, New Jersey, 1997]. Also try Jonathan Pond's *Financial Management Guide: Retirement Planning for Asset-Rich Individuals* [Prentice-Hall, Paramus, New Jersey, 1993].

The most valuable tool for retirement planning is a compound-interest table. This may be found in any number of financial books or at your local bank or stock-brokerage office.

For heirs with special needs, as discussed in *Problem*

13, read *Planning for the Future: Providing a Meaningful Life for a Child with a Disability after Your Death* by L. Mark Russell and Arnold Grant [American Publishing Company, Evanston, Illinois, 1995]. To order, you can call 800-247-6553.

PART 2

LONGEVITY PROBLEMS

FOR THE BEST overview of the challenges of living too long, read Gail Sheehy's *New Passages,* cited on the previous page.

Jeff Sadler's book, *The Long-Term-Care Handbook* [the National Underwriter Company, Cincinnati, Ohio, 1996], is written primarily for the insurance industry. However, this is an excellent resource for professionals and nonprofessionals alike. It covers the financial burdens of aging, as well as the policy provisions preferable in long-term-care insurance.

Another resource for the professional is by Dana Shilling, JD, *Financial Planning for the Older Client* [the National Underwriter Company, Cincinnati, Ohio, 3rd edition, 1997]. Also, read *How to Protect Your Life Savings from Catastrophic Illness and Nursing Homes* by Harley Gordon [Financial Strategies Press, Boston, 3rd edition, 1996].

PART 3

BUSINESS SUCCESSION PROBLEMS

THE LITERATURE IN the area of business succession planning targets professionals such as attorneys, accountants, and financial planners, including insurance agents. The best resources, by Donald F. Cady and Stephan R. Leimberg, are mentioned in the estate-planning section above. Noninsurance professionals should especially read Leimberg's *The Tools and Techniques of Life Insurance Planning.*

INVESTMENT PROBLEMS

THERE ARE MANY good books about investing. Start with a basic book, such as *Ten Steps to Financial Success: A Beginner's Guide to Saving and Investing* by W. Patrick Naylor [John Wiley & Sons, New York, New York, 1997]; also, anything written by Peter Lynch, such as *Beating the Street* [Fireside, New York, New York, 1994]. For a well-written explanation of the investing approach of Warren Buffett, read *Buffettology* by Mary Buffett and David Clark [Scribner, New York, New York, 1997]. For an excellent book on the technical side, read *The Mathematics of Investing* by Michael C. Thomsett [John Wiley & Sons, New York, New York, 1989].

The best text for illustrating investment returns is the *Chase Investment Performance Digest*.

The two best newspapers for investors are the *Wall Street Journal* and *Investor's Business Daily*. The *Journal* can be found on your computer (as well as your doorstep) at: http://www.wsj.com. *Investor's Business Daily* can be found at: http://www.investors.com.

Investing information can also be found at the following Websites:

- **New York Stock Exchange:** http://www.nyse.com
- **NASDAQ:** http://www.nasdaq.com
- **American Stock Exchange:** http://www.amex.com
- **Bloomberg Personal:** http://www.bloomberg.com
- ***Barron's:*** http://www.barrons.com
- **Securities and Exchange Commission:** http://www.sec.gov.

On choosing advisers, read Lynn Brenner's *Smart Questions to Ask Your Financial Advisers* [Bloomberg Press, Princeton, New Jersey, 1997]. Financial advisers should read Mary Rowland's *Best Practices for Financial Advisors* [Bloomberg Press, Princeton, New Jersey, 1997].

For a listing of financial advisers in different disciplines:

◆ **CFPs (certified financial planners).** Contact the CFP Board of Standards, Inc. in Denver, Colorado, at 888-237-6275, or visit their Website at: http://www.cfp.board.org/.

◆ **CLUs (chartered life underwriters)** or **ChFCs (chartered financial consultants).** Call the American Society of CLU & ChFC in Bryn Mawr, Pennsylvania, at 610-526-1000, or contact them at their Website at: http://www.agents-online.com/ASCLU/index.html.

◆ **Telephone Preference Service,** Directing Marketing Association, Dept. S, P.O. Box 9014, Farmingdale, NY 11735-9014.

◆ **Mail Preference Service,** Directing Marketing Association, Dept. S, P.O. Box 9008, Farmingdale, NY 11735-9014.

PART 5

FAMILY PROBLEMS

FOR A LISTING of arbitration practitioners, consult the American Arbitration Association (AAA) in New York, New York at 212-484-4100, or contact them at their Website: http://www.adr.org/. This Website also allows you to access persons in your area who practice through the AAA.

A good resource for funding education expenses is Kristin Davis's *Financing College* [Random House, 1996]. It details how to qualify for financial aid and how to get the software to help with the process. You can call the Department of Education for software to complete the Free Application for Federal Student Aid (FAFSA) form at 800-801-0576.

Jeff Sadler has written a good text for professionals entitled *Disability Income* [the National Underwriter Company, Cincinnati, Ohio, 2nd edition, 1995].

PART 6

LIABILITY PROBLEMS

FOR AN OVERVIEW of the legal side of asset protection, read *Asset-Protection Planning* by Michael N. Brette, JD [Griffin Publishing Group, Glendale, California, 1997]. For basic books on insurance, read Brian H. Breuel's *The Complete Idiot's Guide to Buying Insurance and Annuities* [Simon & Schuster, New York, New York, 1996] or Janet Bamford's *Smarter Insurance Solutions* [Bloomberg Press, Princeton, New Jersey, 1996].

For a listing of chartered property casualty underwriters (CPCUs) in your area, consult the American Institute for Chartered Property Casualty Underwriters, 720 Providence Road, P.O. Box 3016, Malvern, Pennsylvania 19355-0716 (610-644-2100). Their Website address is: http://www.insweb.com/educator/aicpcu-iia/.

PARTS 7 AND 8 have been ommitted from this section because you'll find that they are their own best resource.

INDEX

[NOTE: Page numbers for entries occurring in tables are suffixed with a *t*.]

ABOUT BLOOMBERG

Bloomberg L.P., founded in 1981, is a global information services, news, and media company. Headquartered in New York, the company has nine sales offices, two data centers, and 80 news bureaus worldwide.

Bloomberg Financial Markets, serving customers in 100 countries around the world, holds a unique position within the financial services industry by providing an unparalleled combination of news, information, and analytic tools in a single package known as the BLOOMBERG® service. Corporations, banks, money management firms, financial exchanges, insurance companies, and many other entities and organizations rely on Bloomberg as their primary source of information.

BLOOMBERG NEWS℠, founded in 1990, offers worldwide coverage of economies, companies, industries, governments, financial markets, politics, and sports. The news service is the main content provider for Bloomberg's broadcast media, which include BLOOMBERG TELEVISION®—the 24-hour cable television network available in ten languages worldwide—and BLOOMBERG NEWS RADIO™—an international radio network anchored by flagship station BLOOMBERG NEWS RADIO AM 1130℠ in New York.

In addition to the BLOOMBERG PRESS® line of books, Bloomberg publishes *BLOOMBERG® MAGAZINE* and *BLOOMBERG PERSONAL FINANCE*™.

To learn more about Bloomberg, call a sales representative at:

Frankfurt:	49-69-920-410	San Francisco:	1-415-912-2960
Hong Kong:	852-977-6000	São Paulo:	5511-3048-4500
London:	44-171-330-7500	Singapore:	65-438-8585
New York:	1-212-318-2000	Sydney:	61-29-777-8686
Princeton:	1-609-279-3000	Tokyo:	81-3-3201-8900

ABOUT THE AUTHOR

Brian H. Breuel has been in the financial-services industry since 1968. He has a B.A. degree from Princeton University, a law degree from the University of Florida, and masters degrees in both management and financial services.

He has earned both the ChFC and CLU designations, been a member of the Florida Bar Association, and been active in the Estate Planning Councils, organizations of estate planning attorneys, CPAs, and CLUs.

His career experience includes owning his own pension design and administration company, owning his own fee-based planning firm, and being a senior executive with a major life insurance company. He has had a securities license for several decades, including a principal's license.

From 1990 to 1995, Mr. Breuel enjoyed a midlife sabbatical, living on a yacht in the Caribbean and flying around the world for "the experience."

This is his second financial-planning book. He has spoken at numerous functions across the country on financial subjects, as well as on his sailing/travel adventures.